PRAIRIE VOICES

Iowa's Pioneering Women

PRAIRIE VOICES

Iowa's Pioneering Women

Edited by
Glenda Riley

Iowa State University Press / Ames

For Donald R. Whitnah,

who has encouraged my work on Iowa women since 1969,

long before it was fashionable to do so.

GLENDA RILEY is the Alexander M. Bracken Professor of History at Ball State University in Muncie, Indiana. She is the author of *Frontierswomen: The Iowa Experience,* as well as numerous books and articles about women in the American West. Riley is a member of the Iowa Women's Hall of Fame.

Authorization to photocopy items for internal or personal use, or the internal or personal use of specific clients, is granted by Iowa State University Press, provided that the base fee of $.10 per copy is paid directly to the Copyright Clearance Center, 27 Congress Street, Salem, MA 01970. For those organizations that have been granted a photocopy license by CCC, a separate system of payments has been arranged. The fee code for users of the Transactional Reporting Service is 0-8138-2595-4/96 $.10.

♾ Printed on acid-free paper in the United States of America

First edition, 1996

Library of Congress Cataloging-in-Publication Data

Prairie voices : Iowa's pioneering women / [compiled by] Glenda Riley. —
   1st ed.
      p. cm.
     Includes bibliographical references and index.
     ISBN 0-8138-2595-4 (acid-free paper)
     1. Women pioneers—Iowa—History. 2. Women pioneers—Iowa—Biography.
  3. Iowa—History. 4. Frontier and pioneer life—Iowa.
  I. Riley, Glenda
  F621.F76   1996
  977.7′02′082—dc20   96-24258

Last digit is the print number: 9 8 7 6 5 4 3 2 1

Contents

Preface

DURING the past two decades, a fascination with women's history has emerged in the United States. Iowa's pioneer women have received a fair share of the attention. But now, with the current resurgence of curiosity regarding the development of the nineteenth-century West, interest in Iowa's early settlers has mushroomed.

Books and articles telling these women's stories, as well as museum exhibits, lure Iowans who are intrigued by their past. Still, women's own words and memories often narrate pioneer Iowa most poignantly and explicitly. Consequently, this volume presents a representative sampling of women's writings and reminiscences arranged in three sections: the quest to establish a new home, daily life and family cares in pioneer Iowa, and women's activities and paid employment outside the domestic world. Within each section, the selections are arranged chronologically.

White women with some degree of education wrote all these selections. This does not indicate that uneducated women, non-English-speaking women, and women of color were not present. It simply means that such women did not typically leave written documents behind them and that historians, archivists, and interviewers did not have the prescience to collect what such women did leave. Today, scholars are trying to reconstruct the lives of these women through the use of census records, family Bibles, marriage licenses and wills, advertisements for black runaway indentured servants and similar sources.[1] As the painstaking work goes on, these women's more literate sisters tell the story for all.

Another significant omission in women's writings is the underside of pioneer life. Such topics as spouse and child abuse, alcoholism, divorce, prostitution, rape, and murder are seldom mentioned. Yet police ledgers, divorce records, doctors' accounts, and other similar resources indicate that our forerunners were people like us, full of human foibles, short of temper, and subject to sometimes irrational needs.

For example, when the U.S. Congress authorized the Bureau of the Census to compile marriage and divorce statistics, the resulting 1889 report revealed that the American West had the highest divorce rate in the nation—and thus in the world. Iowa contributed a sizable share and continued to do so until the next report in 1906. Between 1867 and 1906, Iowa recorded 34,874 divorces as compared to 15,646 in neighboring Minnesota; 22,867 in liberal Wisconsin; 16,711 in Nebraska; and 18,904 in Kansas.[2]

Despite such hard evidence, we harbor a nostalgic picture of our ancestors as calm, family-oriented, noncontentious people. Although it was there, Iowa pioneer women seldom mentioned strife. Only one of the selections presented here includes murder and mayhem; one other touches upon social class divisions and alcoholism. Like the epic of uneducated women and those of color, the history of women in crisis has yet to be written.

Among those who contributed to this book and deserve my thanks are Laura Moran, acquisitions editor at Iowa State University Press, who suggested this project; Marvin Bergman and Christie Dailey of the State Historical Society in Iowa City, who supplied permissions; Raymond E. White, chair of the Department of History at Ball State University, who graciously made staff and computer time available; and Theo Roseberry and Jan Dragoo who helped transfer material to disk.

NOTES

1. For an advertisement of a black runaway indentured servant, see Ruth A. Gallaher, "Wanted—A Servant Girl," *The Palimpsest* 7 (April 1926): 116–19. For sources indicating the presence of other types of women in Iowa, see *Manual for Emigrants to America* (London: F. Westley and A. H. Davis, 1832); *The Annual Report of the Colonization Society of the State of Iowa, with the Proceedings of the Second Anniversary, in the Capitol, January 23, 1857* (Iowa City: Sylvester, Harrison & Brother, 1857); and Iowa Land Office, *Prairie versus Bush: Iowa as an Emigration Field* (Davenport: Cook & Sargent, 1859).

2. Department of Commerce and Labor, *Marriage and Divorce, 1867–1906* (Westport, Ct: Greenwood Press, reprint edition, 1978), 62. See also Glenda Riley, "Divorce in Linn County, Iowa, 1928–1944," *The Annals of Iowa* 50 (Winter 1991): 787–800.

PART ONE
Seeking a New Home

Homeseekers began trickling into Iowa in the late 1820s. The first white woman to settle in Iowa was probably Maria Stillwell. In 1828, Maria, along with her husband Moses, illegally "squatted" on land in the government-owned Half-Breed Tract near Keokuk. In 1829, Hannah and Dr. Isaac Galland followed. Hannah bore a daughter who is remembered as the first Anglo baby born in Iowa.

In 1832, when the Black Hawk Purchase Treaty moved the Sauk and Mesquakie Indians from eastern Iowa, the trickle of migrants soon became a deluge. By 1840, Iowa claimed 43,112 residents, not including Native Americans. This grew to 192,214 in 1850; 674,913 in 1860; and 1,194,029 in 1870.[1] It is little wonder that Iowa achieved statehood in 1846 and the Bureau of the Census declared the Iowa frontier closed in 1870.

In reality, of course, portions of Iowa experienced frontier conditions after both these events. The so-called Spirit Lake Massacre occurred in 1857, well after state-

1

hood. Less cataclysmic clashes between natives and migrants occurred with regularity. When conflict did not exist, settlers feared it. Therefore, rumors and alarmism were rife, even after land had been apportioned and most Indians removed farther west.

Today, we look back with a judgmental eye at western settlers. Yet, if we place them in the context of their own times, we must remember that most nineteenth-century people believed that they had the right—even the God-given mandate—to displace Native Americans from their homes and land.

In addition, settlers exploited land and other resources. This fails to jibe with today's environmental awareness and concerns, but pioneers also believed that God had provided such riches for their use. They would have also have argued for the natural renewal of resources and would have been incapable of envisioning either depletion or the huge number of people who would come westward in search of everything from subsistence to great wealth.

This is not to argue that pioneers were right, only to place them in their historical context. We also disparage nineteenth-century attitudes toward women, for they generally had less awareness and regard for women's roles, labor, and contributions than we do. The traditional legend of westering women, for example, tells us the trail was an excruciating trip which wrenched women from their homes and communities, thrusting them into chaos and even death. As contemporary scholars study the westward trail experience, however, they are finding evidence that numerous women chose to migrate, or at least supported the venture, and were stalwarts on the trail and in their new homes. Numerous women even migrated on their own—to teach school, to find other jobs, or to become wives.[2]

On the Iowa-bound trail, women typically continued their domestic chores, persisted as religious and cultural forces, and held their families together during this critical period of transition. After all, most were farm women who had the requisite skills for trail life. Along the way, women honed their abilities and prepared themselves for actual settlement. Trail women also bonded with other women travelers, with whom they shared recipes, work, childcare, and reassurance.

In some ways, then, trail women faced less disruption than men, who found themselves torn from their land, businesses, and usual activities. Instead, they had to drive stubborn oxen, ford swollen rivers, hunt strange game, and, most of all, remove native peoples from their paths.

When they reached Iowa, the situation frequently reversed itself. Women had to live and work in shelters ranging from the covered wagons in which they had made the trip to primitive shacks, cabins, and sod huts. While the men resumed known routines by going into the fields or establishing businesses, women had to provide their families with a plethora of goods, despite nonexistent or crude work spaces, equipment, and help.[3]

The Iowa women's accounts that follow range from the 1840s to the 1870s. They indicate similarities in motives for migration, problems encountered along the trail, and hopes for the new land. They also reveal that Iowa's pioneer women possessed a good measure of grit, determination, and ability to cope with drastic change and an unknown environment.

NOTES

1. *Iowa Historical and Comparative Census, 1836–1880* (Des Moines: n.p., 1883). Also helpful is Isaac Galland, *Galland's Iowa Emigrant: Containing a Map, and General Descriptions of Iowa Territory* (Chillicothe, Ohio: Wm. C. Jones, 1840), 3–17.

2. An early "personal" advertisement is found in "Pioneering Handicap," *The Annals of Iowa* 26 (October 1944): 89.

3. For more information, see Glenda Riley, *Frontierswomen: The Iowa Experience* (Ames: Iowa State University Press, 1981, 1994); "Women Pioneers in Iowa," *The Palimpsest* 57 (March–April 1976): 34–53; "Images of Frontierswomen: Iowa as a Case Study," *The Western*

Historical Quarterly 8 (April 1977): 189–202; " 'Not Gainfully Employed': Women on the Iowa Frontier, 1833–1870," *Pacific Historical Review* 49 (May 1980): 237–64; "The Frontier in Process; Iowa's Trail Women as a Paradigm," *The Annals of Iowa* 46 (Winter 1982): 169–97; and "Prairie Partnerships," *The Palimpsest* 69 (Summer 1988): 52–63.

THE DIARY OF
Kitturah Penton Belknap

ITTURAH PENTON BELKNAP, one of Iowa's first
frontierswomen and surely one of its most positive-
thinking and innovative, was born in a log cabin in
Hamilton County, Ohio, on August 15, 1820. Her parents, John and Magdalene Penton, were hard-working, religiously
oriented people who reared their children with love, a modicum of
education, and respect for the teachings of the Bible. At age nineteen, Kitturah left the family farm to marry George Belknap in
Allen County, Ohio. On October 17, 1839, only two weeks after
their marriage, the young couple sought a new home in what, at
the time, they regarded as the "Far West."

The couple migrated by covered wagon in company with four
other members of the Belknap family. After a tedious journey, during which the group considered and rejected Illinois, they finally
settled in one small cabin near the Des Moines River in Iowa
where they attempted to wrest a living from the prairie. Here Kitturah learned to function effectively as a frontier wife, bore four
children (three of whom died), actively engaged in church work,
and helped build the family's first real home.

As was typical of the early waves of settlers, the family decided to move yet farther west. After spending over a decade in
Iowa, during which time they often turned to religion as a source
of strength and had established a permanent home, the Belknaps
succumbed to "Oregon Fever," presumably at least partly in hopes
of improving Kitturah's and her son Jessie's health. On April 9,
1848, they loaded another covered wagon and began the long trek
to the Oregon country. Kitturah nursed her ill four-year-old child
on this trip while expecting a fifth baby.

After reaching Oregon, Kitturah bore five more children (two
of whom died of typhoid fever), helped her husband with his various farming and ranching ventures, and continued her religious
activities. Despite her own frequent bouts of illness, she lived a
long and active life. She died peacefully after an illness of one
week's duration in Coquille, Oregon, in 1913, four days after her
ninety-third birthday.

The portion of Kitturah Belknap's diary regarding her Iowa
years is presented here with the kind permission of her granddaughter, Doris Belknap Harem, of Corvallis, Oregon, and the
State Historical Society of Iowa. The spelling and grammar have
been slightly changed to facilitate reading, but the substance of the
diary is unaltered.[1]

On October 17, 1839, we gathered up our earthly possessions
and put them in a two-horse wagon and started to find us a home in
the Far West. We had heard of the prairie land of Illinois but we had
never seen anything but heavy timber land so we set our face westward. There were no railroads then. We traveled thru part of Ohio
and across Indiana and Illinois and crossed the Mississippi at Fort
Madison into Iowa. Was four weeks on the way and saw prairie to
our heart's content. Verily we thought the half had never been told.

We camped out every night, took our flour and meat with us and
were at home. Every night cooked our suppers and slept in our
wagon. We had a dutch oven and skillet, teakettle and coffee pot, and
when I made bread I made "salt rising." When we camped I made
rising and set it on the warm ground and it would be up about midnight. I'd get up and put it to sponge and in the morning the first
thing I did was to mix the dough and put it in the oven and by the
time we had breakfast it would be ready to bake. Then we had nice
coals and by the time I got things washed up and packed up and the
horses were ready the bread would be done and we would go on our
way rejoicing.

When we wanted vegetables or horse feed we would begin to
look for some farmhouse along towards evening and get a head of
cabbage, potatoes, a dozen eggs or a pound of butter, some hay and
a sack of oats. There were not many large towns on the way and there
was no canned goods to get then. Where there were farms old enough
to raise anything to spare, they were glad to exchange their produce
for a few dimes.

We stopped at Rushville, Illinois, and stayed four weeks. Expected to winter there but we heard of a purchase of land from the Indians west of the Mississippi and again we hitched up. Mid-winter as it was, we started never thinking of the danger of being caught on the prairie in a snow storm.

The second day we had to cross an eighteen-mile prairie and in the afternoon it turned cold and the wind from the northwest struck us square in the face. We had bought some cows at Rushville, had some boys driving them, and they would not face the storm so I had to take the lines and drive the team while my husband helped with the stock. I thought my hands and nose would freeze; when I got to the fire it made me so sick I almost fainted.

We came to a little house with a big family of children and they had plenty of wood for there was a point of timber run down into the prairie and in after years there was a town there called Westpoint. We got there about four o'clock in the afternoon. Had our provisions cooked up for the trip so we thawed some out a little and made coffee, and the kind lady put a skillet in the corner and made us a nice corn cake. We had bread, butter, good boiled ham and doughnuts. With good appetites we ate and were thankful.

When we had cleaned up, the woman hunted up the children and said, "Now children, you get off to bed so these folks can have a show to make down their beds for if they cross that twenty-mile prairie tomorrow they will have to start early and that little woman looks all pegged out. Now Honey, the best thing for you to do is to get good and warm and get to sleep." But, the "little woman" had the toothache, so she was not much sleepy. There was another family with us. Four of them and us two and eight of the household. We furnished our own beds and made them down on the floor. Tomorrow we cross the Mississippi into Iowa.

Up at four o'clock in the morning. Got our breakfast before the family was up. Crossed the river in the afternoon, traveled till about four o'clock then came to another eighteen-mile prairie and put up for the night. The next day started as soon as it was light. I had to drive the team again today and face the wind. It commenced snowing before we struck the timber. It was hard round snow and it seemed every ball that hit my face would cut to the quick. That night we had plenty of wood and a room to ourselves and the next day we went thru patches of timber and, oh my, but it was cold!

Now we're skirting the timber on the Demoines River and its

tributaries. Thought we could not quite make it so we camped again. The next day we got to the place about noon. Found the family living in the house yet to hold the claim. The house was a double, hued-log house. They let us have one room, and the two families of us lived in one room and we unloaded and commenced business.

The folks we bought the claim of went back to Missouri so we made trades with them and got ploughs, fodder, chickens and hogs. Made us some homemade furniture and went to keeping house. We had a quarter section [160 acres] of land. We thought that sounded pretty big but it was not paid for yet. The land had just been bought of the Indians and had not been surveyed so it was not in the market yet. We could settle on it and hold our claims and make improvements, but we must have the cash to pay when it was surveyed and came in to market or some land-shark was ready to buy it from under us. Then we would lose improvements and all so we had to get in and dig to have the money ready. The first thing was to get some land fenced and broke.

Our timber land was two miles from the prairie. I would get up and get breakfast so as to have my husband off before it was fairly light, and he would cut rail timber all day in the snow and bring a load home at night. Would take his dinner and feed for horses. He came in at night with his boots froze as hard as bones; strange to say he never had his feet frozen.

Now we must save every dollar to pay for our land. We had clothes to last the first year, and we got a dollar's worth of coffee and the same of sugar that lasted all winter and till corn was planted. We did not know anything about spring wheat then so our crop was all corn. Then while the corn was growing my husband made some rails for a man and got some more groceries. He had hauled the rail cuts and scattered them along where he wanted the fence and split the rails odd spells and laid up the fence when the frost was coming out of the ground. We had twenty acres of broke land fenced to plant to corn the first spring. Then we hired a man with a prairie team to break ten acres that was put into sod corn for fodder. It was not tended any, did not get very big, was cut up in the fall and fed out ears and all. The breaking team was five yoke of oxen with a man to hold the plough and a good-sized boy with a long whip to drive the oxen.

Now it is spring and we have got a few sheep on the shares and they are sheared. All this winter I have been spinning flax and tow to make some summer clothes. Have not spent an idle minute and now the wool must be taken from the sheep's back, washed and picked and sent to the carding machine and made into rolls, then spun, colored and wove ready for next winter. Our part of the land had no house on it so we still live in the little kitchen. Father Belknaps live in the other room.

Now it's harvest time. George is off swinging the cradle to try to save a little something, while I am tending the chickens and pigs and making a little butter (we have two cows). Butter is 12 1/2c a pound and eggs 6c a dozen. I think I can manage to lay up a little this year.

This year is about out. We sold some meat and some corn. Fresh pork is 5c a pound, corn 12 1/2c per bushel in the ear. Did not have to buy any clothes this year so we have skimped along and have $20.00 to put in the box (all silver). We will put the old ground in wheat this fall and break some more land for corn. Will have twenty acres of wheat in.

Now it's the spring 1840. The work of this year will be about the same. I have been spinning flax all my spare time thru the winter. Made a piece of linen to sell. Got me a new calico dress for Sunday and a pair of fine shoes and made me one homemade dress for everyday. It was cotton-warp, colored blue and copper and filled with pale blue tow filling so it was striped one way and was almost as nice as gingham. It is now May and the sheep are sheared and the wool must be washed and picked and got off to the carding machine.

So my summer's work is before me. It is corn planting time now so the men have their work planned till harvest. Now that the corn is layed by, George and I are going to take a vacation and go about ten miles away to a camp meeting. There are four young men and two girls going with us, but I made them promise there should be no sparking and they should all be in their proper places in time of service (for they were all members of the church). If they did not set a good example before the world and show which side they were on they could not go with me and they behaved to the letter.

This was the first camp meeting west of the Mississippi as far as I know. People came from far and near and I think there were about twenty clear conversions. Both the girls were married to two of the young men in the fall and lived to raise families who made good, useful men and women in church and state.

Now we have had a rest and have got strengthened both soul and body so we will go at it again. We have thought of trying to get things together this year to build a house next summer as we have about all the land fenced and broke that one man can handle. The crops are fine; our wheat is fine. Will have wheat bread now most of the time. The hogs did so well, can have our meat and quite a lot to sell. We more than make our living so we will have quite a lot to put in the box this year. We will get our wheat ground and get barrels to pack the flour in. Then will have to haul it sixty miles to market.

I think we got $3.00 a barrel. We took it to Keokuk on the Mississippi, then it was shipped off on steamboats.

It is now 1841 and we have most of the material together for the house. It will be a frame house, the only one in sight on this prairie. The coming generations will wonder how we built a frame house with no sawmill within fifty miles. Will have to go that far for nails as we cannot get any large quantity at the little stores here. "Where there's a will there's a way." The timber is all hued out of oak trees that grew on Lick Creek four miles away. Everything from sills to rafters are hued with the broad axe. The timber is very tall and fine. Oak and hickory trees make as many as three or four rail cuts and it splits so straight we can make anything we want of it. We found a carpenter who had some tools and he got to work for two days and layed out the work.

Then George and his father worked at it after the corn was layed by till harvest. Got the frame up and the roof on. There was one of our neighbors going to Burlington after goods for a man who was starting a store in a little town on the Demoines about four miles from us so we got them to bring us some shingle nails and we had made shingles in the winter. While I spun flax George brought in the shaving horse and shaved shingles and we burnt the shavings and both worked by the same light. We now have the roof on and it can stand awhile.

It is now August and the harvest is over and we have the sweetest little baby girl. Call her Hannah. We will now work some more on the house. While my husband is staying round he will be putting on the siding. He made that himself. Cut the trees and sawed off cuts six feet long. Then he split them out and shaved them with the drawing knife to the proper thickness. Put it on like weather boarding and it looks very well. The house is twenty-four feet long and sixteen feet wide. Will take off ten feet and make two bedrooms. The balance is the living room with a nice stone chimney and fireplace with a crane in one end to hang the pots on to cook our food. The house is to be lathed and plastered. Will get the lath out this winter. There is plenty of limestone and some men are burning lime kilns.

It's October. At the house again. Have it all enclosed and rocks on the ground for the chimney. Now it is time to gather the corn so when it is dry they will be husking corn as it is all cut and shocked. It will be husked out and stood up again and the fodder fed to the hogs.

November. Froze up and snowing. Will have winter now till the first of April. We will spend another winter in the little log house.

December. Cold and have had good sledding for six weeks. The upstairs drifted full of snow twice. The roof is put on with clapboards and weight poles. Father Belknaps live in the large room of the same house we do.

We have meeting [church services] there. The tenth was quarterly meeting. Saturday night it snowed and blowed so the upstairs was full of snow Sunday morning that we had to shovel it out and build big fires to get it dryed out so it would not drip before meeting time. We took up some of the boards and shoveled snow down and carried it out in the washtubs (barrels of it). Our room was not so bad. We had spread the wagon cover over it to keep out the cold so we rolled it up in a pile in the back corner and got breakfast in our room. The two families, the presiding elder, and two preachers all joined in prayers and then all took breakfast in that little room. I think it was fourteen by sixteen feet. No one seemed crowded or embarrassed and by the time breakfast was over the congregation began to gather. We opened the middle door and the preacher stood in the door and preached both ways for both rooms were crowded.

It was a grand meeting. By night the roads were broke and both rooms were crowded till there was not standing room. Had meeting again Monday and Tuesday nights. It was a happy time.

Time passes on and now it is time for the holidays. What will we have for Christmas dinner? For company, will have Father Belknaps and the Hawley family and most likely the preacher, twelve in all. And now for the bill of fare. What shall it be? No fruit for mince pies, no red apples to eat, no nuts to crack. They think I'm too young to get up a big dinner under the circumstances. All have gone to bed so I will make out my bill of fare.

Firstly; for bread, nice light rolls; cake, doughnuts; for pie, pumpkin; preserves, crab apples and wild plums; sauce, dried apples, meat first round; roast spare ribs with sausage and mashed potatoes and plain gravy; second round; chicken stewed with the best of gravy; chicken stuffed and roasted in the Dutch Oven by the fire, for then I had never cooked a meal on a stove. I think I can carry that out and have dinner by two o'clock if I get up early. I will cook in my room and set the table in the big room and with both of our dishes can make a good showing

Everything went off in good style. Some one heard the old folks say they had no idea Kit could do so well.

May, 1842, Van Buren County, Iowa. About the same routine of last year. Plant corn and tend it. We will be through planting this month then by the first of June what was planted first will need to be tended for it won't do to let the weeds get a start. They will go thru it with the one horse plough, two furrows between every row and two or three boys with hoes to clean out the hills and pull out all weeds (quite a tedious job if you have fifty or sixty acres). But now it is all thru and the sheep must be sheared.

Today the neighborhood all turns out to make a sheep pen on the bank of the Demoines River whither they will drive their flocks to wash them before shearing. And now the fun begins for all the men and boys are there to help or see the fun. There were five men with their sheep and their boys. George's were the first ones in the pen (thirty). They were taken one at a time out in the river where they could not touch bottom with their feet. Then the men hold their heads out of the water with one hand and with the other rub and souse them up and down till the water looked clean when they squeezed it out of the wool. Then they took them out to a clean apartment and when they got one man's done they sent the boys home with them and put them in a little clean pasture to dry and so till all was done. They all took their dinner and had a regular picnic.

Now it is June. The men are back in the corn except the sheepshearers. The sheep will be sheared this week, then the wool will lay out a few days to get the sheep smell off, then my work will begin. I'm the first one to get at the wool (sixty-five fleeces). Will sort it over, take off the poor short wool and put it by to card by hand for comforts. Then will sort out the finest for flannels and the coarser for jeans for the men's wear. I find the wool very nice and white, but I do hate to sit down alone to pick wool so I will invite about a dozen old ladies in and in a day they will do it all up.

Have had my party. Had twelve nice old ladies; they seemed to enjoy themselves fine. Had a fine chicken dinner. For cake I made a regular old-fashioned pound cake like my mother used to make for weddings. Now my name is out as a good cook so am alright for good cooking makes good friends.

July. My wool came home from the carding machine in nice rolls ready to spin. First, I will spin my stocking yarn. Can spin two skeins a day and in the evening will double and twist it while George reads the history of the U.S. Then will read some in the Bible together and have prayer and go to bed feeling that the sleep of the laboring man is sweet.

My baby is so good she don't seem much in my way. Time moves on and here it is September and the new house is about ready to live in this winter. Have been having meeting in it this summer so it's been dedicated and we will try to say "as for me and my house we will serve the Lord."

November. Everything is about done up and we have moved in our own house. Have not got much to keep house with but it is real nice to have things all my own way. Have got my work for the winter pretty well in hand. Have made me a new flannel dress colored blue and red; had it wove in small plaid. I am going to try and make me one dress every year then I can have one for nice and with a clean check apron I would be alright. I made some jeans enough for two pairs of pants. And have the knitting done so we have two good pair of stockings for all.

It seems real nice to have the whole control of my house. Can say I am monarch of all I survey and there is none to dispute my right. I have curtained off a nice little room in one corner so we can entertain the preachers and they seem to enjoy it. Our house is right at the crossroads and they say it is such a handy place to stop. It is right on the road going any direction so I try to keep a little something prepared.

March, 1843. The years have been much the same. This has been the most tedious winter I ever experienced.

April 1st and everything frozen solid yet. We have a nice little boy now and I don't see as two babies are any more trouble than one. I put them both in their little cradle and the little girl amuses the baby till he gets sleepy. Then I take them out, give the baby some attention while the little girl plays round the house and after they have exercised their muscles I fix up the little nest and lay the baby down to go to sleep. Then the other comes running to be "Hept in to by-by baby to seepens" and they are both soon asleep. I fix one in each end of the cradle and shove it to one side and then I just make things hum for they are both babies. The oldest is only a year and a half old.

We have got fixed up very nice in our new home. Have a good well close to the door and a nice little natural grove on the west (crab apples and wild plums). The crabs are large and fine for preserves and the plums are fine too. Back of the house north is a piece of very rich soil. It is called Hazel Ruff. It has hazel bushes all over it but when grubbed out is very fine land. There we have prepared a place to raise melons and we have them in abundance.

Now I want to tell you how I make a substitute for fruit. Take a nice large watermelon, cut it in two and scrape the inside fine to the hard rind. It will be mostly water and when you get a lot prepared, strain it thru a sieve or thin cloth. Squeeze out all the juice you can, then boil the juice down to syrup. I then took some good musk melons and crab apples, about half and half, and put them in the syrup and cooked them down till they were done, being careful not to mash them. Put in a little sugar to take the flat off and cook it down a little more and you have nice preserves to last all winter (and they are fine when you have nothing better and sugar 12 1/2c a lb. and go forty miles after it). On the east end of the house we have a garden.

November, 1843. I have experienced the first real trial of my life. After a few days of suffering our little Hannah died of lung fever so we are left with one baby. I expect to spend this winter mostly in the house but as we have meeting here at our house I can see all the neighbors twice a week for we have prayer meetings Thursday

evenings. Have commenced to build a church on our land; it will be
brick. We are going to have quarterly meeting here about Christmas.
If it gets very interesting will protract it thru the holidays.

January, 1844. The meeting is over and the house cleaned up.
We had a good time and the house was packed every night. Good
sleighing, and everybody seemed to be interested. We had two beds
in the house and a trundle bed that we could shove under one bed.
Then in the evening I would put both beds on one bedstead and take
the other outdoors till after meeting, then bring it in and shift the beds
and make it up for the preachers. The one that was left in was used
for a seat and to lay the sleeping babies on while the sisters were
helping carry on the work. It was no uncommon thing for the noise
to become so great that it would rouze some of the babes and a man
would take it up and pass it along to the fireplace where there was always a warm corner reserved for the sisters with little ones.

The meeting lasted for ten days. Had over twenty conversions,
and I thought that was about the best time I ever had. I cooked by the
fireplace and our one room served for the church, kitchen, dining-
room, bedroom, and study for the preacher. Sometimes we had three
or four as they came from adjoining circuits to help us thru the work.

January, 1845. We have another little boy born December 23,
1844. We call him Jesse Walker. The first name for his grandfather
Belknap, the second for our family doctor who was also a local
preacher, a fast friend, and good neighbor. We are still taking up the
subject of building a church. Have the lot on the west corner of our
land near the burying ground. We gave five acres for that and two for
the church. It is to be of brick. Tonight we have company. Three
neighbors and their wives have come to spend the evening and while
they are talking about the amount of brick it will take to build the
church, I am getting a fine supper in the same room by the same fire.
Took the chickens off the roost after they came and will have it ready
about ten o'clock. Had fried cakes (had fresh bread), stewed chicken
and sausage and mashed potatoes. Had a fine time. Had prayers before they left at fifteen minutes after twelve.

June, 1848. Summer comes again with its busy cares. They
have got to work at the church and I am boarding three men to get
money to pay my subscription of $10.00 to the church. I have had to

pass thru another season of sorrow. Death has again entered our house. This time it claimed our dear little John for its victim. It was hard for me to give him up but dropsy [excess water] on the brain ended its work in four short days. When our pastor was here a week before he said he thought that child was too good for this wicked world but he little expected to be called to preach his funeral in less than one week. A bad cough and pain in my side is telling me that disease is making its inroads on my system.

October. We have got thru our summer work and now we are preparing for winter. Have raised a good crop but will have to feed it all out this winter; will have a lot of hogs to fatten.

November. Have had a month of cold, frosty nights and now we expect a freeze up; cold northwest winds prevail. I'm going to stay at home this winter and see if I will take so much cold. We have another baby; such a nice little girl. Only six pounds at first and though it is a month old is not much bigger than at first. It has never been well so we have two children again for a while; neither of them are very strong.

The church is not finished but the roof is on so it will stand over winter and meeting will still be at our home. We are fixed nicely in our home now. Have had a very pleasant winter and now it is springtime (1847) again and they all think I had better go on a visit to Ohio. The past winter there has been a strange fever raging here. It is the Oregon Fever. It seems to be contagious and it is raging terribly. Nothing seems to stop it but to tear up and take a six months trip across the plains with ox teams to the Pacific Ocean.

May, 1847. Some of our friends have started for Oregon. They will meet others at the crossing of the Missouri River and make laws and join together in a large company.

Husband and I and two children start for Ohio to visit my father and mother. We go by wagon to Keokuk. There we take the steamer on the Mississippi to St. Louis, thence to Cincinnati. There we get a team to take us out six miles to my sister's. Stayed there one week, then they took us out to Hamilton thirty miles to another sister's. Stayed there three days, then took the canal boat for St. Maries'. Got on the boat Monday evening and got off at the landing at three o'clock Tuesday morning.

There was a little shack there and as there was no one on the stir we had to stay there till daylight. I took our wraps and made a bed for the children and we nodded till people began to stir. Then we hunted up the town and found the hotel and got breakfast. While we were eating we saw an old man just on the other side of the table and we recognized Mr. Jones, one of our old neighbors. We kept our eyes on him and when he left the table we made ourselves known to him. He said, "And this is little Kittie Penton that you carried off from us a few years ago. Well! Well! She has got to be quite a woman." He said he had just been in with a load of oats and was going home empty so he could take us to our journey's end. It was twelve miles to my father so we thought we were in luck.

We got to Mr. Jones' at noon so we stopped and fed the team and got a good warm dinner. Then had about four miles to go yet so we hitched the horses up again and about four o'clock we drove up to my father's gate. They were greatly surprised as we had not written them we were coming. We all seemed to enjoy the trip. The children seemed to be much better than when we left home but I was no better. Everyone would say how changed I was till I really thought I was sick and going into consumption [tuberculosis], but my baby seemed better.

I knew it would be the last visit I would make there whether I lived or not but I kept all these thoughts buried in my own breast and never told them that the folks at home were fixing to cross the plains while we were away. Taking it all around we had a good time. We were there a month, then it came time to say goodbye. The last few days the baby was growing weaker and I wanted to get home where it would be more quiet. All the friends have visited us and Sunday we had a good social meeting and said goodbye to all the friends. It was hard for me to not break down but they all thought in about two years we would come again.

On Tuesday, June 1st, we were ready to start for home. We went by wagon twenty-five miles to Springfield and there we struck the railroad that was just being built from Cincinnati to Columbus, Ohio. It was not finished any further than Springfield so we stayed there all night and in the morning got on the car for Cincinnati. That was our first car ride and the first railroad we had ever seen. We got to ride seventy-five miles. Our little boy was asleep when we got on and when he woke up he looked all around surprised and said, "Where is the horses?"

At noon we were on the bank of the Ohio River. If we had gone with a team would have taken three days. There we found the same old steamboat that brought us down. It had made its trip and was just steaming up to leave the wharf so we got on board again for home. Were on the water two days and one night.

Then we were at the mouth of the Desmoines River where we had arranged to get off and meet a team to take us home (about forty miles). It was a fine level road and by getting an early start we could make it in a day. Now we had been gone a month and traveled all kinds of ways. Just as we landed Father Belknap drove up to meet us. We had friends there so we stayed all night with them and the next day we went home. They thought I looked better for the trip but the baby was failing all the time.

We found the folks all excitement about Oregon. Some had gone in the spring of 1847. Four families of our connection and many of the neighbors but they had not been heard from since crossing the Missouri River. All was excitement and commotion. Our home was sold waiting our return to make out the papers.

It was all fixed up for us to live with Father Belknaps as the man wanted the house on our place. Ransom's and Father's had not sold yet. It did not suit me to live with them so I told them it was out of the question. For the first time since our marriage I put my foot down and said "will and won't" so it was arranged for us to go and live in their house till it was sold. I knew it would use me and the little sick baby up to be in such a tumult. There was nothing done or talked of but what had Oregon in it and the loom was banging and the wheels buzzing and trades being made from daylight till bedtime so I was glad to get settled.

My dear little girl, Martha, was sick all summer and October 30 she died, one year and one month old. Now we have one little puny boy left. So now I will spend what little strength I have left getting ready to cross the Rockies. Will cut out some sewing to have to pick up at all the odd moments for I will try to have clothes enough to last a year.

November, 1847. Have cut out four muslin shirts for George and two suits for the little boy (Jessie). With what he has that will last him (if he lives) until he will want a different pattern.

The material for the men's outer garments has to be woven yet. The neighbors are all very kind to come in to see me, so I don't feel lonely like I would. They don't bring any work, but just pick up my sewing, so I think I will soon get a lot done. Then they are not the kind with long sad faces but always leave me with such pleasant smiling faces that it does me good to think of them and I try not to think of the parting time but look forward to the time when we shall meet, to part no more.

Now I will begin to work and plan to make everything with an eye to starting out on a six month's trip. The first thing is to lay plans and then work up to the program. The first thing is to make a piece of linen for a wagon cover and some sacks. Will spin mostly evenings while my husband reads to me. The little wheel in the corner doesn't make any noise. I spin for Mother Belknap and Mrs. Hawley and they will weave. Now that it is in the loom I must work almost day and night to get the filling ready to keep the loom busy. The men are busy making ox yokes and bows for the wagon covers and trading for oxen.

Now the new year has come and I'll write (1848). My health is better and I don't spend much time with housework. This is my program. Will make a muslin cover for the wagon as we will have a double cover so we can keep warm and dry; put the muslin on first and then the heavy linen one for strength. They both have to be sewed real good and strong. I have to spin the thread and sew all those long seams with my fingers then I have to make a new feather tick for my bed. I will put the feathers of two beds into one tick and sleep on it.

February. The linen is ready to go to work on and six two bushel bags all ready to sew up. That I will do evenings by the light of a dip candle for I have made enough to last all winter after we get to Oregon. Now my work is all planned so I can go right along. Have cut out two pairs of pants for George (homemade jeans). A kind lady friend came in today and sewed all day on one pair then took them home with her to finish. Another came to buy some of my dishes and she took two shirts home to make to pay for them.

Now it is March and we have our team all ready and in good condition. Three good yoke of oxen and a good wagon. The company have arranged to start on the 10th of April. I expect to load up the first wagon. George is practicing with the oxen. I don't want to leave my kind friends here but they all think it best so I am anxious to get off. I have worked almost day and night this winter. I have sewing about all done but a coat and vest for George. He got some nice material for a suit and had a tailor cut it out and Aunt Betsey Starr helped me two days with them so I am about ready to load up. Will wash and begin to pack and start with some old clothes on and when we can't wear them any longer we will leave them on the road. I think we are fixed very comfortable for the trip. This week I will wash and pack away everything except what we want to wear on the trip.

April 5th. This week I cook up something to last us a few days till we get used to camp fare. Bake bread, make a lot of crackers and fry doughnuts, cook a chicken, boil ham, and stew some dryed fruit. There is enough to last us over the first Sunday so now we will begin to gather up the scatterings. Tomorrow is Saturday and next Tuesday we start so will put in some things today. Only one more Sunday here. Some of the folks will walk to meeting. We have had our farewell meeting so I won't go. I don't think I could stand it so George stays with me and we will take a rest for tomorrow will be a busy day.

Monday, April 9th, 1848. I am the first one up. Breakfast is over and our wagon is backed up to the steps. We will load at the hind end and shove the things in front. The first thing is a big box that will just fit in the wagon bed. That will have the bacon, salt and various other things. It will be covered with a cover made of light boards nailed on two pieces of inch plank about 3 inches wide. This will serve us for a table. There is a hole in each corner and we have sticks sharpened at one end so they will stick in the ground. Then we put the box cover on, slip the legs in the holes and we have a nice table. When it is on the box George will sit on it and let his feet hang over and drive the team. It is just as high as the wagon bed. Now we will put in the old chest that is packed with our clothes and things we will want to wear and use on the way. Then there is the medicine chest. There will be cleats fastened to the bottom of the wagon bed to keep things from slipping out of place.

There is a vacant place clear across that will be large enough to set a chair. Will set it with the back against the side of the wagon bed and there I will ride. On the other side will be a vacancy where little Jessie can play. He has a few toys and some marbles and some sticks for whip stocks and some blocks for oxen. I tie a string on the stick and he uses my work basket for a covered wagon and plays going to Oregon. He never seems to get tired or cross (but here I am leaving the wagon half packed and getting off on the journey).

The next thing is a box as high as the chest that is packed with a few dishes and things we won't need till we get thru. And now we will put in the long sacks of flour and other things. The sacks are made of homemade linen and will hold 125 pounds. There are four sacks of flour and one of corn meal. Now come the groceries. We will make a wall of smaller sacks stood on end; dried apples and peaches, beans, rice, sugar and coffee, the latter being in the green state. We will brown it in a skillet as we want to use it. Everything must be put in strong bags; no paper wrappings for this trip.

There is a corner left for the washtub and the lunch basket will just fit in the tub. The dishes we want to use will all be in the basket. I am going to start with good earthen dishes and if they get broken I have tin ones to take their place. Have made four nice little table cloths so am going to live just like I was at home. Now we will fill the other corner with pick-ups. The ironware that I will want to use every day will go in a box on the hind end of the wagon like a feed box.

Now we are loaded all but the bed. I wanted to put it in and sleep out but George said I wouldn't rest any so I will level up the sacks with some extra bedding, then there is a side of sole leather that will go on first, then two comforts and we have a good enough bed for anyone to sleep on. At night I will turn my chair down to make the bed a little longer. All we will have to do in the morning is put in the bed and make some coffee and roll out.

The wagon looks so nice. The nice white cover is drawn down tight to the side boards with a good ridge to keep from sagging. It's high enough for me to stand straight under the roof with a curtain to put down in front and one at the back end. Now it's all done and I get in out of the tumult. Now that everything is ready I will rest a little then we will eat a bit. Mother Belknap has made a pot of mush [corn-meal porridge] and we are all going to eat mush and milk to save the milk that otherwise would have to be thrown out. Then we have prayers and then to bed.

Tuesday, April 10, 1848. Daylight dawned with none awake but me. I try to keep quiet so as not to wake anyone but pretty soon Father Belknap's voice was heard with that well-known sound, "Wife,

wife, rise and flutter," and there was no more quiet for anyone. Breakfast is soon over. My dishes and food for lunch are packed away and put in the proper place. The iron things are packed in some old pieces of old thick rags. Now for the feather bed; I nicely folded the two ends together and lay it on the sacks. The covers are folded and the pillows laid smoothly on, reserving one for the outside so if I or the little boy get sleepy we have a good place to lie. Now my chair and the churn and we will be all done.

Our wagon is ready to start. I get in the wagon and in my chair busy with some unfinished work. Jessie is in his place with his whip starting for Oregon. George and the boys have gone out in the field for the cattle. Dr. Walker calls at the wagon to see me and give me some good advice and give me the parting hand for neither of us could speak the word "farewell." He told me to keep up good courage, and said, "Don't fret; whatever happens don't fret and cry for courage will do more for you than anything else." Then he took the little boy in his arms and presented to him a nice Bible with his blessings and was off.

NOTE

1. Glenda Riley (ed.), "Family Life on the Frontier: The Diary of Kitturah Penton Belknap," *The Annals of Iowa* 44 (Summer 1977): 31–51.

AN AUTOBIOGRAPHY
AND A REMINISCENCE
Mary Ann Ferrin Davidson

ONE OF IOWA'S early frontierswomen, Mary Ann Ferrin Davidson, moved even more frequently than Kitturah Belknap. Apparently, she did so without reluctance. In fact, she described herself as "fond of adventure." After reading her account, one might more accurately describe her as courageous and determined.

Born in Vermont in 1824, the second oldest of seven children, Mary Ann migrated to Blackford County, Indiana, in 1837. Five years later, she married Joseph Carper Davidson, originally from Ohio. During the winter of 1845–46, the couple moved to Iowa. They became the first white settlers in Marshall County and lived among Mesquakie Indians. In their thirteen years, the Davidsons learned how to till the land, watched the government remove the Indians to a reservation in Missouri, and lamented the destruction of the land's natural beauty.

The Davidsons moved again in 1859, this time trekking overland to the Willamette Valley in western Oregon with their four sons and one daughter. In 1890, Mary Ann and Joseph relocated one last time—to Woodland, Washington, on the Lewis River south of Portland. They continued to live in Woodland until their deaths. Joseph died on January 12, 1909, from a cold complicated by advanced age. Mary Ann followed nine days later on January 21 as a result of failing health, asthma, and the stress of losing Joseph.

The following is Mary Ann's story, written in 1902. She not only recorded her experiences as an Iowa settler, but noted the first white marriage in the county, the first white baby born, and even the activities of various Indian groups. The unabridged autobiography is reprinted here with permission of the State Historical Society of Iowa.[1]

I WAS BORN in Ludlow Township, Windsor County, Vermont, August 5, 1824. My father's name was John Ferrin, and my mother's maiden name was Mary S. Davis; and both of them were born in Vermont. My parents had seven children, three sons and four daughters. I was their second child and eldest daughter. My eldest brother died when he was nine years old of scarlet fever; also my second brother aged three died two weeks later of the same disease.

When my father was a young man, he enlisted and served during the War of 1812, which lasted three years. He was in several hard battles, but escaped without being wounded in any of them. My father learned the hatter's trade, but did not follow it, as he preferred farming for a livelihood; therefore, I was brought up to work as other farmer's daughters usually were in those days. I attended school six months of the year, from age of seven until I attained my thirteenth year.

In the fall of 1837, my parents emigrated to the state of Indiana, bought a piece of land and settled on it, three miles south of the town site of Montpelier in Blackford County, fifty miles of Fort Wayne. Blackford and several adjoining counties were then a backwoods country and sparsely settled. Wild animals of most kinds, such as inhabit these western states, were quite numerous; and the report of the huntsman's gun was often heard throughout the day, and coonhunters and their dogs could often be heard throughout the fall and winter months. Bears were plentiful in this section of the country. We often saw deer and wild turkeys in large flocks near our premises, and often partook of their delicious meat. Large gray-wolves often howled so near our house that it was terrifying to hear them. Wild bees were plentiful and many gallons of honey were obtained from trees in which it was deposited. There were many [maple] sugar orchards in the community, and we had good times eating warm sugar every season in the spring of the year.

Several families from Vermont had come and settled in the vicinity of Montpelier. Mr. Abel Baldwin, a man from Windsor County, Vermont, laid out the town and called it Montpelier. The greater number of inhabitants in this section of the country were Hoosiers, and their mode of talking was quite different from the Yankees which caused no little mirth and observation for both parties.

We often had social gatherings in the neighborhood called chopping parties and sewing bees. The host would have chopping or railsplitting for the men, and the hostess would have quilting or sewing for the women to do. All came early and worked till night, then after partaking of a sumptuous supper they would join in dancing, and seldom dispersed until morning. They did not dance quadrilles or round dances, for those had not been introduced in this vicinity at that time; but those kinds which were called contradances—French Four, jigs, etc., and those were danced without being called off.

It was at one of those parties I met and was introduced to Joseph Carper Davidson, a young man twenty-one years old. He was born in Freeport Township, Harrison County, Ohio, December 30, 1819. He was of fair complexion, with blue eyes and goldish hair. We afterward became acquainted and within a year from that time were engaged to be married.

I only attended school four months after we came to Indiana. The summer that I was eighteen, I was employed to teach a three months subscription school[2] (which included thirteen weeks) in the Greenland district, about four miles from Montpelier. I taught for one dollar a week and board, which was considered good wages in those days for times were very hard.

The following Christmas, 1842, I was married to Joseph C. Davidson and soon went to housekeeping in a new log cabin which my husband built on a piece of land that we owned adjoining my father's. We lived there until the winter of 1845. We then sold our place and removed to the state of Iowa.

We then had one child, a healthy rosy-cheeked, blue-eyed and golden-haired little boy, one year and a half old. He was my parents' only grandchild, and the first baby that had made my sisters aunts and my brother an uncle; and of course they all thought he was the nicest baby in the land; and it was very grievous for them for us to go so far away as Iowa as they could not see us again soon. Initially the time arrived for us to take our departure, and we bade them all good bye with many tears.

We journeyed by land as far as Cincinnati; and there went on board the "Tobaccoplant," a large and commodious steamboat from the lower Mississippi; and steamed down the Ohio to its mouth; then, up the Mississippi to St. Louis which was as far as the "Tobaccoplant" went. We then took passage on board the "Boreas," a crazy old packetboat; but it took us safely to Keokuk, which was as far as we wanted to go by water. We were then in Iowa, and as there were no railroads in the state at that time, we employed a teamster to take us to our destination in Washington County, a distance of eighty miles over the beautiful prairies dotted here and there with groves and farmhouses. John Havens, my husband's nephew by marriage, was then living near Richmond in Washington County, and Jonathan S. Davidson, my husband's youngest brother who was then a single man, was living there with them, so we stopped with Havens' six weeks.

Now, at that time there was a large section of country where the land was yet unclaimed lying along the Iowa River, about one hundred miles above Iowa City, which had not long been purchased from a tribe of Indians called the Musquakees, belonging to the Sac and Fox tribes. A party of men from Mr. Havens' neighborhood had gone up there to take a look at the country before we arrived. They came back highly pleased with their discovery and set forth its extra advantages in glowing colors.

Mr. Thomas Bennett, a neighbor of Mr. Havens who was one of the party, came and asked us if we would not like to go up there that Spring and select a claim to settle on. He said that the place he liked best was in Marshall County some thirty miles above any whites settlement; and as he had a wife and several small children, he was very anxious to have us go up there with them. We told him that we would, for we thought it would be better to go that spring if we went at all, for then we could have first choice of prairie and with timberland adjoining; which would be a great object to us.

Finally the time came for us to go; but we were few in number. Mr. Bennett, brother Jonathan, and my husband were the only men. Bennett had concluded not to take his family that spring as he thought it would be better for him to go first and build a cabin and do some breaking [of ground for planting] and then return for his family; so, I was the only woman in the company. I was fond of adventure and preferred to go with my husband and on the 10th of May we started for our future home in Marshall Co., Iowa. The greater part of the way was over a wild and trackless prairie. We forded the streams that was on our route, though one was so deep we had to bridge it before we could cross it.

On the last day of our journey when we were within eight miles of our destination, after having some difficulty crossing quite a large stream that Bennett called Raven Creek—he said that one of the party of surveyors shot a raven near the creek and that gave rise to its name. We camped to let our cattle graze and to prepare dinner. Just as we had got our vituals ready to be eaten, Mr. Bennett exclaimed, "See, yonder comes a Musquakee!" We looked in the direction he pointed, and sure enough, there was "lo, the poor Indian," riding down the creek under cover of bushes, within bowshot of us. I felt rather nervous and asked Mr. B. if he thought the Indian would come to our camp. He replied that he surely would and we would have to ask him to eat with us, and while we were talking the red man of the prairies rode up, dismounted and tied his pony to a sapling nearby. He appeared to about thirty years old, tall and well-formed. His blanket hung gracefully over his left shoulder, leaving his brawny chest and right arm exposed to view. He came striding up and greeted us by saying, "How-dy-do." Mr. B. returned the salutation, and invited him to dine with us. He replied by saying, "How," which meant yes, and seated himself on the ground near our humble table. Mr. B. asked him a few questions in the Musquakee tongue which sounded very queer to me. He stayed with us until we were ready to move on again, and then he piloted us for two miles on to the next creek; and after waiting to see our wagons fairly safe across, he laid whip to his pony and soon disappeared in the distance beyond.

This creek we named Indian Creek and it was ever afterward known by that name. After we crossed Indian Creek, we traveled two miles and a half over a level bottom lying along the Iowa River, then our route led over a hill. When we had arrived at the upper part of this bottom, we were surprised to see a small town of Indian huts and some forty or fifty Indians of all ages running to meet us; some of the younger boys were entirely nude, and nearly all had bows and arrows. I had never seen such wild savages before and my heart palpitated so that I could scarcely speak for I expected that they intended to murder us all right there and then would have our scalps drying around the fire in their council lodge before the next morning; for there was no alternative but to submit to our fate.

They soon approached us, and a stalwart Indian demanded us to stop, and we obeyed at once. He asked in broken English where we were going. Mr. B. told him as well as he could that we were going up the river about three miles from there and was going to build a house, plow up the prairie, and make a farm, and grow corn. They all listened very attentively and seemed to understand what he said; but to our surprise they made no objection. They asked if we had flour and bacon to swap for "sonnio" (money). Mr. B. told them we had not. We then moved on and I felt somewhat relieved when we passed out of sight of them and over the hill; but the scene which we had just witnessed had considerably changed my romantic idea of going into a new country into a reality; and I began to feel timid and lonesome for it appeared we had gotten a long ways into the western wilds of America.

Before we had got half-way to where we wished to stop, the sun had set, and the gloomy shades of night were fast surrounding us; but Mr. B. knew the course we wished to travel, and we trusted all to him. We slowly rolled along, and at last we drove down into a bend close to the river and stopped on a sandy bank near a beautiful grove. Mr. B. said that was the grove he had told us of, and that it was the best place for the present to camp.

The oxen were soon released from the wagons and turned out to graze, a fire was made, and a pail of water brought from the river; the supper was prepared of which we all partook with a good relish, and then we retired to our wagons to sleep. But it was some time before I could close my eyes to sleep for fear of the Indians; and as I lay awake I listened to hear any strange noise; but I heard nothing except an owl hooting in the distance, and the gentle murmuring of the stream.

The next morning was delightful. The sun shone resplendently over the eastern hills. The groves were clothed in green, and the birds cheered us with their various songs. The beautiful rolling prairies covered with luxurious grass lay stretched to the south and west of us as far as eye could reach, with here and there a belt of timber which marked some watercourse meandering to the river. All was unmarred by the avaricious white man, and, therefore, appeared the more lovely to us.

We were well pleased with the country where we were, both in regards to prairie and the nice grove of timber which lay joining it on the west; and there was no need of looking further for a better situation for a home in Marshall County. So there we stuck our stakes on the 16th day of May, 1846, one mile north of where the town of LeGrand is now situated. Mr. Bennett took his claim at the next grove, one miles and a half west from our claim, and brother Jonathan took a claim adjoining ours on the west in Tama County.

The following day we selected a building site, and my husband and his brother went to work preparing logs to build a cabin; and Bennett began breaking prairie for us. The next day after our arrival eight or ten stalwart Indians came to our camp and stayed quite awhile. They looked sullen and did not have much to say; and we were glad when they mounted their ponies and rode away. We were not annoyed by having any more visits from them for several days. But before we had got our cabin made, six grim looking warriors came riding up and dismounted. Their faces were painted in various colors, and their heads were ornamented with feathers and carved bones. We saw by their looks and manners that they were greatly displeased. They came striding up and seated themselves upon the ground close to our camp; then one of them— probably their best orator—began speaking in a loud authoritative style, making gestures and marking lines on the ground with his knife. Mr. Bennett looked chopfallen. We asked him what the trouble was; he replied that the Indian said we were trespassing upon their grounds; that the white man's land was eight miles down the river near Raven Creek, and that we must go away immediately. Now we were satisfied that what the Indian said was not true for Marshall County had been surveyed and sectionized; so we told them plainly we would not go away from there, for this land belonged to the white man. Finally when they saw they did not scare us much, they said we might stay and raise corn and oats for their ponies to eat; but no more white people should settle there.

We proceeded with our work and soon had our cabin rolled up as high as we conveniently could for want of more help and covered with clapboards, bound on by weight of poles; and we were glad to take shelter within its rough walls, without having a chimney or floor made in it; for there came a heavy rain storm that lasted nearly a week. A few days after the rain subsided brother Jonathan returned to Washington County where business called him; then our number was one less and we felt pretty lonely; but within a few days after brother left us, two men came from Bear Creek thirty miles below where we were living. They had two stout breaking teams and were going across the Iowa River to take up claims and do some breaking for themselves which was not far from where Freedonia is now situated. But the river was out of its banks caused by the recent rains and they could not cross it with their teams, so we employed them to break twenty acres of prairie for us. We then had thirty acres broken up, and part of it planted in corn, pumpkins and watermellons which grew to perfection. We had mellons enough to supply the Musquakee tribe. They carried them away by ponyloads in sacks. Mr. Bennett, to be doubly sure of not trespassing upon Indian grounds, left his claim and went back two miles beyond Raven Creek and took up another claim on a small creek in Tama County, broke a few acres of prairie and then went home to bring his family out. We named that creek Bennett's Creek and we believe the name has been perpetuated.

The river still remained so high that those men could not cross with their teams after they had finished breaking for us, so they went down to Raven Creek and took some claims, did some breaking and then went home.

We then were left alone, to the mercy of our Musquakee neighbors, thirty miles beyond any white settlement; and thus we remained five weeks without seeing or hearing from any white person; though, not withstanding our lonely position, we enjoyed ourselves very well for awhile. Nearly every day we would take a stroll to view the picturesque scenery, for the landscape was new and pleasing to us; the verdant groves and the magnificent rolling prairies adorned with grass and brilliant flowers of various colors waving to the breeze one swell after another till lost from view like the placid waves of the ocean, were delightful to behold; and all was untrampled and unmolested, save by a few Indian ponies that could be seen grazing here and there, or their owners galloping in the distance in search of them when needed.

The Indians more or less of both sexes came nearly every day to our house and the most of them were friendly. We had learned a few of their words so we could talk some with them which helped to pass away the monotonous hours through the day; and the hum and stings of millions of musquetoes and the shrill notes of the whippowils, bore us company through the night.

At last we were visited by that terrible Foe, chills and fever, which attacked ourselves and baby Lucien every day with grim vengeance; and as we had no one to wait upon us, our suffering and loneliness was hard to bear. The fever which raged very high scarcely left us from one chill to another; nevertheless, we had to rally ourselves every evening to prepare some little refreshments and milk our two cows. Our nearest access to water was the river and our best way to get there was three-quarters of a mile from our cabin; and

as we could not get along without water, my husband was obliged to
go that distance every evening for a pail of water. He was so weak
that be had to lie down several times to rest himself by the wayside
before reaching home. Thus the time passed for two weeks. Finally my husband was
taken dangerously ill of a sinking chill; baby and I were sick in bed.
I heard him say, "Oh, I'm so sick I fear I cannot live!" He was then
vomiting very hard. I got up immediately and prepared some hot teas
which he drank to no avail; he still continued vomiting and purging,
and was becoming very weak. I did all I could to help him, but nothing seemed to relieve him, that I could give him for we had no doctor's medicine in the house. I was greatly alarmed. Night was fast
setting in and a terrible thunderstorm was approaching from the
northeast; and ere long the rain was pouring down, accompanied by
heavy winds. The fire was about to be put out by the rain—we had
no stove at the time—and there was no wood in the house nor none
in the yard to replenish it. What was now to be done? I could not let
the fire go out; for the only way I could keep my husband alive was
by giving him something warm to drink. I quickly thought of the
hickory-pole bedstead the men had occupied while they were stopping with us, chopped it to pieces and placed some of them on the
fire and covered them with bake-kettle lids, and by that way I managed to keep the fire from being put out by the rain.

The vivid flashes of lightning and the loud peals of thunder
were terrifying, and the rain poured down as if the heavens were
opened. The wind and rain blew through the crevices of the cabin so
hard that I could not keep a light burning; but the room was illuminated by flashes of lightning most of the time. Our baby being sick
and frightened cried so hard, that I had to hold him in my arms a long
time before I could get him composed to sleep.

The storm raged till after midnight. My husband had become so
sick and weak that he could not be moved without fainting and could
not speak above a low whisper. His limbs were cold and his visage
wore the aspect of death. At last, he was taken with the cramp; I then
thought he was dying and redoubled my efforts to save him. I rubbed
his limbs with all my might and applied hot flannels wrung out of
strong mint tea to his stomach and bowels. I also continued giving
him ginger tea to drink; but he threw it up immediately after swal-
lowing it, though it seemed to be the only thing that kept him alive
for it warmed his stomach. The rain sprinkled his face where he lay

and helped to keep him from fainting. Four hours I anxiously watched over him expecting every minute he would breathe his last. About three o'clock in the morning his sickness took a turn for the better; he rested easier and went into a doze of sleep.

Thus I went through that dreadful night all alone, with no one to speak a sympathizing word to me, no one to call on for redress in that lonely cabin, thirty miles from any white person, and not even an Indian within three miles of us, of whose company I should have been more than thankful.

Daylight came at last and I rejoiced that my husband was still alive; but if he had been dead he could not have looked more like a corpse than he did that morning. While he rested and our baby was asleep, I hastened to the river for some water which we were obliged to have.

After all that I had gone through during the night, I expected to have a very hard chill by ten o'clock, as that was the usual time for my chill to come on; but was happily surprised by not having a symptom of a chill that day. Probably it was the shock my system had undergone during the night that had broken the chills on me, for I did not have another chill that season.

My husband gradually gained strength and in a few days he was able to be around, for his chills were also broken up.

We remained alone about ten days longer, when one morning our longing eyes beheld a covered wagon coming over Indian Town hill two miles away; and our joy can better be imagined than described when we saw as it came nearer that it was brother Jonathan's. The cause of his long absence was that he too had been sick of a bilious fever,[3] and as soon as he became able to drive he started for our place with a load of provisions, which if we had not been sick we should have been out of before, for we had no way of obtaining any.

Brother informed us that Mr. Bennett and his family were sick of the chills and fever and concluded not to move up to their claim until the next spring.

Fall came and we were anxious to save our crop of corn which we had raised that summer, so we could winter our stock, for we intended to stay there. My husband overworked himself in cutting the corn fodder, and was taken very sick again of a fever. For eight days he did not taste food, and it seemed doubtful if he ever would recover, but finally he became a little better and could eat some very light food but we gave up the absurd idea of trying to winter there, so far from the settlement and late in October. As soon as my husband was able to be moved, we bade good bye to our home in Marshall County where we had lived five months without seeing a white woman—and not but a few white men—and returned to Washington County to spend the winter.

My husband remained ill all winter; he had the third day ague[4] and was not able to chop our firewood. In the spring he gradually regained his health, and on the 11th day of May 1847 we started again to our home in Marshall County, accompanied by Mr. Bennett and family, brother Jonathan and Samuel Davidson, my husband's nephew, who was a single man 19 years old and had lately arrived from Blackford County, Indiana. Bennett stopped on his claim in Tama County, and we proceeded on to ours ten miles further on up the river.

We found our cabin as we had left it, but a party of surveyors who had camped there a few weeks in the winter, had used up five or six bushels of our potatoes which we carefully buried for seed, and had fed nearly all of our corn that we left stacked and nicely covered with prairie hay to their horses, which was quite a loss for us being so far from any settlement.

That spring soon after our return, there were three families by the name of Asher who came to Marshall County from Flint River, Henry County, Iowa, and took up claims on Linn Creek, ten miles west of us and went to farming. Samuel Davidson took a claim one mile and half southwest of us, on what is now called Davidson Creek, and got five acres broken up that spring. He took his claim for his father, William Davidson, my husband's eldest brother, who was then living in Indiana.

We got along very well that season, although we were sick a good deal during the summer of chills and fever. We raised about eight hundred bushels of corn, some potatoes, and a good many garden vegetables that season so we had plenty to live on through the winter, besides having some corn to sell to our neighbors.

The Musquakee Indians kept coming back from their reservation in Missouri till there were five or six hundred congregated in and around their town that summer. Some of them were saucy and impudent and all were more or less troublesome. There was scarcely a day for several months without some of them being at our house; and their ponies molested our cornfields a good deal, for sickness had prevented us from getting our field enclosed. But fortunately for us

those Indians all went away from that section of the country long before winter set in, as it was customary for them to do every fall, and
go where they could get provisions more Plentifully; but returned
early the next spring to make sugar, and prepare their patches of
ground for growing corn and beans.

In the month of July brother Jonathan and Samuel Davidson
went back to Washington County for a load of provisions and we
were left alone for three weeks, but we did not feel nearly so lonely
as we did the first summer, for now we had white neighbors within
ten miles of us.

Bennett's folks were sick a good deal of the time that summer
with the ague. One day while our boys were gone, an Indian informed us that Bennett and all of his family were very sick, and my
husband went down to see how they were getting along; he found
them so sick he remained over night with them and did not get home
until afternoon of the next day. I stayed alone within three miles of
six hundred Indians, except for our little baby and the dog. I felt
rather lonesome but no harm happened to me.

During that summer we dug a well 46 feet deep and obtained
good water which proved to be lasting; and made our cabin comfortable for the winter.

Mr. Bennett and wife became so discouraged that they moved
back to Washington County that fall, and left their claim for all time.
In November brother Jonathan and Samuel Davidson also went back
to Washington County to spend the winter where they could get work
to do, as they needed the money to help them along. So we were left
alone to pass the winter the best way we could, isolated so far from
white people.

The Mr. Ashers came a few times during the winter to buy corn
and would stay all night with us. Brother Jonathan came once during
the winter, and brought us some pork and groceries, but he only
stayed a few days; and the rest of the time we spent alone. But as we
bad pretty good health and the winter was mild, we got along well;
although we experienced a good many lonely hours.

Mrs. Bennett was the only white woman that we saw for several
months and I only saw her while she stayed here, excepting Mrs.
Booker. She and her husband were going on a visit to her parents,
Mr. and Mrs. Isaac Asher, and stopped over night with us. Mrs.
Booker had flaxen hair and blue eyes. Our little boy asked me why
that woman had "blue" hair. He had never seen a woman that had

light colored hair, since he could remember. Mrs. Bennett and myself had black hair and eyes.

In April 1848, Brother Jonathan came up to see us and brought some more groceries and flour, but did not stay long; being a single man he had concluded to give up his claim and return to Richmond, Washington County and work at cabinet making, which trade he had been learning the past winter; and Sam Davidson had also concluded to stop near Richmond and work at the nursery business.

So we were left alone, but there were a good many white men who stopped with us that season, as they were out looking for claims in Marshall County to settle on.

We plowed and planted over twenty acres that spring, and raised a fine crop of corn, potatoes and beans, besides lots of turnips, pumpkins, and a good garden. We did all the work ourselves, with only one yoke of young oxen, and as they were not used to plowing I had to drive them, for there were neither man nor boy that we could hire in the county.

That summer there were fully twelve hundred Indians in and around Musquakee—several hundred of the Winnebago and Pottawatamie tribes had come [with] the Musquakees that season, and we were annoyed a great deal by them for as many as sixty on an average came to our house nearly every day; but the most of them were friendly to us. There were two men by the name of Haskel and Abbot came and stopped with us for several weeks that summer and sold provisions, tobacco and calico to those Indians, which made them still more troublesome; for these men kept their goods in our house, and they would flock in by the dozens.

In June 1848, there was born to the wife of Isaac Asher a son, and on the 19th of October of the same year, we were presented with a little daughter, and they were the first white children born in Marshall County.

The winter of 48–49 was very severe. Snow fell on the 22nd and 23rd of December to the depth of two feet, and it snowed several other times during the winter to the depth of six or eight inches in a single night, and the ground was not entirely bare until the 10th of April. There was no travel in the section of the country for two months excepting on snowshoes. We were five weeks and two days at one time without seeing a white person. Our white neighbors as well as ourselves had to do without bread except what we pounded corn to make. It was next July before we had bread because the high water prevented us from going to a mill as the streams were not bridged.

A few families of the Winnebagoes were camped for the winter near the mouth of Timber Creek, which was about three miles west from our piece; and some of them came to our house nearly every day to buy corn; and as we could talk with them, they helped to pass away some of our lonely hours.

One day that winter my husband had an altercation with a bad-tempered Indian, which ended in a frightful scuffle. He was a tall stalwart Indian, about thirty-five years old, much superior in size and strength to my husband, besides my husband was quite lame of rheumatism in his shoulders. He came with his squaw and several other Indians, to "swap" some buckskins for corn. We traded satisfactorily with them and all tied up their sacks and went away excepting this one Indian. His squaw asked him to tie up his sack; he said, "No," and then told my husband to give him some more corn for his buckskin; he told him plainly that he would not. The Indian then snatched the skin, and said he would take it and the corn too. My husband seized hold of the skin at the same time, and each tried to jerk it from the other; the Indian became so exasperated that be soon relinquished the buckskin and seized hold of my husband's hair and jerked him down onto his knees with great violence upon the floor.

I was much frightened, and stood motionless for a few seconds, but presently became roused to action. Seizing a large wooden poking stick I aimed a blow at his bead; but the scoundrel saw me and warded off the blow. At the same time he threw his big arm around me, clinched hold of my hair and held me tight as a vise against his left side; still bolding his grip on my husband's hair, and keeping him bent down nearly to the floor; so it was impossible for him to defend himself in such a situation. A furious struggle ensued; for the savage was trying to hold us both, so we could not get away from him, and we were trying to disengage ourselves from his iron embrace, so we could defend ourselves if possible. I still held the stick in my hand and managed to strike his head several times; but he soon managed to stamp the stick out of my hand. I then began to scratch his face and eyes but he quickly put a stop to that fun, for he managed to catch hold of my hand with his teeth and hold it tightly. He bit my hand so hard that the scars remained for some time. I then could do nothing but submit to my fate.

Presently my husband succeeded in grasping the poking stick firmly with both hands and soon would have broken the Indian's legs with it, but he saw his danger and immediately let go his grip from both our heads, and jumped backwards a few feet, and stood watching our movements like a panther. We then expected that he would kill us all, for he had a large knife sticking in his belt; but to our happy surprise he made no further attempt to injure us, neither did he demand any more corn; but stood there looking at us, and appeared to regret that he had pulled so much hair from my head; for presently he said he would bring me a pair of moccasins. We told him we did not want any of his moccasins and bade him to take his sack and leave the house, which he did without any further hesitation, and never came into our house afterwards. His squaw was waiting outside the door for him, and they quickly disappeared out of our sight over the hill.

When the Indian seized hold of my husband, his squaw ran to him and plucked him by the coat, and said something in an excited manner; but he heeded her not. She then ran out of the house and hallooed for the other Indians to come back; but they had gone out of hearing. Our little baby girl was lying asleep in a rocking chair pretty close to the fire near where we were scuffling and the chair came very nearly being turned over several times. The squaw seeing that the child was in danger, moved the chair to the back part of the room. Probably our baby would have been killed had it not been for this kind-hearted squaw. Our little boy, who was then four years and a half old, screamed and cried, still he had presence of mind, for during the fracas he took the fire shovel and struck the Indian on the back several times with it. He said that he did not want to hurt him very much, but be wanted him to let papa and mama alone.

We did not see another Indian for several days; finally, there was quite a crowd of them came, and among them were some of the oldest men in their camp. We felt rather discouraged at seeing them for we thought, probably, they had come down to make us some more trouble, and perhaps they would take possession of our corn crib. But we soon saw they did not intend to be uncivil toward us, and they spoke very indignantly of the Indian who had so badly misused us, and said he was a bad Indian, and often quarreled and fought with his own people. They asked if we would sell them some corn; and when we told them that we would, they were much pleased and said they were afraid that we would not "swap" any more corn to them, since that bad Indian fought with us. Ever after that the most of them treated us kindly as long as they stayed there. We had had several quarrels with other Indians since we had been living there, but none so fearful as this one.

Thus we passed that long, cold and dreary winter, a winter ever to be remembered by us. But spring came at last, and we rejoiced to hear the birds sing and see the prairies covered with green grass once more. But as the streams remained high, there was but very little travel until July; therefore, we did not see many white people until late in the season.

In June, 1849, brother William Davidson arrived at our place with his family. They stopped several weeks with us until they could get some corn planted and a cabin built on the claim that their son Samuel had taken for them in the spring of 1847.

There were several other families that came and settled in Marshall County that season; but none nearer than Timber Creek, seven miles above us.

In the fall of 1849, Mr. Isaac Asher and family left their claim and came down and settled on the claim that brother Jonathan had left in Tama County. They had two grown daughters still living at home with them. Frances the elder was twenty years of age and Ann the younger was eighteen. They were both nice girls and were a great deal of company for us, as they often visited at our house, and often assisted me about my work, so the time passed quite pleasantly with us that winter.

Now in the progress of time, Samuel Davidson and Miss Ann Asher became acquainted with each other. Their love was reciprocal and they were married on the 18th of July, 1850. Their marriage was the first one consummated in Marshall County.

We were not troubled by the Indians during the winter of 1849–50, for they all went away in the fall but returned in the spring as usual to grow corn and beans. They were civil toward the white people and gave no cause whatever to frigten them in regard to taking their lives and plundering their houses; however, the people who were living on Timber Creek and Linn Creek became very much alarmed; for someone of their neighbors had seen an Indian with his face painted black and they considered that was a sure sign of war; so they set to work at once to build a temporary fort on Timber Creek and while the fort was being built, they heard that a party of Indians were encamped on Iowa River, only a few miles above them, and several families became panic-stricken, and said it would not be safe for them to stay there longer. So they threw their heaviest cooking utensils into the hazel brush so as to hide them from the Indians— and where, it was said, they could not find all of them after they returned—and loaded up their wagons with their lightest household effects and made tracks as fast as possible for the settlement on Skunk River.

One man suggested that someone ought to let Davidsons know of their impending danger; another replied that there was no time to lose; for this was a case of life, and death, and everyone must look out for himself. Though the next day after the panic, a young man from Timber Creek came to our house and requested my husband to go with him to the Indian village and have a talk with the Indians. My husband complied with his request, and saw no signs whatsoever of hostility. They all appeared just as friendly as usual; and when he spoke of the alarm among the people of Timber Creek, they were perfectly surprised and said the white men were "heap mean" to raise such a lie on them.

Nevertheless, those people who were living on Timber Creek that had courage enough to stay molded bullets, and finished building the fort and moved into it, and stayed there ten days. Finally as no Indian warriors had made their appearance, they concluded that it was a false alarm; so they left the fort, returned to their homes, well satisfied that there had been no bloodshed, although they had had several quarrels among themselves.

That same spring and summer, there were about twelve hundred Indians living in Indian town and vicinity, and we were all becoming tired of them; for they were damaging the timber. They chopped the sugar trees, and peeled the bark off valuable trees to make their wickiups, and were a nuisance in many other respects; besides they were preventing the country from being settled near their town, as most white women were afraid of them, and could not bear the idea of living in that vicinity.

So the white people petitioned the Government to have them removed; and in the latter part of July the Dragoons [soldiers armed with short muskets] came and took them away to their reservation in Missouri.

In the year of 1850 there was a Post Office established at Timber Creek; before that time we had no Post Office closer than thirty miles.

In 1851, people began to settle up Marshall and Tama County very rapidly, and in a short time town sites were located, flouring mills and sawmills built, bridges built across the Iowa River and minor smaller streams; churches and schoolhouses erected and the prairies were broken up and disrobed of their natural beauty. There was a good flouring-mill built on the Iowa river, within a quarter of a mile of our place; so we no longer had to pound corn to make our bread.

Brother Jonathan Davidson named our home in Marshall county "Mooshane" which is an Indian name signifying "Morning Sun," and it was a very appropriate name, for our place lay sloping to the East and there was a beautiful grove above on the West side.

We lived at Mooshane thirteen years, then sold our place to Mr. Ami Willett, a neighbor of ours, and on the 15th day of May 1859, we bade adieu to Mooshane, and started on our long journey across the plains for the Willamette Valley in western Oregon.

NOTES

1. Mary Ann Ferrin Davidson, "An Autobiography and a Reminiscence," *The Annals of Iowa* 37 (Spring 1964): 241–61.

2. Each scholar subscribed, or paid, an agreed upon amount of corn, other produce, or money for a prescribed term.

3. Technically, bilious fever results from a liver ailment. Usually, the term meant something like the flu, with headache, indigestion, nausea, and a high temperature.

4. A fever characterized by regularly recurring chills.

Grandmother's Story
THE MEMORIES OF
Mary Elizabeth Lyon

M ARY ELIZABETH LYON migrated to Iowa in 1852 when she was only eight years old. The family planned to buy land with the land warrants that Mary's grandfather had earned by service in the War of 1812. Two years later, however, her family moved again in search of richer land in which to invest the warrants. It was a more comfortable trip than Mary Ann Ferrin Davidson experienced, for Iowa, which had achieved statehood in 1846, now offered some roads and other conveniences to settlers. Still, Iowa migrants feared conflict with Indians. One of Lyon's clearest memories is a rumored "uprising" that came to nothing.

Fortunately for later generations interested in early Iowa women, Mary Elizabeth's granddaughter, writer and amateur historian Bessie L. Lyon, preserved her grandmother's memories. During World War I, as her grandmother sat and knit stockings for the Red Cross, Bessie, her brown-eyed namesake, settled down by her knee. Bessie begged her grandmother to tell "about your coming to Iowa." When her grandmother replied, "It is a long story and I hardly know where to begin," the young woman urged her to go on.

Bessie Lyon later wrote down her grandmother's words; they first appeared in *The Palimpsest* in 1924. They are reprinted here in slightly abridged form by permission of the State Historical Society of Iowa.[1]

T HE COLONY travelled very comfortably, though not rapidly, across Ohio, Indiana, and a part of Illinois. Desiring to strike the Mississippi at Keokuk they left the Cumberland Road, and came across country by whatsoever roads or trails they could find, fording streams, wading through mud, and enduring untold hardships. I remember the great bows of the old ox-drawn wagon, and can feel yet the lurch and chug of the big wheels, as they struck the ruts and hummocks along the way.

Usually mother drove a part of each day, thus letting father walk behind, while brother William rode our faithful horse, Jim, and drove old Spot and Whitey and the young cattle which we were bringing to our new home. There were three of us children old enough to run along behind or ride Jim and we took turns in herding our live stock, which frequently paused to graze by the wayside.

Once, shortly before we reached Keokuk, there was a terrible downpour of rain which delayed us for several days. Pushing on through the deep, black mud of Illinois, we finally came to drowned land that seemed scarcely passable. As our team was in the lead, father urged his oxen on. "Get up, Buck! Go long, Dime!" he coaxed, and with final application of the ox goad he bravely sought to cross the swamp. Buck and Dime did their best—but at last, puffing and panting, they stopped dead still.

The wagon was hub deep in the mire, there was no dry land near, and the wagons behind were too far away to help us escape. Father crept out on the wagon tongue, unyoked the oxen, and headed them back to the edge of the swamp. Mother, with the baby in her arms, mounted old Jim, William crept up behind her, while sister Nan and I each climbed on father's shoulders—for by this time he had waded in up to his knees. "Go on, Jim, pull us out," he said, as he grasped old Jim's tail. Jim seemed to know he was saving the family, for with great care he threaded his way back to firm ground. Another horse was taken from one of the other teams and he and Jim pulled the heavy wagon out, backwards.

When we reached the Mississippi we waited our turn to be ferried across to Keokuk. To our childish eyes, the sight of the great, seething mass of water brought terror indeed. Father and Mother spoke so reassuringly, however, and even the animals walked on to the boat so calmly that our fears subsided.

Our family stayed two years in Louisa County but my father felt that the land must be richer away from the river, so he went to investigate north central Iowa before he invested grandfather's land warrants. In Hamilton County he located land for himself along White Fox Creek in Cass Township. He also preempted[2] several other farms for relatives who had money as well as warrants to invest. A farm that sold for sixty thousand dollars just before the war boom was one that he took up from the government for my grandmother Stengher.

I remember well his preparations for that trip—how mother looked after every button on his coat, and how she sewed a peculiar band inside his shirt. In this was stitched the money with which the relatives who had no land warrants wished him to pay for their land.

Late one cold day in March, 1854, we arrived at Newcastle, now Webster City, and pushed on as rapidly as possible in hope of reaching the log cabin up on White Fox Creek, which was to be our new home. How anxiously we children scanned the unbroken prairies, looking for that log hut! The roads were muddy and Buck Creek was very high, so we had to leave our goods on the bank that night. The family with a few conveniences were successfully ferried across on old Jim, however, and by dint of walking and carrying many bundles, we made the last two miles of our journey on foot.

But alas for our high expectation! The log cabin was utterly desolate, and it gave ample evidence of having been used as a stable, rather than a human dwelling place. Small wonder that my mother, remembering the pretty little white house back in Ohio, sat down and wept.

But pioneer women spent little time in crying and mother soon had a fire going. Somehow we got settled. The old hut was made cheerful by being papered with clean newspapers. We children went to the woods, dug up gooseberry bushes, and planted them in neat rows. How much good we got from those old bushes! We started a wild plum grove near the house, and Father had some young apple trees sent from Louisa County.

Mr. P. W. Lee, now one of the substantial citizens of Webster City, says that the first apple he ever saw or ate was one I gave to him when he and his father, J. W. Lee, came to visit us. His father was our school master, who had come from Ohio with us and whom we held in high esteem, and it is probable that I plucked some of the first fruit of our young trees to give to little "Willie."

But the greatest event I can remember of our early life on White

Fox Creek was the first fair held in Hamilton County. As I said before, we brought old Spot and Whitey from Ohio, and they and their offspring furnished us with milk and butter. Down under the bank of the creek was a shelving rock, beneath which a wonderfully cool spring flowed. Here my mother managed to keep the milk and butter cool even in the heat of summer. In the fall of 1857, everyone was urged to exhibit products at the fair and I can see yet the roll of butter, daintily marked and as smooth as marble, that mother sent to the fair. She won first prize on it, too.

The next year news came of an Indian uprising. With the terror of the Spirit Lake massacre [1857] vividly in mind Mother and we children hastily grabbed a few belongings, packed a basket of food, and Father took us in the wagon to Webster City[3]. From there a regular train of wagons, loaded mostly with women and children, started for Boonesboro. Father returned to our home, determined to defend it.

The party got as far as Hook's Point, now Stratford, where darkness compelled a halt. There was no shelter save one cabin, so the wagons were drawn into a circle, a fire built, and everybody sat up and talked all night. The following morning messengers came bearing the good news that the alarm was false, and so the whole company turned around and reached home that night, tired but safe. ...

We all ran and grabbed him, fairly weeping with joy. It meant so much to us that Father was safe, and that this Iowa home was safe too, for we had just found out that we loved our new home in this great new State of Iowa.

NOTES

1. Bessie L. Lyon, "Grandmother's Story," *The Palimpsest* 5 (January 1924): 1–8.

2. According to the Distribution-Preemption Act of 1841, settlers could stake prepurchased claims on most surveyed lands. They later bought up to 160 acres for the minimum government price of $1.25 an acre—or, in this case, the equivalent in land warrants given for military service. Default lands were frequently available for preemption as well.

3. It was common to take protective measures against Indians, who were understandably upset and "hostile" about the loss of their former homes. Bessie Lyon later wrote that, "The best means of escape, according to a prevalent idea, was to hide in a

hollow log. ... Laura Cooper Treat, who came from Pennsylvania to Webster City when she was twelve years old, relates with what trepidation she and her mother embarked down the Ohio River in 1857. She had been told that the wind blew over the vast prairies of Iowa so hard that people had to lie down and clutch the tall grass to keep from being blown away. As for the Indians, she made up her mind that three hollow logs should lie in their yard—one for each member of the family." From Bessie L. Lyon, "Prospecting for a New Home," *The Palimpsest* 6 (July 1925): 325–26.

A PRAIRIE DIARY
Mary St. John

THIS DIARY was written by twenty-year-old Mary St. John. In 1858, she came from Walton, New York, to Iowa with her family: father Isaac, fifty-two (1806–1883); mother Rhoda Lindsley, forty-eight (1810–1871); brothers Aaron, seventeen, Benjamin, ten; and sisters Esther, twenty-two, and Emma, eighteen.

Isaac St. John farmed the family land near Walton, but in the 1850s he sold the farm to enter a partnership in a Walton tannery. Within a few years the partnership dissolved and he decided to seek more productive farmland in the West. Hearing of a land sale at Osage, Iowa, in the spring 1857, Isaac set out as an "advance agent" for his family. When he reached Iowa, he located near the Seely family, former neighbors from Walton, and with their help purchased a suitable piece of land at the head of Crane Creek, three miles northwest of Saratoga (between Riceville and Cresco).

Mary's diary spanned the year 1858, but she made scant mention of the family's travel preparations. On February 23 she recorded that they began to assemble things to pack and on February 25 she noted that "Father had an auction for the purpose of selling our furniture ... most of them sold as well as could be expected."

The St. Johns left their New York home around the first of March. They "took the cars" (railroad) for the West. "Today is the first time I was ever in a car in my life," Mary wrote. "I like riding in them first rate." The St. Johns, who took the opportunity to visit friends and relatives along the way, rode the "cars" to Chicago, Milwaukee, and finally to Prairie du Chien. On March 31 they crossed the Mississippi River into Iowa by wagon and ferry.

Due to Isaac's firm belief in education, all the older children had received schooling back in New York. Mary obtained a teaching certificate shortly after arriving in Iowa. Sometime around the first of June, 1858, Mary left for Round Grove where she taught and was "boarded." A second writer continued the diary without interruption, probably Mary's sister Esther or her mother, judging from internal references to other family members. The change in handwriting indicates that Mary took over again in the fall but soon turned the diary back to the second writer. Mary later married Charles D. Cutting on September 3, 1863, and gave birth to her only child, William, on February 11, 1865. If she kept other diaries between 1858 and her death at the early age of 31 on June 3, 1869, they unfortunately are not extant.

Because this document contained entries for almost every day of each month, it gives a remarkable feel for the repetitious nature of women's domestic labor, which had to continue even as the family established a new home. Of course, young single daughters like Mary and her sister did their share, for every member of a family was also a worker. The diarist herself sometimes seemed wearied by the unending routine. She wrote "baking and so on this morn," "mopped the floor of course," or simply "etc., etc."

Mary had joys as well. She used exclamation points for things like especially nice weather, the Fourth of July, or the novelty of several wagons passing by the St. John homestead at one time. Frequent visitors and the arrival of letters also seemed to provide a welcome break in the tedium.

Mary's description of building a family home also offered a number of insights. She indicated that the field and crops came first, the home second. When renovation of the existing house finally began, even Mary's mother participated, including performing such heavy work as "lathing," or putting siding on the house. Throughout the preparation of both the fields and the house, labor sharing with neighbors played a critical role.

The Iowa portion of the 1858 diary is presented here with the kind consent and cooperation of Mary St. John Cutting's granddaughters, Merle Cutting Bohnet and Verna Cutting Lusher of Rancho Cordova, California, and the State Historical Society of Iowa. It has been slightly altered and condensed to aid readability.[1]

APRIL

1 Thursday. We started from Decorah this morning and rode till a little in the afternoon and we stopped at New Oregon [later named Cresco] for dinner. Got stuck in the mud about a mile from Mr. Seely's and Emma and I walked to the house.

2 Friday. Father has been after his oxen today and the rest of us staid to Mr. Seely's.

3 Saturday. Esther, Emma and I went up to S. W. Seely's today. Esther is going to stay all night. Emma and I came down home with Mr. D. Seely.

4 Sunday. Father, Mother, Emma, Benny and I are here to Mr. Seely's today. The wind has blowed very hard all day.

5 Monday. Have not been out of the house but once today and then Emma and Emma Seely and I went up to meet Father and had a ride after the oxen.

6 Tuesday. All came over home this morning except Mother and she staid to S. W. Seely's. Unpacked some of our things and made up two beds.

7 Wednesday. It has rained most all day. Mother has come over today. Esther, Emma and Aaron and myself staid in our house alone last night.

8, 9, 10, Thursday, Friday, Saturday. [No entries]

11 Sunday. We have all been at home all day today. It has been very cold and it has rained all day, thundered some.

12 Monday. Have washed today but it rained so we had to put our clothes a soak.

13 Tuesday. Father and Aaron have made some stools today and a Drag.[2] It has rained some. The wind has blowed pretty hard all day but it looks some as if it might clear off tonight.

14 Wednesday. Today we hung our clothes and they got dry. Father and Aaron went out to look around on the farm and Aaron shot a Badger. I have written to Abbie, Sylvia and E. M. Ogden today. It has been a very pleasant day.

15 Thursday. Mrs. Ann Seely and Charley, Mrs. Allen and Emma Seely have been here visiting to day. Mrs. Seely drove the oxen.

16 Friday. Father and Aaron have been over to Mr. Spencer's today and did not get home till most night. E. and B. and I picked a nice mess of flowers today.

17 Saturday. We set out our current bushes this forenoon. Aaron is dragging this afternoon and Father has gone down to Mr. Field's.

18 Sunday. We are all at home again today and it is raining very hard. The stage driver and one passenger came here this morning and said they lay out on the prairie all night.

19 Monday. Aaron has been down to the city today but he did not get any mail. Father has made some cucumber boxes today.

20 Tuesday. Today we have washed and baked some bread.

21 Wednesday. Father went to Mr. S. W. Seely's after the mail, got one letter and I got one from Charley.

22 Thursday. Done our ironing today and baked and in the afternoon tried to keep the stove warm. The wind blew very hard.

23 Friday. Father, Aaron and Ben have been over to S. W. Seely's.

24 Saturday. Father, Aaron and Benny have been down after some wood today. Shot one chicken while they were gone.

25 Sunday. [No entry]

26 Monday. Father started for New Oregon this morning. Aaron went down to the city. Got one letter for Father from Uncle Aaron.

27 Tuesday. Father has not come home yet. There are prairie fires most all around us tonight.

28 Wednesday. Last night about twelve o'clock Father came home from New Oregon. They have been ploughing some today and dragging some.

29 Thursday. Father has ploughed the garden today and commenced sowing his wheat. We had a call from Mr. Patterson tonight.

30 Friday. Father, Aaron and Benny have been down after some wood this afternoon. Father got a letter from Uncle Aaron and I got one from Aunt Maria.

MAY

1 Saturday. Father went to help move Mr. Torcey's house this forenoon and went from there to Mr. Canaday's and brought home some corn.

2 Sunday. We have all been at home all day today.

3 Monday. We have not washed today on account of rain. It has rained very hard all day.

4 Tuesday. Father and Aaron have been over to Mr. Torcey's after lumber.

5 Wednesday. We have washed today. Smith Seely came over here this morning. Father, Aaron went after wood and Benny went home with Mr. Seely. Two gents called to get a drink of water.

6 Thursday. Father and Smith Seely have been to Mackintires after oats today. Mr. Seely stopped here to tea.

7 Friday. Mr. Seely came over here this morning about five o'clock after some oats and Esther went home with him. Father and Ben went over to Capt. Bennet's and Emma and I rode up to ridge and went to Mr. Seely's.

8 Saturday. Father went down to Saratoga this morn and the boys went after wood. Esther got a letter from Mr. Patt and one from Edwin yesterday and Mr. P. wrote some to B.

9 Sunday. Mr. Hallet came here today to see if we had seen his cow.

10 Monday. Father started for Decorah this morning with Salmon and Mr. Allen and his wife. Mr. A. and wife are going east. Aaron has been dragging today. We washed today.

11 Tuesday. Ironed this morning. Father came from Decorah this afternoon.

12 Wednesday. Father has sowed some wheat and Aaron has been dragging.

13 Thursday. Mr. Chamberlain called here this morning to tell us that Sally Sigler was dead. Father has been down this afternoon to attend the burial. Father got a letter from Uncle Aaron, Esther got one from Em Berry.

14 Friday. J. Seely came over here this morning. S. W. and Charley came to bring her.

15 Saturday. Jennie is here yet and just at night we all went to take a walk.

16 Sunday. We have all been to meeting today but Mother and Benny. Colonel Sanders read a sermon and we elected S. W. Seely superintendent of the Sabbath School and Mr. Gibbons librarian.

17 Monday. Washed this morning but did not hang up the clothes on account of rain. Charles Cutting [her future husband] called here this forenoon. Father and Ben have been after a load of wood today.

18 Tuesday. It is a very pleasant day today or at least was this forenoon. Father has been over to Mr. Gough's after a cow and calf today.

19 Wednesday. It was very pleasant this forenoon but has rained most all the afternoon. Father has been over to Mr. Smith Seely's this afternoon.

20 Thursday. Father started for Decorah this morning with Salmon. Aaron went down to the Post Office and got four letters and one paper. Mother went over to S. W. Seely's this morning and Emma and I went after her at night.

21 Friday. [No entry]

22 Saturday. Father came home today. Mary, Emma and Benj. went down to Saratoga to meet him.

23 Sunday. Had a heavy rain and thunder shower last night. Very warm during the day. All went to meeting. Only sixteen present. The creek was so high that people could not cross it.

24 Monday. Washed and mopped. Em. Seely spent the day. Mr. D. Seely and Mr. White came just before dinner. Mr. Chamberlain here to tea. Mary and Emma have gone home with them.

25 Tuesday. Father and Benjamin gone to Riceville. Brought home a pig and a kitten. Mother and E. went down the creek for a walk in the afternoon.

26 Wednesday. Rinsed and hung up the clothes, baked bread, mopped, etc. Benj. went for the girls, missed them, they came home first. Planted garden and corn in the afternoon.

27 Thursday. Ironed. Father and mother brought home three letters, some crackers, potatoes, etc. this afternoon.

28 Friday. Mrs. Seely and Sandin, Mr. White and Salmon visited here today. Baked bread, cake and pies. Mr. W. stays all night.

29 Saturday. Rain today. Churned, mopped and so on.

30 Sunday. Rained so hard we could not go to meeting. Father went down afoot, but no one else came and there was no meeting.

31 Monday. Washed a good big wash, mopped, and baked. Had a platform fixed before the door, dug stone. A call from Mr. Fox in morn.

JUNE

1 Tuesday. Ironed. Mary, Emma and Benj. went to Saratoga. Mary stays down to get a [teacher's] certificate. Raining at bed time.

2 Wednesday. Baked bread, Mary came home this morning. Has rained much today. Had a call from Mr. Rice.

3 Thursday. Another heavy thunder storm last night, creek very high this morn. Aaron went to Mr. Ricker's to get boots mended. Mary has gone to her school. Mr. Huyck called a little while. Mr.

White is here to stay all night. There is a heavy fog to night. *4 Friday.* Cloudy and showery this forenoon. Mr. White and Benj. went a fishing. Mr. W. left afternoon. Mr. S. W. Seely here to breakfast. Father and Aaron have dug stone some. Es., Em. and Ben. went out for flowers this eve. Clear sunset!! *5 Saturday.* Have baked, mopped etc. Father and Aaron dug and drew stone in forenoon. Went after wood this afternoon. Sent for the N. Y. *Evangelist.* Has been pleasant all day though rather windy. *6 Sunday.* Cloudy with a little rain. All went to meeting. 25 present. Reading of 2nd Lecture in "Jay's Christian Contemplated" by Mr. Sanders. Subject, "Christian in the Closet." Plenty lightning with some thunder and rain and wind this eve. *7 Monday.* Clear but windy. Washed and baked bread. Mr. White and Mr. Chamberlain came up in the morn. Too wet to break.³ Aaron has been dragging. Planted corn this afternoon. Mr. W. and C. gone. Went to gather flowers after tea. Folded clothes for ironing. *8 Tuesday.* Ironed. The men are dragging and planting. Benj. went and carried Es. and Em. part way to Mr. S. W. Seely's. Es. stayed all night. Lamed the ox. Has been pleasant though cloudy in the afternoon. *9 Wednesday.* Rain, rain, rain. Creeks very high. *10 Thursday.* Aaron went over to S. W. Seely's and from there to the city. Stayed with George Huyck all night. Two letters and a paper in the P. O. *11 Friday.* Father went over to Duria today. Aaron and Emma went after Mary this afternoon. Has been pleasant though cool. *12 Saturday.* Baking and so on this morn. Mother and Benj. went to Saratoga for Es. Father has been hoeing and planting garden some this afternoon. Mary and Emma have been fishing and picking flowers. *13 Sunday.* A pleasant day. All went to meeting. There were 32 present. More than any Sabbath before this season. Subject of the discourse read, "The Christian in the Family." Had four classes in the S.S. Took a collection for the "Child's Paper." Raised enough to get 15. *14 Monday.* Washed but did not hang up the clothes. Father has been dragging and planting today. Aaron went to carry Mary to her school this morn. Mr. Page has been over to look at a large rack. Think he can split it for our cellar wall. Have had a pleasant day, not very warm for the season.

15 Tuesday. Had a very heavy thunder shower this morning. Our folks finished planting before this rain. Have baked bread and cake, and churned. Father and Mr. Huyck went over to Mr. Gough's this afternoon. Mr. H. is here to night.

16 Wednesday. Aaron went to Saratoga and brought the mail, had letters from B. D. Mr. H. left this forenoon. Chamberlain came over about noon to get A. to help him break. Has been pleasant all day. Have rinsed the clothes and done some ironing. F. has been at work in the cellar drain.

17 Thursday. Father wrote letters to Uncle A. and N. S. G. Plowed some and went to Saratoga. Brought home two letters and a paper. And two letters for Chamberlain. We have churned and finished ironing. Has been a very warm day. A great deal of wind. Ther. 75 after sunset.

18 Friday. Father has been with Mr. G., Mr. H. and G. H. to Mr. Gough's, Benj. went over to Col. Sander's farm after dinner. Mr. Seely, Huyck and George H. here to supper. We have baked bread and pies today. Very warm, though some cooler than yesterday. Father has gone to dragging just at night. Hr. Huyck stays all night.

19 Saturday. Father and Mr. H. have gone to Mr. Hallet's to look at a piece of woodland. Mary came home with them. We have baked bread, cake, and pies to day. Has been very warm.

20 Sunday. The whole family have been to meeting. Only 21 there. Had a very interesting sermon read from the text, "What shall it profit a man if he gain the whole world and lose his own soul." Has been very warm, with quite a breeze most of the day.

21 Monday. Mr. Huyck and Page here to work. Chamberlain here to board. Father carried Mary to her school this morn, paid for his wood lot and brought home a load of wood. Went to Saratoga this afternoon for powder. We have washed and baked bread and made a boiled dinner.

22 Tuesday. Our folks getting out stone and digging the cellar. Had a call this morn from Mr. Sanders and Seely. Have baked bread, cake and pies, rinsed the clothes and prepared for ironing. We all went over to the large rock this afternoon and had a shower while gone.

23 Wednesday. Out door and in door labor has gone on as usual to day. Have had or rather are having a heavy thundershower this evening. It lightens almost constantly.

24 Thursday. Has rained by spells all day. Aaron went to the city this morn and brought home a letter and some crackers. Have been baking, ironing, etc. They have worked in the cellar and getting out stone what they can. Rain and mud, rain and mud, mud in doors and out.

25 Friday. Father has been to Jamestown to day. Messrs. Sanders, Seely, S. W. Seely, and G. Huyck made us a call and brought letters and a basket of crackers. G. H. stays with us all night. Still worked at the cellar. We have baked bread and cake and churned. There have been a few showers.

26 Saturday. Still working at the cellar. Had a call from Chamberlain this morn. Mr. Huyck gone to Mr. Gough's this afternoon. Mr. Page gone home to spend the Sabbath. Have baked bread and pies and mopped. Hoed garden a little to night, cut wood, etc. It has been very warm this day.

27 Sunday. A very warm day. Only sixteen present at our meeting. None of the Sunday School officers there. Subject of discourse read, "The Christian in the Church." Mr. Huyck came up just at night.

28 Monday. Father left very early this morn for Howard Centre. Mr. Page, Mr. Huyck and Aaron working at the cellar. Have washed, baked pie and cake, mopped, etc. Mr. Chandler called just at night to see if he could hire a teacher. Did not give him any encouragement. Excessively warm.

29 Tuesday. Ironed and baked bread. Father came home a little after sunset, walked from Howard Centre. Have been drawing out stone, and splitting them and digging the cellar. More air astir than yesterday.

30 Wednesday. Working in the cellar and cutting stone. Chamberlain came up in the forenoon and attempted to break, found it too wet still. Have baked bread and puddings, and churned. There was a shower about noon and after. Emma had a letter from Coz. Ephraim. Page gone home.

JULY

1 Thursday. Mr. Page did not come back. Father and Mr. Huyck work in the cellar. Aaron and Chamberlain gone to break on Col. Sander's lot. Benj went over after noon. Rain about five P.M. Baked bread and pumpkin pies. Warm and sultry part of the time. Once in a while a fine breeze.

2 Friday. Rain this morning. Working in the cellar. Much cooler towards night than it has been for days. Mr. D. Seely took tea with us. Mr. Huyck went away with him. Aaron went after Mary this afternoon.

3 Saturday. Churned, baked, etc. Father and Aaron hoed in the garden some. Mr. Huyck came over early in the morning. Mr. Ricker here to dinner. Father and Mr. H. went over to R's afternoon. Mary, Emma, Aaron and Benj. have gone to Saratoga. M. and E. to stay all night. Aaron brought home a load of wood. Rec'd our first *Evangelist* of June 24th.

4 Sunday. Rather a cool pleasant breeze most of the time. Nineteen present at our meeting to day. Subject of lecture read, "The Christian in the World." Have the promise of preaching[4] next Sabbath if nothing prevents. There is a meeting appointed on Sat. for forming a church and other needful business.

5 Monday. Washed and baked bread and cake. Jenny and Emma S. and Mr. Chamberlain were here to dinner and tea. Mr. Page and Huyck here to work. All went over after tea to see the rock blasted. Had a glorious fourth at home!

6 Tuesday. Cutting stone, hoeing corn, etc. Aaron working for Chamberlain. Esther and Benj. carried Mary to her school. Ironed part of the clothes and baked bread and biscuit. Mr. Page went home tonight. S. W. Seely came over with our plow just at night.

7 Wednesday. Out doors work moving along about as usual. Have finished ironing. Baked bread and cake. Commenced a sack[5] for Benj. Had a hard thundershower with some strong wind this evening.

8 Thursday. Baking, etc., etc. Father went away to get help to raise the house. Messrs. Seely, Sanders, and Salmon were here to tea besides our own workmen. Have had a very comfortable day for the season. Rec'd a letter from Sarah St. John.

9 Friday. Cloudy and lowering[6] all the morning and commenced raining before noon. Rained hard nearly all the afternoon. They began putting the underpinning down but were obliged to stop. Chamberlain and Aaron came home just after noon.

10 Saturday. Outdoors and in doors work moving on as usual. Father, Mother, Esther and Mr. Huyck went down to meeting according to appointment, but did not find Mr. Windsor there, was hindered by the heavy rain of yesterday. Had a short meeting of consultation and prayer. Found a letter and an *Evangelist*, June 17, containing a receipt.

11 Sunday. A cold day for the season. Went to meeting. Had quite a good congregation, 32 present. Listened to a discourse of H[enry] W[ard] Beecher's printed in the *Independent.* Rec'd an *Evangelist* and *N. Y. Rural* and a letter from Mr. Pattingill.

12 Monday. Washed, baked, etc. Mr. Page came about ten o'clock. Mr. Huyck here. Aaron and Chamberlain on the Col's breaking. Mr. Beers came over for our plow to use a few days.

13 Tuesday. Quite a pleasant day. Father drew over our door step this morn. Chamberlain gone to Riceville. Work in doors about after the usual routine. Ironed part of the clothes. George Huyck over a while this afternoon. Mr. Beers brought the plow home today. It did not work very well.

14 Wednesday. Commenced raining before five A.M. and has lightened, thundered and rained nearly all day. There has been some high wind also. Finished the ironing this morning, baked bread, etc., etc.

15 Thursday. A fair day for outdoors work. They have been laying the steps in the cellar way, placing the underpinning and door step. Aaron and Chamberlain breaking on the Col's lot. Have not been drove with house work to day. Baked some cake.

16 Friday. Baked bread, mopped the floor, etc. S. W. Seely and wife came over before noon and brought five letters and two papers. S. W. cut Father's and Huyck's hair after dinner. Mother and Benj. went after Mary this afternoon. M. called at Mr. Banks'. Mr. Page went home to night.

17 Saturday. Washed some calicoes this morn. They have been plowing and leveling around the house to day. Mr. and Mrs. Seely and Mr. Carver from St. Charles were here to tea. Father went down to Saratoga this morn. Mr. John Windsor is at Mr. Seely's and is going to preach for us tomorrow.

18 Sunday. All went to meeting and enjoyed it very much. Had an excellent sermon from Mat. 28th 20. There were twenty-eight present. We received our first number of the *Child's Paper,* also seven letters and a paper.

19 Monday. Aaron went with Mary to her school this morning. It rained quite briskly when they started but did not continue long. We washed and put our clothes a soak. Chamberlain came up just before noon and has been breaking here this afternoon. Father and Mr. Huyck have been writing letters to day.

20 Tuesday. Had a heavy fog this morn. Mr. Page came this

morning to finish getting out stone for the drain. We rinsed the clothes this morn and ironed some calicoes. Baked bread and pies. Folded the clothes for ironing.

21 Wednesday. Finished ironing this morning. Mr. Page completed his work and went home this afternoon. Father has been plowing corn with the oxen since tea. It has been warm and has looked like showers but they do not come yet.

22 Thursday. Father sowed and dragged in some buckwheat to day. Have had more appearances of rain, but only a few drops have fallen. Father and Mr. Huyck have been plowing and hoeing corn and potatoes. Aaron and Chamberlain breaking.

23 Friday. They have dragged some ground for turnips to day. Breaking and hoeing corn as usual. Have baked cake, custard, pudding, and bread this day. Emma has a sore eye.

24 Saturday. Finished breaking and measured the ground before noon. Have finished hoeing before tea. Mr. Huyck and Chamberlain have gone for good. Father went to Saratoga after tea. Found a letter and paper in the office. We have baked, mopped, etc.

25 Sunday. Mother and Emma did not go to meeting today. Had rather a thin meeting—fourteen present. Subject of discourse, "The Christian in Prosperity." Only part of the discourse read. Had some papers from the office. Mr. Coleman and Mr. Windsor propose to be here two weeks from yesterday and to day.

26 Monday. Washed and baked today. Father went to Riceville after some lumber. Aaron and Benjamin worked some in the cellar mudding it up. Brought in the clothes and folded for ironing. Has been cloudy most of the day.

27 Tuesday. Ironed most of the clothes and baked bread. Aaron shot a duck this morn. We cooked it for dinner. Had a call from Mr. Doolittle this morn and one from Mr. Thayer afternoon. Geo. Huyck came over after our wagon to day. Father and Aaron have been at work in the cellar some. Small showers through the day.

28 Wednesday. Showers again. G. Huyck came back with the wagon and stayed to dinner. Aaron went back with him to stay all night. Emma and Benj. went a fishing, caught a few and cooked for supper.

29 Thursday. Father and Aaron cut some grass today. Mother, Esther and Benj. went to Mr. Seely's and Sander's visiting. Found one letter in the office. Had showers in the afternoon. Baked bread, etc.

30 Friday. Our folks have been cutting grass. Baked a cake and a custard. It commenced raining before 8 P.M. and is at it hard at bedtime. Some hail and constant thunder and lightening.

31 Saturday. Had a hard thunder storm all night long. The creek this morning is much higher than it has been since we have lived here. Baked bread and cake. Mary washed some calicoes. Some rain through the day.

AUGUST

1 Sunday. All went to meeting. Eighteen present. The remainder of last Sabbath's discourse read. Bridges gone so that the creek people did not come. Has been cloudy most of the day and looks like rain.

2 Monday. Washed and baked bread. Father went to carry Mary to her school and get a load of wood. Did not get back till two P.M. Aaron gone to Saratoga to help put up the bridge. Got home about eight P.M. Have folded clothes for ironing.

3 Tuesday. Ironed most of the clothes. Father and Aaron both down to Saratoga all day. Baked custard and cake.

4 Wednesday. Baked bread, mopped, etc. Father and Aaron gone again. Received a letter, also three papers.

5 Thursday. Father is cutting his wheat today. It is not worth thrashing. Finished ironing the starch clothes. Rec'd two letters and a paper and sent two letters to the office.

6 Friday. Father has raked up his wheat and put it in heaps. Baked two pies, two cakes, and two loaves of bread. Cooked chicken and duck, peas, beans and new potatoes for dinner. Benjamin caught some good nice fish this afternoon. It has been a very warm day.

7 Saturday. Had an early dinner and went to Saratoga hoping to find ministers there according to appointment, but lo, it is again a disappointment. We had a season of prayer, 15 present. Showers during the afternoon.

8 Sunday. Very warm today. All went to meeting except Aaron. Had a very full attendance, 42 in all. No preaching. Subject of lecture, "The Christian in Adversity." Mr. Patterson's people here to tea. Mary came over and went back with them.

9 Monday. Father has been cutting hay. Went to Saratoga after wood and provisions. Have washed and spread the clothes down to bleach. Took them up at night and put them a soak. It has been excessively warm all day.

10 Tuesday. Haying out doors before noon. Ironing, baking and so forth indoors. Father, Mother, and Esther went to S. W. Seely's in the afternoon. Showers during the afternoon and evening.

11 Wednesday. Had a heavy shower last night, but pleasant through the day. Father has been making a hay rigging to day. Have finished ironing, been mending, etc. We had baked ducks for dinner.

12 Thursday. Baked bread, mopped and so on. Father has finished his rigging and done a little of several things. There was another hard shower this morning. We had a boiled Indian pudding,[7] potatoes and beets for dinner.

13 Friday. Father has cut some grass, tried to get some dry that was cut before. We had baked duck and chicken and new potatoes for dinner. Rather pleasant but warm.

14 Saturday. Baked custard pies and custard and bread, mopped, etc. Father went down to Saratoga in the afternoon and brought a paper and two letters from the office. Aaron has been putting up hay.

15 Sunday. All went to meeting as usual. Twenty-four present. Sermon from the *Independent* by H. W. Beecher. Subject, "Special Providences of God." A very pleasant day.

16 Monday. Father has built a [hay] stack today. S. W. Seely has been helping him. Have washed, baked bread and custard. Boiled an Indian pudding, potatoes and beets and fish for dinner. A very pleasant day.

17 Tuesday. A good hay day. The wind has blown hard some of the time and there is constant blaze lightning in the south this evening. Have ironed a part of the clothes, the rest have been bleaching.

18 Wednesday. Still at haying. Baking, rinsing clothes, etc.

19 Thursday. Finished ironing. Worked at the hay in the morning. Looked like rain before noon so they quit. Aaron and Emma went after a load of wood and brought home some crackers.

20 Friday. Baked cake, bread and biscuit, mopped, cooked artificial oysters and potatoes for dinner. Father has worked in the hay field all day. Threatens rain in the morn but came off pleasant before noon. Cattle uneasy. Three wagons passed here today!!!

21 Saturday. Working in the hay field as usual. Cool and high wind some of the time. Baked custard pies, also two Johnycakes[8] for dinner, boiled potatoes and fried chicken. Mopped the floor of course. A very pleasant evening.

22 Sunday. Went to meeting as usual. Nineteen present. Subject of the lecture read, "The Christian in his Spiritual Sorrows." Quite cool all day.

23 Monday. Still at work in the hay field, making a new stack today. Washed in the forenoon. Baked bread, and a Johnycake for dinner, cooked beets and potatoes and corn. Has been rather cool again today.

24 Tuesday. Our folks have cut hay today. We have put on a quilt today. Find ourselves in rather close quarters. Looks some like rain.

25 Wednesday. Baked bread, worked on the quilt, etc. Father drawed a load of hay this morn before breakfast and finished drawing before noon.

26 Thursday. Father and Aaron have been mowing weeds this forenoon. Benj. went to S. W. Seely's in the morn and went with Father after wood this afternoon. Brought home three papers, a ham, and sack of flour. Finished the quilt before night.

27 Friday. Cold and windy. Father and Aaron have smoothed off the cellar bottom. Baked bread. We have had a good smart fire all day to keep warm. Mary brought home some black berries.

28 Saturday. Baked two pies, two loaves of bread and a fowl and 2 Johnycakes, churned, mopped. Mary washed some calicoes, rinsed our white clothes, ironed some of them. Father and Aaron cut weeds in the slough, cold yet.

29 Sunday. All went to meeting. Thirty-two present. Subject of lecture read "The Christian in his Spiritual Joys." Quite cool but pleasant. Some frosty this morning.

30 Monday. Did not wash because we have no soap. Baked bread, churned, mopped, ironed, made emptyings, etc. etc. Father and Benj. went to take Mary to her school and brought home a load of wood. Aaron has been working for S. W. Seely.

31 Tuesday. Father went to New Oregon this morning. Aaron has been mowing grass. Cool and pleasant.

SEPTEMBER

1 Wednesday. Aaron cutting grass yet. Father brought back a sack of flour, provindes [supplies], and groceries. Raining this evening. Mother washed the windows today.

2 Thursday. Washed, baked, boiled dinner, etc. Father and Aaron have cut weeds and done chores. Cool and high winds during the day. Had a hard shower in the night.

3 Friday. Father and Aaron have been to Riceville. Rinsed and ironed the clothes, baked cake and burned [roasted] coffee after tea. Showery. Heard tonight that Mr. Coleman and wife are in town and there will be a meeting tomorrow to organize a church.

4 Saturday. Baked bread, cake, pies, mopped, churned etc. Father, Mother, Esther and Benj. went to Saratoga to meeting. Organized a church with ten members. Expect more to join us soon. Mr. and Mrs. Coleman are with us tonight.

5 Sunday. Had two services today and omitted S.S. Three more joined us making all thirteen members. Had a sermon in the morning on "Church Polity." A short one in the afternoon after which Mr. Banks' child was baptised and the communion service attended to. Forty-two present.

6 Monday. Washed this forenoon. Had a call from Mr. Huyck. Father drew two loads of hay, had an early dinner and went to Riceville for lumber. Attended a school meeting where they voted taxes for building school houses.

7 Tuesday. Rained by showers through the day. Our folks have been lathing. Baked bread in the morning.

8 Wednesday. Benj. went to S. W. Seely's this morning and borrowed two hammers. Lathing today. Aaron has been plowing this afternoon. Pleasant and cool. Dried the clothes and folded for ironing.

9 Thursday. Baked bread and cake, ironed, etc. Lathing all day. Rained most of the time.

10 Friday. Have cut corn for drying today, been lathing, etc. Father went after Mary this afternoon. Her school is out. Brought home two papers. Quite cool tonight.

11 Saturday. Father and Aaron went to draw hay for Uncle Darius today. Did not get back till late in the evening. Baked bread and a chicken pie, mopped, etc. There has been a high wind most of the day.

12 Sunday. Went to meeting. 25 present. Mr. D. Seely read the lecture, entitled "The Christian in Death." Rec'd a letter and a paper from the office. A very pleasant day though cool. A little frost this morning.

13 Monday. Washed and dried and folded the clothes. Father went to Riceville after lumber. Aaron has cut wood. Rained in the forenoon, wind has blown hard some of the day. Had a Johnycake for dinner. Cooked a chicken, potatoes and beets for supper. Baked bread.

14 Tuesday. Ironed, mopped, cut corn for drying, cooked potatoes for dinner. Rained before noon. Aaron has been plowing this afternoon, went off hunting for a nooning. Have had five chickens to dress. Mr. Griffin here to dinner.

15 Wednesday. Father and Aaron went to draw sand, got sloughed [stuck in mud] and came home without any. Mrs. Seely and Charley spent the day. S. W. here to tea, Mary and Emma gone home with them. Baked bread, pies and biscuit, cooked chickens, onions and potatoes for dinner. Made a custard.

16 Thursday. Father and Aaron went to New Oregon this morning. Mother, Esther and Benjamin spent the day alone. Mary and Emma came home just at night. Cool and pleasant. Fires comfortable to sit by.

17 Friday. Cool and pleasant again, considerable wind. Cooked potatoes and corn for dinner. Our folks have not come home yet. Cut corn for drying.

18 Saturday. Baked bread, cake and pies and an Indian pudding. Churned, mopped, cooked potatoes and corn for dinner. Father and Aaron came home about four P.M. Brought two papers and a letter.

19 Sunday. All went to meeting but Mother. Only eighteen present. Lecture read, "The Christian in the Grave." Very pleasant and warm.

20 Monday. Washed, baked bread and mopped. Did not hang up the white clothes till night. Father and Benjamin went to Riceville. Had a call from Mr. Patterson in the morning. Smoky and misty and cloudy and sunshiny by turns.

21 Tuesday. Ironed the calicoes. Father and Aaron went after sand in the morning and Aaron after noon. Have shot four pigeons today. Had chicken and biscuit and potatoes and beets for dinner. Cloudy most of the day.

22 Wednesday. Finished ironing, baked bread and a cream pudding. Cooked a chicken pot pie, corn and potatoes for dinner, mopped, etc. Mrs. Seely came early in the morning. Aaron has been drawing sand. Mary and Emma went to S. W. Seely's for the cows tonight. Have dressed 12 pigeons and 8 chickens today.

23 Thursday. Father and Aaron have been to Riceville again. Baked bread, cake and an Indian pudding, cooked pigeons and potatoes. Mr. Seely and Chamberlain here to tea. Mrs. Seely has gone home to night and Mary and Emma have gone to Saratoga.

24 Friday. Father made a riddle [coarse-meshed sieve] in the morning and has been sifting sand all day. Aaron has been drawing

sand. Benjamin gone to S. W. Seely's to drive oxen. Have dressed
nine pigeons, made cake, ironed two pieces of new cloth, etc., etc.
Mary and Emma came home afoot tonight.

25 Saturday. Father has been slacking lime all day, have to heat
the water in the house. Baked bread and a custard, mopped just at
dusk. Benjamin came home to night.

26 Sunday. All went to meeting. Thirty present. The last lecture
in the course was read, "The Christian in Heaven." Very strong wind
all day. Mr. Banks and wife and cousins took tea with us.

27 Monday. Did not wash. Our folks finished mixing morter.
Aaron went for wood this afternoon. Mary, Emma and Benjamin
went with him to gather hazel nuts. Mr. Fields came just before tea,
is going to stay and do some joiner work. Baked bread, 6 pigeons and
1 chicken.

28 Tuesday. Had a large wash. Baked the pigeons, cooked potatoes and beets for dinner, baked bread, mopped, etc. Aaron has been
plowing. Father and Mr. Fields getting out timber to finish the chambers. Folded the clothes for ironing.

29 Wednesday. Ironed the clothes, baked bread and cake,
cooked ham, potatoes and an Indian pudding for dinner. Mother has
been lathing, Father and Mr. Fields carpentering, Aaron plowing.
Had a chicken to dress.

30 Thursday. Have been lathing all day. Aaron has been to
Riceville for lumber. Cooked potatoes and turnips and baked chickens for dinner. Very pleasant now days.

OCTOBER

1 Friday. Lathing again today. Aaron plowed this forenoon, and
went to Riceville for nails this afternoon. Benjamin went to S. W.
Seely's of an errand in the morning. Baked a Johnycake for supper.

2 Saturday. Baked bread, cake and a pudding, mopped, etc.
Have been lathing some and doing a variety of carpenter jobs. Are
not quite ready for the mason yet. Aaron has been plowing, are all
tired and glad it is Sat. night. Warm and windy.

3 Sunday. Went to meeting as usual. Twenty present. Sermon
read entitled "The Brevity of Life," by J. S. Pattingill. Mr. Seely
brought up four papers and five letters. Comfortably warm to sit
without fires in the middle of the day.

4 Monday. Washed, baked bread and Johnycake, cooked beets,
an Indian pudding and potatoes for dinner. Father has been carpen-

tering, Aaron plowing. Folded clothes for ironing. Churned and mopped. Cold this evening. Had a call from Mr. Banks today.

5 Tuesday. Ironed the clothes, baked bread and an Indian pudding, had chickens, potatoes and cabbage for dinner. Aaron has been plowing. Father carpentering some. Cut corn, etc. Frost to wilt vines this morning for the first time.

6 Wednesday. Rained more or less all day. Father finished a letter to Mr. Jennings. All in doors most of the time. Has come off cold tonight—the wind blows hard.

7 Thursday. Father and Benny went to Saratoga. Mr. Fellows came to plaster the house this morning—commenced in Mother's bedroom. Chicken, ham, biscuit, potatoes, beets for dinner.

8 Friday. Benny went to Saratoga with Esther and Emma— came home about noon, brought one letter and three papers.

9 Saturday. Aaron and Benny went with Col Sanders after the onions over to Dr. Chandler's. Brought home three chickens. Fellows finished plastering.

10 Sunday. Mr. Fellows went home early this morning. Father, Aaron, and Benny went down to meeting. It has rained some all day. Had meeting at Mr. Seely's house.

11 Monday. Father went to Saratoga after a load of wood. Have cleaned house all day today. Aaron cut wood in afternoon.

12 Tuesday. Aaron went after a load of wood. Father attended election. Cleaned house again today.

13 Wednesday. Aaron and Benny digging potatoes. Father has been ploughing. Cleaning house.

14 Thursday. Washed and folded clothes for ironing. Washed two bed quilts. Aaron and Benny digged potatoes. Father ploughed. Mr. Banks came to look for his cattle.

15 Friday. Ironed in the forenoon. Benj. went to S. W. Seely's and Father after him. Mr. De Moss brought 50 lbs. of beef. Had one letter and a paper from the office. Baked bread.

16 Saturday. Baked pies and cake and cleaned up some. Father painted the cellar wall outside.

17 Sunday. All went to meeting. Wind blew hard all day. Eighteen present. Had one paper from the office. Prairie fires burning this afternoon. A smart shower this evening.

18 Monday. Washed and cleaned Mother's bedroom and regulated the battery, folded clothes for ironing and drove some nails in the closets and hung clothes. Aaron has been painting the cellar, father plowing.

19 Tuesday. Ironed, moved the bed into the bedroom, regulated some up stairs, baked bread and biscuit, etc. Emma S. came here in the stage this afternoon. Have been plowing, painting cellar and so on.

20 Wednesday. Baked pies. Father, Mary, Emma and Emma Seely went to Saratoga in the afternoon. Aaron plowed in the morning. Made some pasteboard. Had one letter and one paper from the office.

21 Thursday. Finished putting things to rights in the chambers. Father is making a door frame. Aaron plowing. Churned and mopped. Very pleasant weather now days.

22 Friday. Baked bread and cake, mopped, etc. Father, Aaron and Benj. went to Saratoga and plowed and burned around Uncle Aaron's house. Had one letter from the office. Delightful weather.

23 Saturday. Baked pies and churned and cleaned up for Sunday. Father went to Jamestown in the morning, bought some corn, covered and plowed over the ditch in the afternoon.

24 Sunday. All went to meeting but Mother. Wind very strong. Twenty present. Had one letter and two papers. Prairie fires burning in sight for the first time this fall.

25 Monday. Washed, cleaned up the cellar, baked bread, mopped, cooked beef, potatoes and an Indian pudding for dinner. Aaron has been plowing some. They are making a wood box this evening, goody! Strong wind, fires on every side.

26 Tuesday. Ironed the calicoes this morning. Father and Aaron went to the woods for timber for a barn. Esther, Mary and Emma and Benj. took a short walk at dusk.

27 Wednesday. Cut squash for drying, mopped, etc. Cooked potatoes for dinner, baked an indian pudding. Father and Benj. went to the woods, Aaron has been digging post holes. Father is minding the tea kettle. Rained some today.

28 Thursday. Baked bread and pies. Rained more or less through the day. Father went to S. W. Seely's just at night.

29 Friday. Baked pies and Indian bread, mopped, cloudy and unpleasant, some rain. Father went to Saratoga for timber for a barn. Rec'd two letters and three papers.

30 Saturday. Baked bread and cake, mopped, hung up the clothes and so on. Father and Aaron went to the woods for rails. Mr. and Mrs. Seely and Charley came here with some vegetables to store in the cellar. Stayed to tea.

31 Sunday. Pleasant to day. All went to meeting. Twenty three present. Lecture read, "The Worth of the Soul, A Reason for Early Piety." Rec'd two letters and two papers.

NOVEMBER

1 Monday. Ironed last week's washing, mopped, boiled an Indian pudding and potatoes for dinner. Father and Aaron have been working on the barn all day.

2 Tuesday. Snowed this morning and has done so most all day. Very tedious out yet they have worked at the barn most of the time.

3 Wednesday. Washed and mopped, baked an Indian pudding and cooked potatoes for dinner. Baked a Johnycake for supper. Father started for New Oregon this morning and Mother went down to Mr. Seely's. Rained and snowed some.

4 Thursday. Aaron and Benjamin worked on the barn. Cooked a chicken pot pie for dinner. Rained a little. Stewed squash for pies.

5 Friday. Baked three pies and four loaves of bread. Father and Mother came home about four P.M. Brought one letter and one paper. Rinsed and hung up the clothes, folded for ironing.

6 Saturday. Ironed, baked cookies, churned, and mopped. Had beef, potatoes, carrots, bread and butter and pie for dinner. Father and Aaron have worked at the barn. Had a few flurries of snow.

8 Monday. Washed, mopped, etc. Did not hang up the clothes because the wind blowed so hard. Has snowed some.

9 Tuesday. Rinsed the clothes and hung them out. Father and Aaron went to Saratoga for wood in the afternoon. Had three papers from the office. Commenced a new sack of flour. Baked bread.

10 Wednesday. Ironed today. Cooked beef, potatoes and an Indian pudding for dinner. Aaron went after wood. Father has made a cellar door.

11 Thursday. Father has made another door and hung it. Aaron went after rails, has gone to S. W. Seely's to stay all night. Put some walnut and larch in the ground to day. Mopped.

12 Friday. Snowed till afternoon quite fast. Father went to Riceville after corn. Aaron came home at noon. Geo. Huyck with him. Stays all night. Baked cake.

13 Saturday. Father went to Saratoga, timber for wood. Baked bread, mopped and so forth. Thermometer stood at 20 below just before sunrise.

14 Sunday. All went to meeting. Thirty-one present. Rev. W. Windsor preached twice. Text in the morning from Heb. 9th 22nd., afternoon Job 28, 28. Mr. Windsor came home and stayed all night with us. Had a beautiful evening.

15 Monday. Mr. Windsor left for home this morning. Washed and hung up the clothes. Still and comfortable. Father banked the house with hay before noon, went with Aaron after wood and to the office. Churned.

16 Tuesday. Father went after wood. Benjamin went with him and went after the mail. One paper. Father, Mother, Esther and Benjamin went to S. W. Seely's just at night to spend the evening. E. stayed all night. Baked bread.

17 Wednesday. Aaron went after wood today. Cold and blustering most of the time. Mr. Chamberlain and Truax and Emma Seely came up just at night and stayed all night. Did the ironing.

18 Thursday. Father and Benjamin went to Saratoga afternoon. A beautiful moonlight evening and very good sleighing.

19 Friday. Thermometer stood 8 below zero at sunrise. Aaron went after wood this morning. Mr. Gough brought 210 lbs. of beef today. Baked bread. Clear and pleasant.

20 Saturday. Baked cake, mopped, tried out the tallow, made brine for the beef. Father went after wood this morning. Quite warm and pleasant this evening.

21 Sunday. Went to meeting as usual. Twenty present. Lecture read, "The Love of God and of Jesus Christ, A Reason for Early Piety." Two papers in the office. Mild and pleasant.

22 Monday. Washed, mopped, baked bread, prepared meat for mince pies. Mr. Suttiff here to dinner. Father has drawn two loads of wood. Aaron has been in the woods chopping all day.

23 Tuesday. Father and Aaron went west for wood today. Baked four mince pies and cookies, churned.

24 Wednesday. Aaron went after wood. Father made two leaves for our table. Baked three carrot pies, a tin of biscuit and two loaves of bread. A stranger called while eating supper and wished to stay all night. His name is Foot.

25 Thursday. Thanksgiving day. Mr. D. Seely and wife, S. W. and wife and Charley, Mr. Sanders and wife spent the day here. Had a very pleasant time. They brought six letters and one paper from the office.

26 Friday. Father went west to get some corn. Did not get but a little.

27 Saturday. Father and Aaron went to Crane Creek to get timber for wood. Aaron stayed and went to Saratoga for mail, found none. Snowed so hard afternoon that Father did not go back. Baked bread.

28 Sunday. All went to meeting but Mother. Snow drifted some. Sixteen present. Esther stayed down. Mrs. Seely is sick.

29 Monday. Washed. Very windy, did not hang out the clothes. Father went west after wood, found it, hard going.

30 Tuesday. Father and Mother, S. W. Seely and wife went over to Mr. Bank's visiting. Aaron went after Esther in afternoon. Mary and Emma went home with Mr. Seely. Have rinsed the clothes, brought them in this evening.

DECEMBER

1 Wednesday. Father went to or started for New Oregon this morn. Snow and considerable wind this afternoon.

2 Thursday. Mr. Seely brought the girls home this morning. Very cold all day and blustering in the afternoon.

3 Friday. Father came home tonight. A cold day. Baked bread, mopped and baked cake.

4 Saturday. Took down the bedstead in the bedroom and set it up in the chamber. Set up a new one in the bedroom. Baked pies, mopped, etc. Our folks have made a sled for Benjamin.

5 Sunday. Snowed last night. Snow all blowed up in heaps this morning. None of us went to meeting. Seems like a long day to spend all at home. Clear but cold.

6 Monday. Washed, churned, mopped, etc. Father went over to election today. Mr. Buckbee here to dinner, supper and to stay all night. He brought three papers and a letter for us from the office.

7 Tuesday. Aaron went this morning with Mr. Buckbee to help him over the prairie. Father went to S. W. Seeley's to help him butcher but did not attempt it. Baked bread and ironed some. Ther. today below 16 degrees at 9 this evening.

8 Wednesday. Finished ironing, mopped, etc. Father went over to help butcher again and is not home tonight. Clear, cold and pleasant. Ther. this morn at sunrise 25° below zero—this eve at 9 it is 23° below.

9 Thursday. Father came home early this morning. Mr. Seely has been over to help him butcher. One pig weighed 152 lbs., other 206 lbs. Father brought home one paper and one letter. Ther. 26° below zero this morning.

10 Friday. Have cut up the pork, cleaned the souse,[9] tried the lard, churned, mopped, etc. Weather has moderated very much. Ther. this morn was 15° above zero.

11 Saturday. Baked bread and pies, fried cakes, mopped. Weather about as yesterday.

12 Sunday. All went to meeting but Mother. Fourteen present. Had a wedding at intermission. One letter and one paper in the office for us. Rained some this afternoon.

13 Monday. Washed, mopped and made souse. Did not hang up the clothes. Father and Aaron went after wood in the afternoon.

14 Tuesday. Rinsed and hung up the clothes, cut and pickled the cuttings, mopped, etc. Father went after wood again A.M. Aaron came home this morn, brought three letters and two papers. A beautiful day. S. W. Seely and family and Aunt Mary here to stay tonight.

15 Wednesday. S. W. and family went home about 9 A.M. Aunt Mary stayed till 8 P.M. when Father and Mother started with her for Saratoga. Aaron went after wood thro' A.M.

16 Thursday. Father has gone to N. Oregon. Have ironed, mopped, etc. Most of us have spent the evening in writing letters. Clear and very pleasant.

17 Friday. Baked four pies and two loaves of cake, churned, mended and the regular routine of housework. Father came home tonight with a load of corn.

18 Saturday. Cleaned up for Sunday, made some fried cakes, baked bread. Father went home this morning with the Capt.'s horses. The Capt. and his wife came back with him and dined with us. Weather mild. Had a visit from some wolves about 5 A.M.

19 Sunday. All went to meeting. Preaching in the morn by Rev. Mr. Windsor from Eph. 2, 4–7. Communion service in the afternoon. Thirty-five present. Mr. and Mrs. Windsor came home with us to stay all night.

20 Monday. Father went west after a load of wood.

21 Tuesday. Washed, churned and mopped. Father and Aaron went after wood and Father went on to Riceville.

22 Wednesday. Father, Mother and Benjamin went to Mr. Gibbons for a visit. Have made pies and bread today. Received three papers, two letters tonight.

23 Thursday. Had a visit today from S. W. Seely and family and Mr. Dwight Strong and wife of St. Charles.

24 Friday. Father gone to New Oregon. Rinsed the clothes,

baked bread, mopped, ironed starch clothes, and some coarse ones. High wind this evening. Ther. 4 deg. below zero this morning. *25 Saturday.* All who are at home went to S. W. Seely's and spent the day very pleasantly. Raining quite smart this evening. Father is not home yet. *26 Sunday.* Went to meeting as usual. Found Father at Mr. Seely's. He came in last evening. 21 present. Foggy this evening. *27 Monday.* Still foggy. Could not wash because the boiler has failed. Father and Aaron went to the woods, Father went from there to Riceville. *28 Tuesday.* Has rained moderately all day and has been a heavy fog most of the time. Aaron has been to Riceville, carried over the lime and brought home some lumber. Churned. *29 Wednesday.* Washed but could not hang up the clothes. Baked bread and biscuit, and fried cakes, mopped. Father went to Saratoga this afternoon, brought home two papers. Mr. Lackey here to dinner. Had an invitation to spend New Years at Capt. Bennett's. *30 Thursday.* Prepared mince meat and baked four pies. Father has made a bedstead. Aaron went to Riceville for lumber. Colder and windy this evening. *31 Friday.* Father went to N. Oregon today to purchase a stove. Churned, mopped, ironed some starch clothes, rinsed and hung up some. Swept the chambers.

NOTES

1. A partial version appeared in Glenda Riley (ed.), "A Prairie Diary," *The Annals of Iowa* 44 (Fall 1977): 103–17.
2. A drag was a harrow or similar device with a wooden or metal frame holding spikes or sharpened disks. It was pulled—or dragged—over land to level it and break the clods, and to cover seed after it was sown.
3. Breaking land meant to open the soil and separate it in preparation for tilling of crops.
4. The promise indicated that a regular minister would preside over the service, rather than the laity leading it and reading a printed lesson or sermon.
5. She probably means a short, loose-fitting, straight-backed shirt or jacket, commonly worn by men and boys in that era.
6. Lowering meant to look dark and gloomy.

7. An Indian pudding is a steamed pudding made primarily of corn meal, molasses, and milk.

8. Johnnycake was a type of corn bread usually cooked on a griddle or baked on a Johnnycake board in front of an open fire. It was originally a kind of bread made by Shawnee Indians known as Shawnee-cake.

9. Souse is a pickled food, especially made from the ears, feet, and head of a hog. She probably means they cleaned the parts of the pig in preparation for making souse.

Westward Migration
THE DIARY OF
Mary Alice Shutes

I N 1862 the Shutes family left their relatives and friends in Wyandott County, Ohio, to set out for a new home in Carroll County, Iowa. By this time, state roads, maps, and the beginning of a railroad network had appeared. Neither did Indians pose any threat to the Shutes family as they traveled through south-central Iowa and settled in Carroll County northwest of Des Moines.

The Shutes's small caravan included a covered wagon, a surrey, and several "horse-hackers." Eight people were in the party: G. Hiram, his second wife Ann, his brother Chuck, and the Shutes's children—Charles, Mary Alice, Howard, Archie, and "the baby."

Thirteen-year-old Mary Alice was assigned the task of keeping a diary of the month-long journey. Many years later she noted, "As many of my hours were in the saddle Mother Ann kept the diary in the surrey and made notes as we traveled and she and myself wrote it up evenings so much credit belongs to Ann as she wrote down the things as they happened."

Mary Alice was born on August 11, 1849, in Marion County, Ohio. She and her brother Charles were the children of G. Hiram and Nancy J. McElvy Shutes. After Nancy's death, Hiram married Ann P. Drown in 1855, a union which produced several more children. Some years after the migration to Iowa, a prairie fire burned the Shutes family out of their home. They moved to a farm in Sheridan Township, Carroll County. The local cemetery eventually became the final resting place for Hiram, Ann, Charles, and three other children.

Also in Carroll County, Mary Alice married Enos Mallory (exact date unknown). The Mallorys in turn migrated several more times until they finally settled in Grants Pass, Oregon. It was in Oregon that the old travel diary was eventually brought out and recopied by Mary Alice's daughter, Julia Mallory Curtis. During the late 1920s and early 1930s the two women worked together to produce as accurate a copy as they could. According to Mary Alice, "It is as close to the original as is possible to get. The writing is badly faded and the paper brittle but being the writer, aged thirteen at the time, and a member of the party much of the happenings are totally engraved on my memory. Where reading was difficult or small parts missing they were easily filled in."

Mary Alice Shutes Mallory died on March 3, 1939, at age 89 and was buried in Grants Pass. Her diary is the only surviving family record. Unfortunately, an account written by her father in the 1860s or 1870s was lost or unaccountably destroyed, and the family Bible was destroyed when it accidentally got water-soaked.

The diary is presented here through the generous cooperation of LeRoy L. Shutes, son of Archie and nephew of Mary Alice, and with the consent of the State Historical Society of Iowa. LeRoy Shutes and his wife Mabel covered various parts of the original wagon route by automobile several times, and in 1953 followed Mary Alice's trail all the way to Grants Pass, Oregon. With his permission the diary has been altered slightly in terms of punctuation, grammar, and spelling to facilitate reading, but for the most part the manuscript is Mary Alice's story as she wrote it.[1]

Sunday, May 4. Mother Ann and Pa asked me to make a daily Diary of our migration from Marsailles, Wyandott County, Ohio to Jasper Township, Carroll County, Ioway for our family so I am starting today. This is our last Sunday at Morrell's Tavern where we live and also the last Sunday in Ohio as well. This is close to Marsailles in Wyandott County where Pa had his shoemaker's business. He had his cobbler's business and a small store in town itself, but after knowing we were moveing to Ioway for keeps he sold out his store goods and moved his shoemaker's equipment to the Tavern building which had been our home for several years.

Now the covered wagon is partly loaded for the trip—for a migration to Carroll County, Ioway, Pa estimated it to be a good eight hundred miles and forty days away when our wheels do start bending the grass towards the west. Gerathmil or G. Hiram as he is called is our Pa. Pa had been out to Iowa last fall and bought some land which had all log buildings; there are quite a few settlers not so far away. Mother Ann told us, "we will start early Wednesday morning at the time set by your Pa. And you know your Pa—early means before daylight and plenty early at that."

Pa took Archie, Howard and me in the surrey last night down to say goodbye to grandmother Elsie Shutes at La Rue. Charles rode his horse but Pa would not let me ride mine. He said, "you will get plenty of being straddle of a horse before we get to the end of the journey just ahead of us."

Grandmother Elsie smiled and hugged us, kissed us too, but she did not seem like herself. She did not seem very happy we were going so far away, but we told her we would be back to see her in a year or so. Two of grandmother's daughters were there, Aunt Louisa and Aunt Lydia. Another daughter, Nancy Ann, and a son, William, did not show up. Uncle William is enlisting in the Union Army and just got himself married.

Finally we are on our way home and back to the Tavern to get the job done of finishing loading the covered wagon. There is lots to do. Now here we are—done all we can. Going to bed to try to sleep. See you in the morning.

Monday, May 5. This will be a day of hustle and bustle. We are up with the sun or maybe a bit earlier. Uncle Charley Hatch was here real early for breakfast with the family. He is helping Pa get things fastened to the covered wagon; had to fit it inside so Mother Ann and the baby can sleep inside nights as the baby is only a few months old. Ann and the baby will spend most of their traveling time in the new surrey brought for that particular purpose and sometimes Ann can rest by a nap in the covered wagon.

Uncle Charley is going all the way to Ioway with us. He said "so we would have another good man along and besides I want to see the new country across the Mississippi where the game is free for the shooting, trapping or just catching it."

We are finding it a little rough to have to give away a lot of things we have owned since we can remember; things valuable to ourselves only, mostly sentimental value. The younger kids were haveing the same trouble. They shed tears over some things they hate to part with but no one pays much attention to them for after all they are just babies yet. These kids always seem to be in the way of the older folks but we know they are trying to be helpfull.

The day has ended so to bed to try to sleep.

Tuesday, May 6. Up before the sun on our last day here before the big trip and the last day in this Country. It seems there is so much to do and it's not easy to tell what to do first. Can't see why we can't start today but Pa said, "before daylight in the morning." All the neighborhood kids are here it seems. They promised to be here in the morning to see us off on our trip to Ioway.

We said goodbye so many times to so many people. Some we must have said goodbye several times. Finally supper is over. Mother Ann chased us to bed early but we can't get to sleep.

I slipped around where I could watch the older folks. They seemed to be trying to make the best of something they wished would not happen. A last word with a longtime friend talking how "we will come out to Ioway to see you and the new country." The ones about to leave for Ioway talked about when they would be back for a visit to Ohio. Charles said, "most of them know this will never happen."

After everyone was gone we heard Pa say, "some we won't see again." They seemed to sort of feel a bit sad that this was the way it would be but knew there was nothing they could do about it. Us younger ones just feel a bit different with a good lark ahead of us but it is a bit disappointing for those left behind. They said that they wanted to go to the Indian Country too. Of course we have built up a lot of make-believe about a country we have never seen but we know we have a lot to learn. Just cannot admit it to those folks left behind—not just now anyway.

Pa had slipped away for a last visit with his mother at La Rue. I slipped out and asked Mother Ann why he went when he had been there just last night. She said, "well, a last minute visit between a mother and son who is going a long way off is something you just can't understand now—only the mother and son can."

Mother Ann's parents, Gilbert and Elvira Drown, are here at the tavern for a last visit and goodbye. They are staying all night so as to be here in the morning to see us off for Ioway. So now we are off to bed. Good night.

Wednesday, May 7. Must have slepped better than I thought— likely all of us did. Pa woke us up. It is still very dark. There's not

even a ray of light in the eastern sky and the stars are still out. Uncle
Charley, who likes to be called Chuck or Unkey, had a good campfire going to furnish more light than the lanterns. Their light seems
so puny. It seems like all the neighborhood kids are here but it is so
dark away from the fire you just can't tell who is who. The fire makes
shadows that look funny, some short, some long or fat, but without
the fire we could not see very much of the goings-on.

Breakfast has been cooked and passed out by the neighbors with
the help of the older kids. It is a final display and effort of friendship
and also to save us women who are leaving for Ioway a last cooking
chore.

The younger kids know something unusual is going on but
don't understand it like the older folks do. The older folks seem to
understand some things we younger ones don't grasp. Some of the
older ones seem to welcome the solitude away from the fire. They
have said their goodbyes and are just waiting.

We are all loaded. Uncle Charley is on the covered wagon seat
with Archie. Howard was put in the quilts in the back of the wagon.
The excitement so far has not gotten him wide awake. Charles seems
restless getting on and off his horse. I am dressed like Charles and sit
straddled on my horse. I am to ride straddle like Cow Girls are supposed to out west in the Indian Country. Besides it is the only safe
way as no one wants to fall of their horse and be hurt.

Pa decided to take the cows along but said, "don't know how
long they can take it." They are tied one on each side of the end gate.
Uncle Charley predicted that they will never make it as their hoofs
will split.

Pa is finally in the surrey with Ann but seems he does not like
to give the final order to start although he is more anxious than anyone else to get going. Then he gives a wave of his hand and a shout,
"let's get moving." Uncle Chuck slapped the lines on the horses'
backs, the team starts to move, and the wheels began their turning
that we know will go on for many days and miles. Pa estimated eight
hundred miles and forty days from where we are to our new home in
Ioway. Rainey weather and bad roads were to be expected.

We horse-backers had to punch the cows to get them started.
Cow Boy Charles was the last on his horse. The surrey is the end one.
Our trip to the west and the Indian Country has begun. We are on our
way to Ioway and the folks left behind go back to their homes. We
pass the Church and roll out into the country. There is enough light

now to see the outlines of trees and buildings and the fields can be made out.

The cows are not convinced they can't stop any time but the jerk of their chains on the end gate reminds them to keep moveing. They will try it again. They never learn.

Here we are stopping for our first "cow rest" as we called it. In half an hour we are on our way. Passed through Kenton several hours later. No one paid any attention to us. Covered wagons are too common to attract attention any more. One lone dog barked at the cows but when Charles cracked his whip at them they ran away. Charles had his whip to keep the cows moveing. He plans on carrying it all the way to Ioway.

We are out of town and stopped for annother "cow rest." Uncle Charley built a small fire "to warm the coffee" he said. Had a bite to eat. Then crossed the Scioto River and noticed it flowed south. Moveing again through just plain country. Is the middle of the afternoon. Annother "cow rest" then on our way again. Crossed the Scioto River again. It is flowing north and is not very big. Watered the stock and rested a little. Half an hour later came to a crossroad. Kept moveing a couple of hours. We are at a little village, Holden. Are in Auglazie County. Have passed through Hardin County.

It has been fifteen hours since we started and Pa figured we had gone thirty miles—a good first day. Found a good camping place so we staked out the stock and cooked supper. It tasted smokey but real good anyway. A team and wagon went by but hardly looked our way as we are just annother covered wagon going west to the Indian Country.

Charles is to watch tonight until midnight. The rest of us rolled into our quilts with me under the covered wagon. Charles woke Unkie Charley after midnight. When he crawled in his quilts I did not wake up—more tired than I thought. So our first camp night.

Thursday, May 8. Just started to get daylight. Everyone but Charles and me are ready to go. Horses are even saddled and the cows fastened to the tailgate. Charles and me ate alone and rather fast as we felt guilty for not wakeing up. So here we go getting on our nags. Uncle Charley hollered, "get on your Charger Charles." He liked to joke. Pa said, "the lake shore for tonight but we cannot rush the cows as they might go lame." We passed through Waynesfield. Crossed several cricks and watered the stock at one. Here we are crossing a railroad track. Now annother town, Unionpolis, and on into a bigger town, Wapakonota. At the railroad tracks the cows balked. They had paid no attention to the first tracks—asleep maybe. We are on the regular Stage Coach route from Lake Erie to the big Reservoir. Pa called it St. Mary's Lake. Folks hardly looked our way. Here we are in Molton. "Cow rest." Pa said, "we are doing all right." Next town is St. Mary's. At a crick the stock had their blow as Uncle Chet calls it. We moved on north of the lake to a rather rutted road. The lake looks big to Charles and me as we never saw so much water in one puddle before. We came to a camping place not far from the lakeshore. Grass very scarce so Pa got some hay someplace for the stock. He staked them out. We cooked and ate supper and had a nice campfire. We walked down to the lakeshore, all except Ann and the kids. The men folks arranged about turns for night watch to watch the stock and keep the fire going as a warning for intruders to keep away.

Forgot to mention that Pa, with the help of a clockmaker in Marion, had put together a device to count the revolutions of one of the rear wheels of the surrey. It goes to 9,999 and starts over again so with a correct multiplier that Pa had figured out this was good enough to tell the distance we traveled each day.

Uncle Charley tried to tease Pa about his contraption. He said, "why not put one on each horse?" He knew it was a good idea. Pa just grinned and said nothing. With this Pa can tell how many miles covered and estimate how much we have to go yet. The instrument's real name is an odometer. Mother Ann said, "it will reduce the monotony of the day's travel and Pa will watch it a lot. It might go wrong sometimes but Pa will soon find out and get it working again."

Pa talked to a man about the cows balking at the railroad tracks. He advised tying a cover over their eyes when we come to a railroad so they can't see the rails and won't cause any trouble.

So we are haveing our second night camping on our way to Ioway.

Friday, May 9. Real early breakfast and we are on our way. Daylight is just haveing its way in the east. Soon we are in the town, Celina, at the northwest corner of the lake. At Pa's orders we all stopped in front of a store which already had their lamps lit ready for earley customers. No one else seemed to have shown up yet. Pa and Uncle Chet talked a few minutes. Hiram went into the store. Chet is crawling back on the wagon seat. "I want to get through town before it gets crowded. Besides the cows might get scared," he said. So away we go, all but the surrey with Pa, Ann and the baby. Their horse is tethered to a hitching post in front of the store. No one let us younger folks in on what the secret was from the store for us or as to what Pa was doing in the store.

Uncle Charley said, "we will soon be out of Mercer County then to the State line into Indiana so we will soon be out of Ohio." Soon we are out of town. The road along the river bank looks like a canal. The river has been dredged and straightened. It is the Wabash River we are told. Traveled a couple of hours. Wondered what had happened to the surrey and Pa.

Then here they come and went by us like they did not know us. But we soon found out the secret reason for the burst of speed of the horse and surrey. We came to a small crick and on the other side was the surrey. A campfire was going and Ann had dinner ready to eat. It was "cow rest" time anyway. Pa had bought some nice fresh ham at the store for a treat for all of us. It was realy a fine treat and real good eating besides.

Then Pa told us, "this will be the last stop in Ohio. Indiana is just ahead but Ioway is still a long way ahead." Our wheels are soon turning toward the west again. The Wabash River is on our left. Not very long untill a marker which said Ohio on one side and on the other side the Indiana State Line.

We passed the sign. Charley remarked, "one state behind us." The cows had made it into Indiana with us. We are in Jay County. Looks the same as Ohio to us. Soon at New Corydon then crossed the river into Jay City. The state stage route turns south to Portland but Pa had his plans to go to Marion over in Grant County, Indiana.

We are going on west. The roads are not so good. After a while we reached Limberlost Crick which was a good place for a "cow rest." Pa decided to make this our first camping night in Indiana. The sun is setting red. Uncle Charley predicted "no rain for annother day." Pa and Charles greased the wagon wheels.

Seems the cows have been contrary all day. Unckie had to have his joke. "The cows have not become pioneer-minded yet but will later on" said the man of Joking Wisdom. I am watching camp tonight with Charles "to shorten the night" he said.

Saturday, May 10. We are up early. Breakfast and on our way. The next ten miles we are covering dirt roads. There is a prediction of no rain. Rain would be bad for us and we would be in a mess.

After a couple of hours we crossed a north-south road and came to a crick at West Liberty where we watered the stock and had something to eat. Watered the stock extra as it is warm. Our rest was short and we are on our way again. Crossed several small cricks by fording them. Had annother "cow rest" at a crossroad then kept moveing to Metamora. What a relief. We have come to much better roades. We made twenty miles in nine hours from Pa's counter.

Its after dinner time so we are stopping at Solomon River for a real "cow rest" and cooked dinner. Pa seems in better spirits. Here we go again. In two hours or so we forded annother stream. Pa was determined to go within about ten miles of Marion. Uncle Chuck finally pulled the team off to the side of the road and talked to Pa. It was decided not to push the cows further. We had made more miles than the first day. A sign by the road said "Marion 7 Miles."

Now Pa tells us, "after he started accross on the not-so-good roads he wished he had gone by way of Portland and good roads even if it was a day's more travel. But we won't rush again unless it is almost to the end of our journey to Ioway."

Uncle Chuck told Charles that he did not see how the cows took it. One of them has about quit giveing milk and it is only the forth day so there is some discussion if walking the cows out of milk is happening. Tomorrow is Sunday so we are going on into Marion in the morning then camp untill the next day.

Sunday, May 11. Had breakfast and are takeing it easy for the first morning since we started for Ioway. We are told we will drive right through Marion but the Misissinwa River came first. We turned off into a camping ground and prepared for a day of rest with no traveling. Mother Ann and me rested up by washing up things that needed it. Then Charles and me drove the surrey into town to see what annother Marion that was not in Ohio looks like. Not so much we thought so we drove back to camp to take it easy. Nice day and warm.

Pa had an opportunity to sell one of the cows, the pokeist one, who was hardly giveing any milk anyway. It was swapped for cash as Pa put it. After dinner Pa and Ann went someplace in the surrey and the baby is left with me. The boys are really haveing a big time by themselves. My worry is to be sure they don't go over by the river but they took orders fine so not so bad a day after all.

Pa mailed some letters to his mother Elsie and in some way, he found out who the postmaster was to see if there was any letter for him from his mother. There was a letter that he was looking for. It had come by train. Now we know the real reason that he wanted to come this way and was so determined to come through Marion. Charles and me wondered if Hiram had other Post Office he would be interested in for the same reason but we did not enquire.

From Pa's counter he figured we had gone a bit over one hundred and forty miles since we left Marsailles. Uncle Charley guessed at one hundred and twenty-five miles behind us. So ends our first Sunday on the trip to Ioway.

Monday, May 12. We are up early and had breakfast. Weather very nice. Just warm enough. So here we go. Off early and only with one cow to graze at the end of a rope. We are trying something different to see if it will work. We let the cow graze on the way with either Charles or me on one end of the rope and the cow on the other end. We don't like the idea.

Last night at the campfire we found out that Hiram and Charley had been over this route last fall from Marsailles to Marion, Indiana. That made it easier and faster as we knew where to camp and so on. Us young folks were not in on this but just as well as now we are all new to it and on our own so the country is new to us.

Drove quite a while. A road sign to the left said "Kokomo—west, Tipton—straight ahead." We kept going straight. We stopped at a little crick for a "cow rest" then moved on to annother crick and through a little town called Simms. We went on into Howard County then a little further to a crick where we stopped for a rest and noon meal. On the way again and stopped at a T-road Chuck called it. Tracks to the west did not look as if they were well-travelled. On quite aways we came to a good-sized stream where there was a house or two and a small store. We crossed the river to the south bank and had a "cow rest" which was due any way.

Uncle Chuck took my horse and he and Charles went over to the closest house and talked to a man. The crick is Wild Cat Crick. We found out that the road to Kokomo accross the country was not too good if it rained as it is not graded very well so we are going on south to Tipton. We are now along a stream and a good place to camp. Our sixth camp. Hiram had planned on going through Kokomo so after things quieted down and Charles and me were watching the camp-fire, Pa and Charley were discussing how much they were off the planned route through Kokomo.

They took the saddle horses and went some place to get fixed up for morning. When they returned Pa stated, "we will go on west to Frankfort and there pick up the planned route." So we are to get up early as if we had not been doing that. So now for the quilts.

Tuesday, May 13. We are up early as planned and as usual it is rather dark. Tied the cow back on the end gate. The idea of haveing a cow on one end of a rope and Charles or me on the other end did not work. When Bossy did not want to move a jerk on the rope was not enough to prove to Bossy who was boss. It took the team on the wagon to prove to Bossy who was boss.

After a few hours we crossed a crick. Kept moveing a couple of hours then stopped for an "eat rest." Sky was almost clear. No rain today. What a relief.

Cross annother crick. Rested and watered the stock. On we go and came to a river which was not so big. Pa decided to camp for the night. Frankfort was a short way ahead. Hiram wanted to go through town real early in the morning. Chuck's idea too. So we are rolling in our quilts. See you in the morning.

Wednesday, May 14. A week ago today we started from Mar-sailles for Ioway. So now we are starting our seccond week of camp-ing on the way to the Indian Country out in Ioway. We have sort of gotten on to the hang of a camper's life.

Pa said, "we are sure luckey so far. No rain and no trouble worth worrying about." So off we go through the town of Frankfort which is quite a town. Were a number of roads that crossed the one we were on towards the west. Soon a "cow rest" then on our way again. We came to annother north-south road. The north one was marked "Lafayette."

There is annother immigrant in a covered wagon stopped over by the side of the road. Is talking to a man on horseback. Charley went over to talk to him. The man on horseback said, "the country up north is very hilley so it will be much easier to cross the Wabash River and Wabash-Erie Canal by going to the ferry at Attica or Williamsport. There is a railroad bridge at Attica but I'm not sure if the wagon bridge started a couple of years ago is completed enough so it can be used at all."

But he knew there was a good wagon bridge at Covington further south over the Wabash River and Wabash-Erie Canal. Also he knew the roads towards Covington were real good and used a lot. So we will go west. Don't know what the other man in the covered wagon did. We did not see him go.

Went through Linden. There was a railroad track and Bossy just ignored it or decided it was harmless. Came to a stream and decided it would be the place for our eighth camp. Tomorrow we will have to decide where to cross the Wabash River. So into the quilts for tonight. Pa will have to decide.

Thursday, May 15. We are off early. Everything working fine. After some hours we drove through New Richmond. We took a short rest then went on again to a junction at Pleasant Hill. We are swinging to the northwest. After some time we are takeing a "rest stop" as well as an "eat stop." We are at Newton and it was decided to go the road to the south-west toward Covington and the Wabash River bridge. Of course you had to pay toll on the ferries.

It is midafternoon. We have crossed the Wabash River which was quite a stream or looked so to Charles and me. The Canal was not as big as we thought it would be. So on we go. One more "cow rest" and the Illinois State line is in front of us. Is a good watering place and a fair-looking camp spot so it was decided that our last camp in Indiana would be here so we could look over into Illinois. Illinois will be the last state we will go all the way accross. It has taken us seven days to cross Indiana and no wet weather so far but we thought we would get it several times.

Pa was sure from his counter that we have covered some two hundred and seventy five miles. Might be a little less but anyway an average of close to thirty miles a day. Does not seem possible with cows to slow you down but here we are. So far the roads have been dry and only a few bad ones and not so bad at that. However the men think the roads will get not-so-good especially in annother hundred miles or so. Can't see why worying so far ahead.

But good news anyway. Pa decided to sell our last cow. She is getting pokier all the time and the continual walking does not seem to be good for her. She is almost dry so it was decided tomorrow as we passed Danville over in Illinois that the first reasonable offer will be good enough. Uncle Charley said, "we sure have been pushing our luck and something will go bust if we don't watch out." So in the quilts for us. Early in the morning we will be in Illinois. Night Charles—have a good till-midnight watch.

Friday, May 16. Here we are at breakfast. Its over and we are ready to be on our way. We are used to getting up early. It is warming up.

Here we go into Illinois in a couple of hours or so. Stopped at a farm house not so far out on the north side of Danville. Pa talked to a man after we stopped at a farm house about selling the cow. The farmer thought he knew someone who might be interested to buy and was close. He had talked about buying annother cow. He and Pa went over to see this man. They took Charles and my horse. So to pass the time away we fixed up something to eat. It was not very long untill Pa and two men came rideing up. They left with the cow not ours anymore and Pa said, "he had the cash and me the cow so we just traded or swapped."

Charles and me felt so good we could have hollered Amen but we knew better. Now there would be no cow torturing us like it was the past three hundred miles. Uncle Chet had to have his joke and fun so he said, "when we get out in the Indian Country out in Ioway we will have Buffalo milk."

Pa decided it was time to eat before we had gone very far but we talked him into waiting untill we came to the Vermillion River not so far ahead. The mile indicator says we are seven miles into Illinois. It might be a contraption as Uncle Chuck calls it but it helps to give a good idea on miles traveled and a guess as to how far to go which is important too. We crossed the Vermillion River and camped for a little late dinner. Rested longer than usual and now we are off again.

The wagon don't look right with no cows on the tailgate. No one feels bad though as they were a hinderance in place of a help and gave no milk. Crossed a good-sized crick and met a man going into town. Charles asked him "what branch or river that was." He said, "Vermillion." Must be annother branch. We moved on for some time. Had a rest then for quite a spell. Can't keep from looking at the end gate. No cows.

Crossed a crick. Sign at the corner with an arrow pointing south and said "CONKEYS STORE." So we go that way. Pa had been told about this place close to Salt Fork River. Here we are. Quite a few houses, a general store with C. H. CONKEY on it, a blacksmith shop, and a shelter with a fireplace. It is a good place to camp. It was built for covered wagons and their families like us going west. Our tenth camp. First one in Illinois and best one yet.

There are two other covered wagon families ahead of us. One which has two wagons and four children are going all the way to the Mississippi River. They have a brother there and a place to move right into. This family is in no hurry and expect to take ten days. We hope to make the Mississippi, cross at either Muscatine or Davenport, and make it in close to half that time. The other wagon had one child besides the parents. The boy is about nine years old.

After supper was over and we thought we were ready for the night it began to thunder and lightning flashed accross the sky. Was noisy. The Store Keep came out and told us we better move in under the shelter of the big shed roof as it might get real wet. So we are doing that but one man is staying in each wagon to watch the teams.

There was more noise than rain but it acted like one of those all night rains or drizzles so we are trying to go to sleep but it is rather noisy.

Saturday, May 17. Daylight. Everything outdoors is wet and a light drizzle is falling. Store Keep came out and advised us to stay another day and night for the roads would not be very good to travel on and a bit rough on the horses. We all decided to stay except the man with one boy. He decided to pull out on his own about noon. The drizzle had stopped and he had good huskey horses too. The weather is clearing and the sun is shineing some but not doing much as far as drying the roads goes. There is a warm south wind. Charley said, "let he wind blow and the sun have a chance. Ioway will be waiting for us."

The Store Keep, guess it was Mr. McConkey, is giveing the men directions and a bit of advice about the roads toward St. Joseph and on to Urbana City where he says the town has built a shelter for emigrants like us. There is shelter for covered wagons or whatever you have and also for the horses. Pa told Chet, "guess our cows would not have been welcome here."

The Store Keep said, "they went one better for folks—not only a shelter but a fireplace for cooking arrangements." The shelter has removable sides except the south side which is open. He admitted that this was where he got the idea that "a good shelter would be good business."

The family of three are pulling out on their own. It is just after noon. As to where they were going they did not say. Then of all things a Dr. Wilkins found out, likely from the Store Keep, that we were from Marion County, Ohio and he made himself known to Pa. He said, "I was born in Marion County and practiced there before coming out to the frontier" as he called it. Pa was as pleased as if he had found a long-lost brother.

The next day was Sunday which was our usual day of rest but we had all ready had a day of rest so it was decided to pull out early in the morning if the weather was fit. Our joking Uncle Chuck had to say, "our rabbit foot must still be working for us for this was our only rain in ten days." The two-wagon family decided to go early same as we did and take it easy. Pa and Ann stocked up at the store. Conkey is well-paid for the use of his shelter but it is worth it to us.

Conkey, guess it was, said, "being Sunday I will be over early and we will have a short Christian service here in the shelter." Forgot to mention there is a Post Office here as well as a blacksmith shop. Pa had the team's shoes looked after and everything greased. Here we go into our quilts.

Sunday, May 18. We are up early. Nothing new. Just finished breakfast. The Store Keep, true to his word, showed up and asked for a few minutes. He read a few Bible verses, said a short prayer, and wished us all a safe journey and that all would be well with us in our new home. Nice idea. Made you feel real good.

The family with the two wagons and four children were ready to leave the same time we were. Really enjoyed visiting with them as it was someone to talk to besides yourselves at the campfire. The older boy said, "we are from New Jersey." So they came from a long way off. Our trip is not so big. Uncle Chuck remarked, "Conkey knows what he is doing. He is planting the seed for future customers." Maybe the Store Keep knows folks better than we do.

Nothing happened all the way to St. Joseph. Short rest but not a cow rest. Had our noon meal. It was a hot one which beat cold ones. Stopped at a stream at St. Joseph and watered the horses. Pa decided to go on for a couple of hours and then camp for the night. Roads a bit soft. Must have had more rain here then at Conkey Town.

When we stopped the man with the two wagons and bigger

horses said, "we will see you tomorrow." Pa figured we were in for the night. The man said, "we are going into the shelter in town at Urbana City." Pa figured we were a couple of hours from Urbana City so here we are camped. Is cloudy with a chilly wind.

Monday, May 19. Pa woke up early. It was only starting to get daylight. A cold wind made it chilly and the sky looked like it could rain any time so it was decided we better get started and get to the shelter if we can before it rains and have breakfast there. So we are on our way. The clouds seem to be getting blacker with some thunder and lightning.

Uncle Charley told Pa to get the kids in the surrey and he and Ann to get going fast to try and get into the dry at the shelter. So away they go on the trot. Uncle Chet changed things as he was sure we were in for plenty of wet. He tied Nancy to the end gate and told me to get into the wagon with him. He wrapped a canvas arround most of Charles and his nag to keep them partially dry. Charles would have to trail behind on his "Charger" to see that everything was coming all right. It was steady and wet. Did not mind it but really enjoyed it. Guess because I am in the dry. Now Charles can be a real cowboy with no play. He seemes to be getting a kick out of it. He waves his hand after a fashion.

Must have been over an hour before we arrived where the surrey was in the dry. Uncle Chet drove the team right into the horse shed but it was not deep enough for the wagon. Charles came in beside the team then untied my nag Nancy (named after my mother) and put her under cover. He unhitched the team and backed the wagon out of the way. It is still raining quite hard so with the canvas for a cover Charles and me made for the big shelter.

So here we are in the dry. Let it rain. A warm fire in the cookplace. The two wagon folks ribbed Pa for not coming on in last night. He told them he thought the horses needed a rest. Now we remember we had no breakfast so next in order.

Sure plenty of floor space for blankets and quilts. May not be so soft but is dry. After our eats the men talked it over and decided to stay here a couple of days if there was no complaint. They never expected any complaint. This would give the roads time to dry a bit and some rest for the team. Oh yes, no cows is good. Mother Ann and me will do some washing. The rain barrels are full. It is good to stop traveling for a change and just to be in the dry.

Pa went to the store nearby and got some eggs so we could have bacon and eggs. Everyone has their own bacon but eggs are not very good travelers in a covered wagon despite careful packing. Covered wagons have no springs and our surrey has hardly enough room for the riders so no eggs are wanted or welcome.

In the middle of the afternoon when the clouds were breaking into a sprinkle now and then, a covered wagon pulled up at the shelter. There were two children, both good-sized but looked rather bedraggled. They were dry but cold so we hustled them all into the shelter. Our men took care of their team and told them to get up by the fire and help themselves to the hot bacon and eggs and coffee for those who wanted it. They did not hesitate very long. They knew we meant it and we enjoyed seeing them enjoy it.

Pa said the man's name was Jensen. Its getting dark so that lanterns are lit and between the lanterns and the cookfire it is real cozy. Travelers in covered wagons do not often get such nice treatment. It really helps to forget the rough ones that you expect and generally get.

The rain has stopped and the sky is clear. We are tired of watching it rain and the warm fire makes you sleepy. The man with the two wagons predicted, "going to be a spell of nice weather." He did not say why he thought so. You can notice the days are getting longer and it does not stay chilly in the morning. Anyway everyone is rolling in their bedding. No one cares to sleep in their covered wagon tonight.

Tuesday, May 20. When we awoke it was daylight. The sun was shining. We all ate breakfast together. The mother of the two children said, "you just don't know how we felt to see a warm fire and hot things to eat right from you folks." Mother Ann commented, "this could happen to any of us on a trip like this and someone could do the same thing for us."

The rain barrels are full so we are washing things that need it then hanging them out to dry in the sun and wind. Won't be many places like this to help the weary traveler who is the pioneer. The men bought food for the horses. No grass anymore as there are too many imigrants on the main routes going west.

After dinner the Jensen family pulled out for the west leaving such a nice dry place and a warm shelter. Mr. Jensen told Pa his reason. He said, "I can't get to north-central Illinois by staying here. The relatives are expecting us up along the big river." We wished them luck. And they are on their way.

Someone in authority from Urbana City came to see us all. Wanted to know how we all were doing, if everyone was well, and said that a Doctor was handy if anyone wanted one. No one seemed to need any pills or castor oil as everyone has some of their own remidies but its nice to be asked. It might be they were covered wagon folks not long ago or as Charley said, "They may be really checking for sanitary reasons as well as just for our health." Nice idea anyway.

Charles and me just fooled arround walking. There is lots of rideing straddle still ahead of us. Pa done some tinkering with his counter. Also had a blacksmith look over the horses' feet. Uncle Chet had to have his joke. He likes to rib Pa about his contraption so suggested haveing a bell sound every-so-often on miles. Pa just did not hear him. Charles and me are with Pa and his counter. In fact, Uncle Chet's jokes sometime are getting stale and rusty.

We watched the fire later than usual. Hiram said, "we'll start early in the morning but not too early. Let the sun do more drying."

Wednesday, May 21. Starting our third week on the way to Ioway. Had breakfast. Sun out good. It will be a bright day and warm. No cows so can camp most anywhere now. Pa is converted but don't say so.

The man with the two wagons wants the roads to dry more so will stay annother day. We did not see them just before we left for the west. Sure glad to get going again. Here we go. Rested once then came to the Sangamon River. Crossed into a little hamlet, Mahomet, and went on through town. Stopped for dinner. Gone fourteen miles and here we go again. Crossed a crick and then annother crick into Santa Anna. Good camping place. Gone almost thirty miles. Our fifteenth camp for us. Fixed things for a daylight breakfast.

Thursday, May 22. On our way at daylight after our breakfast. Why the rush? The sky is lighting up and on we go further west.

Stopped for a short rest then came to a crick by a grove and watered the horses. A man came along on horseback. He said something about Buckley's Grove at the crick. I expect this is it. Did not spend much time here but got going. The man said, "nice town, LeRoy, not over an hour ahead." We came to the town with a sign of Boots and Shoes that was so faded that I could not read the name.

Went right through town. Rested west of town and had something to eat. Watered the horses at a crick. On we go for an hour then came to a big crick with a bridge. There is a store close by. A man said, "it is Kickapoo crick, named after the Indians that had lived here." Is a Post Office in the store, a blacksmith shop and several houses, and a building on the crick that looks like a mill. Pa got some fresh eggs at the store and some sugar. He thought the price was high but I don't think so. Man at the store told us there had been a survey just on south for a railroad from Danville to the Illinois River. Charles said there was a sign, Delta, but Pa's map has Priceville on it. I give up.

Store man gave some advice how to go and get to Bloomington so we won't have to go through so much town. Bloomington is big—over ten thousand. He said that at a crick a mile south of town close to a man's barn lot you tell him I sent you and he will let you camp in his barn lot off the State Road for the night. Uncle Charley may know his name for he talked to him quite a spell. Here we are and it is working as the man said. Pa got feed from him so we could get an early start in the morning.

Some boys came by on their bareback horses and came over to our wagon. We told them we were on our way to Ioway. Both said, "never heard of the place." Makeing fun of us of course or maybe they have not been anyplace either.

Must be up before daylight to get through town before people are up. We wish we did not have to go through big towns.

Friday, May 23. Up real early to get through town before the teams and folks can bother us small town folks. On the way quite a spell. Now going west. Soon railroad tracks. Some cars had Illinois Central on them. Seems a lot of town but we hurried fast. Did not see too much. Not so many on the street yet. Some looked at the covered wagon, the surrey, and us horse-backers. Likely we were imagining things. We just don't like big towns and neither does Uncle Chet.

Not long untill we came to more railroad tracks and some engines makeing a lot of noise and puffing out black smoke. The team did not seem to mind but our saddle horses did not like their noise and smoke. Uncle Charley hollered, "watch out for the main line." Don't know which one that is but we are across anyway and on west. What a relief to be across the tracks and through the big town. Asked a man for directions to be sure we were on the State River towards Peoria.

Not so far came to a crick so we watered the horses and took a breather as Charles called it. Must have been an hour to another crick which a boy told us was Sugar Crick. Was a blacksmith shop, a building that looked like a mill, and some signs that said "Twin Grove Mills" and "Kings Mills." Looked like there might been a town here. Sign said "Willesboro Post Office." Stopped to eat. Folks are scarce here. An old sign said "Concord" but we were told the town is now Danvers. Anyway we went through it. Not much town. Came to a crick. Was annother Sugar crick so must be sweet water arround here. Came to a marker "Tazwell County" and a building called Way Side Inn.

Good roads. We watered the horses. Is hilley. Stopped for a bite to eat. On we go. Same old landscape for quite a spell then Mackinaw City. Quite a village. Kept going to the Mackinaw River or a big crick anyway. Crossed at a ford, went north aways, and crossed the same crick twice close together as it is real crooked.

We are camping. This our seventeenth night. Hope to be in Peoria tomorrow night.

Saturday, May 24. Up early as usual. Seems we have gotten off our route some way, the one we were supposed to follow. Going east and north to a settlement, New Castle, then turned west to a crick. I believe it was Deer crick. At a north-south road we stopped for a bite to eat and a short rest for the horses. On we go to a town, Groveland, which is an Amish or Mennonite settlement. Seems all the men have whiskers and some have full beards. A man asked if we had any horses to sell. Pa said no but told him we started with two cows and sold them as they were too pokey. Told them we were on our way to Carroll County, Ioway. We were told about a big Mennonite settlement out in Ioway on the Ioway River in Ioway County. They have thousands of acres and a railroad has just been built through their land to Homestead. The State Road route goes through there and we think we will too. Maybe a lot of whiskers there as here. A lot of nice folks behind the whiskers. We are going through Ioway City for business reasons.

At the store Pa was told it was only two hours or so to the Illinois River. There is a village, Foun du Lac, not far from the south end where the river widens into Lake Peoria. Also there is a wooden bridge accross the river. He said, "better camp for the night on this side of the river." Pa and Ann had planned it that way anyway but did not tell the whiskered folks that.

Pa wants to get a good night's rest before going through the big town. Had special business here. Mother Ann's father had a brother named De Witt Drown who had lived in Peoria many years after he went there in 1839 as Government surveyor. His widow Sarah Drown still lives there and Ann had promised we would see her if we came that way. She lives on third street in the eleven hundred block with her daughter. She knows we are on our way to Ioway.

Arrived at a nice place to camp where arrangements to camp are made and we had to pay. Pa enquired about Aunt Sarah's address and located a man who knew just where it was. He offered to come over to our camp early in the morning and guide them to this address. He would ride with them in the surrey.

I would have charge of the baby and the kids and ride in the covered wagon. Uncle Chuck was to be given instructions how to go after we crossed the bridge and this route would bring us to a place to camp untill Pa, Ann, and this man caught up with us. You could tell Uncle Charley was a bit worried but he did not say so. He does not like big towns. Tomorrow will be Sunday which is our day of rest. There is not so much travel anyway on Sunday so should not be many teams out on the streets.

Pa figured by his pedometer that we had made over four hundred miles and a little more. So we hoped we were halfway to Carroll County, Ioway. Had our supper and talked some. Rolling in for the night now. See you in the morning. Our eighteenth camp.

Sunday, May 25. Up early with the sun. Had breakfast and were ready to roll when the man who was to serve as guide arrived. He had his directions all on paper with a sketch for Uncle Charley. Besides he explained it and gave him some advise. Here we go. Over the wooden bridge which has a draw to let boats through on the river. We are accross. The surrey went on west and we turned north. Did not seem right to go annother way but that was the way it had to be.

Things worked slicker than we expected. Uncle Charley read his directions and it was not long untill we went through some of the downtown. Then out into the residence section again and then into the country. Came to a small stream with shade trees. It was a place we were supposed to wait for the surrey. Seems odd without the surrey. There are five of us besides the baby and I am to be the cook for all of us and have it ready to eat close to noon because the man said, "I will be there with them and it will be close to being that time so expect to be on time." Sure enough.

Sure enough I had things about ready for our meal when here they come in the surrey along with annother man leading annother horse for the good samaritan to ride back home on. Pa wanted to pay them for their good deed but they both said, "we would be ashamed of ourselves if we accepted pay." But they did agree to try my cooking which was a feather in my bonnet I thought. Our good Samaritans are soon on their way. We hope we can help someone else in a similar way sometime.

Ann said that Aunt Sarah Drown was enjoying good health and going on seventy years old this fall. Uncle De Witt had been dead five years. Aunt Sarah was real pleased that she had a chance to visit them. She was so worried they would not come this way as they were the first blood relative she had seen on her side for many years. She did not remember how many years.

Well, takeing the man's advice we moved on several hours and came to Kickapoo crick. A good camping place so here we are. The Mississippi River will soon be our problem.

Monday, May 26. Up early as usual. Some six miles on the way to Edwards Station along Kickapoo crick most of the time. Crossed a crick then turned to the right and saw a sign "Jubilee College." We just kept going to Brimfield. Stopped to eat. Pa's indicator says fifteen miles. Rested only once. No cows. On we go for a couple of hours. Crossed French crick. Good roads. A couple of hours to Spoon River. Hills on both sides and real steep. We all got out and walked and for the first time used a tow rope on the wagon tongue, a wide breast strap on each of the saddle horses and a whiffle-tree arrangement. We had four horses which was a big help for sure and the wagon team needed the extra help. The hill was long as well as rather steep. It would have been real rough doing it all by themselves, that is if they could have made it by themselves. Anyway they did not have to. The first real work the saddle horses had done so far from our viewpoint.

Here we are at Trenton, a small place. Stopped a short time and in about an hour are back by the railroad. Pa decided that with hills and all we better not try for Knoxville today. Made annother fifteen miles. A couple of stops and we camped. Days are getting longer. If the horses could take it we might cover more miles. The roads are good compared to a few miles back. It has been decided that the horses are doing their best so we won't push them. Yet, when the end of the trip is close, maybe then. So here we go into the quilts.

Tuesday, May 27. A good breakfast. Pa seemed extra happy and before we started the wheels turning again towards the west he said, "we are at least halfway to Ioway. Our indicator shows four hundred and seventy five miles. We surely have passed the halfway mark soon after we left Peoria. I think Peoria is close to the middle of our journey." That made us all feel real good. We are on our way. In an hour we were in Knoxville which is the county seat of Knox county. We are stopping at the Court House for some advise on the best place to cross the Mississippi River. Pa had heard about the bad spring floods along the big river about the first of May but was told in Marion, Indiana that the river was dropping fast.

The sheriff at the Court House said, "the ferry camp is in Rock Island. Its been badly flooded but its in use again. You can get over to Davenport all right. Tnen there are the Ioway roades no matter where you cross." Then he added, "while the roades at Drurey's landing and accross the river from Muscatine were badly flooded it is my opinion that the roades from Davenport west would be worse than from Muscatine because the Drurey landing folks and Muscatine officials have been spending much time and money on their roades to keep the ferry folks at Davenport from getting more than their share of the ferry trade." He was really pulling for Muscatine so we don't know where we will cross the river yet. Found out we will not have to go through Galesburg. We are takeing an angeling road toward the northwest. It saves miles besides.

Now crossing a railroad and on north to Henderson crick. Had a rest and a bite to eat. On we go to a sign at our left "New Henderson." Stopped at a store for something. Now on north. Another store. Crossed Pope crick and north into Windsor. Pa got some feed. Going west then north. Rather hilly. Charles came back. He had been scouting ahead looking for a good camping place. Here it is.

There is a man working close to where we are camping. Pa went over and talked to him about the Rock Island–Davenport ferry. He said, "its about twenty miles to the ferry. As to the Muscatine ferry over at Drurey's it is a good day's journey. There is a sort of town on this side, Pines Bluff. Its not a real town. I do not know if one ferry is better or not but the Rock Island one is a day's travel closer from the east so it is used the most."

Uncle Charley said, "Hiram, if we get going early and push things we can be on Ioway dirt for tomorrow night we will be getting some rest on both sides of the river." Pa said, "I think it would be pushing the horses too much but it makes little difference if we travel a little further on this side of the river." Uncle Chet then came up with, "I realy prefer an extra day in Illinois and believe the Muscatine ferry the best place."

This plan is to go west early in the morning and get to Muscatine on this side of the river at Drurey's and camp for the night. How soon we will be on the ferry boat depends on how many are ahead of us. Anyway we will soon be on the same roades over in Ioway in any case. Pa seemed in favor of Rock Island and Unkey for Muscatine. He was likely thinking about more big towns to go through the other way. While the men were deciding where to cross the river Charles was reading my diary of yesterday and argued that we camped on Mills crick not Edwards River last night. Well, we are not going back to find out so he wins.

Heard Ann tell Pa, "I wonder why the Muscatine crossing seems to be the most reccomended over Rock Island and gets the most advertiseing." Pa commented, "even if Rock Island gets the most advertiseing I have about made up my mind to go by way of Muscatine. There's not really much difference. It will be the same on the time to get to Carroll County." Then he added, "as far as I am concerned I want the Mississippi River behind me." One fellow claimed the roads north from Muscatine were smoother but admitted he had never seem them.

Now that brother of mine is arguing that this is our twentieth night. This traveling must be getting him. I told him to stop arguing and to stop reading my diary and that I had settled on Mills crick over Edwards River to please him and he would just have to settle that this is the twenty-first camp, which it is. He just grined like he always does when he knows he is on the short end of his arguments. So we are rolling in for the night.

Wednesday, May 28. Ate early at a daylight breakfast. Pa remarked, " Charley wins. We will cross the river at Muscatine." So off we go to the west. Saw a sign which said "Pleasant Ridge" to the right. Just kept moveing to Edington. We have made fifteen miles. It is ten o'clock. Gave the horses a blow and had a bite to eat. No more eats untill the next town. Stopped for a short rest and typical camp meal. Was told it was not over ten miles to Drurey's Ferry Landing and that it was a good idea to get your name in the pot as soon as you get there for passage early in the morning. Soon on our way. With the excitement of seeing the big river it seemed we were going slow but really makeing good time. Here we are. It is just five o'clock.

Pa had hurried ahead with my horse and I drove the surrey horse for the first time on the trip. Pa was waiting for us. He had a campsite arranged for and our name in the pot for crossing before noon. We are sure there are over a dozen ahead of us so the idea of the man's to get there the night before was a real good one and a good deal for us. Hiram is really pleased and so are the rest of us as we know we can cross tomorrow for sure.

Uncle Charley said, "we will have only two hundred miles to go when we get accross the Mississippi into Ioway." Hope he is right. So we are to spend our last night on Illinois soil and tomorrow we will really be at the begining of the end of the trip to the Promised Land out in Ioway, the Indian Country.

A man came over and talked to us. He remarked, "you should have been here several weeks ago. You would have seen the Mississippi rampaging on the worst of its floods that the old timers can remember. There were no crossings for quite a spell. Not just too much water but too much trash and big trees that would smash anything in their way."

Water is still high but not dangerous. Melting snow up north has caused it. It just warmed up too fast. Might have been nice to see the floods but not to have to wait for it to get safe to cross. Let's go to sleep so see you in the morning.

Thursday, May 29. No hurry as we have lots of time. Charles is disapointed that we would not have to be ferried over on a ferry boat that had horses for drive power or a horse-powered tread mill. Instead we are haveing to be ferried over on a steam-powered ferry. I like the steam power the best. Don't know why Charles was all set for horses for power.

Went down to the landing several times to see the boat being loaded. The boat had a name on it. DE_____ some or other.[2] I should have written it down but maybe someone else remembers it. Are a few houses here. The place is called Pines Bluff. Do not see any pine trees around.

The ferry was on the job as soon as it was light enough to see anything. There is lots of noise. Maybe that is what woke us up early. Might have been the excitement of what we expected to happen. Pa told us to keep back and not get in the way of the men and wagons being loaded on the boat.

Things seemed to work out very well. About eleven o'clock Pa was told to have his outfit at a certain place by about one o'clock so our turn would be soon. It felt good to know you were being taken care of. Had all our stuff ready to move aboard. In fact, Charley said it was only twelve-thirty. The boat is over on the other side unloading. Then we hear the whistle toot-toot and the boat is backing out into the river. Quite a ways over there too.

It is only a little after one o'clock and they are pulling into the landing on our side. The ferry tied up to the landing platform and the big landing apron as Pa called it came down. They did not seem to have any return cargo. A man is walking down the gang plank. Charles insists that is what it is. Looks like an awful wide plank to me so it will be a loading platform to me.

A man talked to Pa and Uncle Charley. Now here we go. Drove to the loading platform. The horses were blindfolded so they would not get excited over seeing so much water or maybe so much churning of so much water by the paddle wheels of propellers. No one is allowed in the wagon or surrey or on the horses. We walked on board. The wagon and surrey wheels are blocked and the horses unhitched.

Pa and Charley are holding the bridles of the team and someone was holding the head of the surrey horse. Charles and me held our own horses' heads and talked to them. It is really exciteing. Nothing like it before for us. Mother Ann has the real job sitting on a chair holding the baby and Howard. I kept hold of Archie's hand with one of mine and the nag with the other hand. Now the whistle screeches. The horses just throw up their heads. Their eyes being covered they can't see anything anyway so won't get scared very easily. Then we find out Charles' horse and my horse are tied extra to a post. They could not have moved very much anyway. Nothing happened anyway all the way over.

The big loading platform has been pulled up. Two more blasts and then puff-puff and chug-chug of the engines and we are on our way from the Illinois landing. We are crossing the Mississippi. Goodbye Illinois and here we come Ioway.

We watched the bubbling and swirling water in the wake of the boat. Guess they are paddle wheels from the covers we can see. Nothing is happening on the way over. Well, here we are pulling into the Ioway side landing before we are ready to stop enjoying it. Is so exciting to cross the big river.

Almost as soon as the boat bumped the landing pier the big

apron came down with a bump. The team was hitched to the covered wagon, the blocks knocked out from in front of the wheels, and the wagon moves off first up on Ioway soil. "Ioway dirt," said Uncle Charley. He grinned like a small boy with a new toy like a top.

The horse is hitched to the surrey, the blocks knocked out, and Pa drove off after the wagon. Then Charles and me followed with our nags but a man had hold of the other side of their bridles untill we were up on Ioway soil, on Ioway dirt. They thought we could not handle them maybe. We are safe anyway. The blinders are taken off the horses after they were on shore.

We are assigned to a camping place back from the river aways so now we can get our things back together, have our eats, and be all set and ready to go to pull out for the west to Ioway and the Indian Country. What a relief to be on the west bank of the big river Mississippi.

Did not waste much time on eating and resting. Uncle Charley said, "not quite three o'clock. Let's get away from this dust and noise." So we are ready for Ioway—our future home—although its quite aways to the west yet, almost to the Missouri River.

We are off through town mostly north and west. Crossed the new railroad in about an hour then moved on. Stopped for a short rest. Weather is nice. Moved on up the road—I mean the trail. We are Westerners now so its a trail. Crossed some cricks. We wanted to get to the ferry over the Cedar River before we camped for the night. Want to cross the river tonight if we can. This is not such a big river compared to the one we just crossed. And we have made it. Our rabbit foot is still working. The ferry man said, "get on the boat." We did and over we go.

The name was Tice's ferry. So here we are on the west bank of the Cedar River and are makeing camp. Tomorrow off for West Liberty and Ioway City where there is a bridge accross the Ioway River. So we eat our first meal in Ioway and are rolling into our quilts. So good-night.

Friday, May 30. Up early and had breakfast. Are ready to start the wheels rolling to the west although it is still a bit dark. When the sun makes enough light to see we will be going on our way. It was like our early days of the starting off of our covered wagon trip through Indiana. But now things have changed. The end is not so far away so we wanted to get going and get there. The Ferry boat man was up early too and was unloading the first emigrant as we pulled out of our camp. It was not quite four o'clock.

The trail angeled to the northwest. In a little while, maybe an hour or so, we crossed a soggy draw with a crick in the middle. It was not very long until we crossed the new railroad tracks. We stopped under a tree. It is real warm. We give the horses a breather. After stretching our legs we resaddled ourselves and moved on. Must have been an hour when we came to a town, West Liberty. In a little while we crossed to the other side of the railroad tracks. Came to another crick and watered the horses. We are moving into Johnson county. Chuck says, "eight o'clock, doing all right."

The trail angeles for awhile then turns west quite a spell then angeles north. Crossed a good-sized crick just south of where two cricks came together. Good place to water the horses and being close to eating time by our stomachs we ate and rested a bit. On our way. In a couple of hours we are at the railroad where it goes into Ioway City. We came to the Ioway River and crossed on a bridge. A man told us it was the Burlington street bridge.

After we had crossed, Pa, Ann, and Charley had a talk and decided we were to continue on several miles to a town named Coralsville. This is where we are to camp tonight. Mother Ann got into the covered wagon with the baby. Pa took the surrey and drove back accross the bridge and into town. He is to get hold of the men that he bought the Carroll County land from last fall. Mother Ann told us that their names are Agnew and Ford.

We arrived at the campsight and were all set up for the night when Pa showed up. He had found one of the men but I don't know which one. He is to be back at their office early in the morning, seven or earlier. We are told, "we are in the Mormon's town where they camped in 1856 and started their handcart trip to Utah from here." Pa had told us this too. He remarked that "we would follow about the same trails they did untill after we passed Des Moines."

Getting dark so we are rolling in. Be up before five o'clock for Pa's early trip into town for his meeting with those two men.

Saturday, May 31. End of May. Our third day in Ioway and our twenty-fifth day on the way from Ohio to the Indian Country out in Ioway. Sounds romantic, don't it? Had our breakfast early so Pa

could meet with Agnew and Ford in town before seven o'clock as
planned. Pa took my rideing horse. He said the surrey was a nuisance
and took too much time.

Pa and Uncle Charley had been over to the black-smith horse-
shoer last night. Unkey and Charles are to get the horses over to the
shop early this morning to get their shoes reset or whatever is needed
to look the wagon over. Pa surprised us and was back right after noon
time. He said, "things worked slicker than expected." He sounded
well pleased with his business visit and with Agnew and Ford. He
talked quite a while with Ann. Charles took my steed over to the
black-smith to get fixed up and get the job on the other horses
speeded up. Wondered why Pa always took Nancy and never
Charles' nag so I asked him. He said, "Nancy just rides with less
jolt."

It was decided that as soon as Charles was back with Nancy
(named after my mother who died when I was five years old) we will
move on. Pa is over at the shop. When the men came back we finished cooking dinner and ate in no hurry. We loaded up and are on
our way toward Homestead which is the Mennonite or Amish settlement of several thousand members and over twenty thousand acres
of land along the Iowa River—so Pa told us.

We are north of the new railroad track that is only a year old.
We are not far from the railroad tracks. The trail is good. Crossed
some cricks. Came to a town, Tiffin, but not much there. Kept moving then stopped at a crick to water the horses and for a rest stop. On
we go. Things sure look neat. Annother depot at Oxford. Forded a
good crick. Not a bad place to camp so we are. Had not gone many
miles but it was late to try for the town of Homestead which is just
ahead so we are rolling in for the night.

Sunday, June 1. A new month. Had breakfast and we are off to
the west. Pa wondered if the Amish would object to us traveling
through their town on Sunday as they are a very religious sect.[3]

Road are very good. Things look about the same. The farms
look well-kept. No farm houses as they live in towns. We are south
of the railroad. Soon crossed over to the north side and then back
again. Here we are in Homestead. It is early, maybe six o'clock, but
there is lots of activity going on anyway. Pa said his counter showed
over six hundred miles and he pointed to a sign "Des Moines 100
miles." Could Des Moines really be that close?

All the men here have beards who are old enough to raise one. Looks odd to us but it seems part of their religious belief. In place of haveing any trouble with the whiskered folks we were very surprised when we were stopping for a rest to have these men and wives stop and ask us what they could do for us. Your respect and admiration for them and their beliefs increased many times over and your thanks to them was real.

So we are off to the west. New railroad grade not far away. Rails for work trains are down so we crossed over and came back over again. In an hour we passed through a town. Kept moving and went through some timber. We see fields with new crops and they showed much care. No wonder Mennonites are so successfull. They are not afraid of work and that was easy to see.

Came to a crick. Stopped and watered the horses. On we go. It is then rest time and we had a bite to eat. We are south of the railroad. Here we are in Marengo. The rails are down and are used by work trains. We moved on close to Big Bear crick then through lots of woods. Now out of the woods for a while then back in and accross a little crick and on and on. Rather hilly so we had to rest the horses more often. Now we are on a more level ground and country. Came to a townsight. Rails are down but are not too level. Now a town on the county line of Poweshiek. A signpost says "Victor." We drove on accross a crick and kept going about an hour or so. Then timber and came to Little Bear crick again. We crossed and made camp. "A good days travel with so many hills," Pa said.

Is rather late for us to make camp. This was our longest Sunday travel, but Pa is getting more anxious to get to Carroll County. So are the rest of us as well so into the quilts for tonite.

Monday, June 2. Off early as usual. Crossed the new railroad. Rails are laid but not very level. On west a few miles. In an hour we turned in through a town. Not much here. Crossed back over the tracks. The men are working on leveling the rails.[4] We crossed Little Bear crick again. It sure looks like the town was here on the crick but the railroad is changing that. We are south of the railroad again. Had to cross the crick twice close together. Soon going south then turned west. Trail sure twists to keep out of the sloughy spots. Annother town, Malcom. We are south of Little Bear crick.

Stumps most anyplace even in the middle of the road or rather the trail. Sometimes they are so close together there is hardly room to drive between them. In fact, this almost caused a fatal accident. Archie must have dropped off to sleep for when going between two stumps one of the front wheels of the wagon hit a stump and Archie rolled off the wagon seat. Thanks to our luckey stars Uncle Charley was alert and saw Archie hit the double trees and bounce off in front of one of the wheels. Uncle Charley said, "I thought he was a goner. I pulled so hard on the lines to stop the team and wagon that it brought the team back against the whiffle trees." But the wagon stopped and when Archie's shoulders hit the ground his head was almost under the wheel. The jar must have brought him wide-awake. He sat up a second in the clear before the horses straightened up and the wheels moved forward over the spot that Archie's head had just left. Am sure luck is with us.[5]

Pulled up a little ways to a good place to stop. Besides Charley was so shaken up with the near accident. Now Pa and the rest of us found out just what had almost happened. Had our noon meal while we all settled down.

The railroad is just accross the crick. Watched it a little while. The rails are laid down too. It is a work train and the men are leveling the tracks but we have to get going on west again. In a couple of hours we turned north a mile or so then west again. Crossed several cricks then a bigger crick. Stopped for a rest and watered the horses. Trail is better. Real warm.

We are on the main State Road from Ioway City to Des Moines. We must have got off the trail when we got mixed up with the stumps. Charley might have dozed off and the team wandered onto the wrong trail. Who knows?

Pa is sure there is a stage stop soon somewhere. He remembers from last year's Ioway trip because this part was by stage. We crossed a crick and decided to make camp. Not as many hills as yesterday so it was easier on the team. Had supper and a nice campfire. No one said a word about Archie's near accident. Pa said, "Grinnell can't be so far away."

Charles is going to take his night watch, his first in Ioway, so the rest of us are rolling in. What a day.

Tuesday, June 3. Up early. In an hour came to a crossroad and a sign "Grinnell" with an arrow pointing towards the north. Crossed a crick. Here are some buildings. Pa thought they looked a bit familiar. He thought it was last year's Stage Coach stop but was not real sure. He said, "I saw so many new things for the first time with just a look." Pa stated, "it is only a little over a hundred miles from here to Carroll County. We have gone over seven hundred miles in twenty-eight days. They are behind us, not ahead of us."

We are in Jasper County. Picked up some supplies and then on we go through some woods to winding road. Turned northwest and crossed a new row of survey stakes where there has been some grading for the new railroad tracks. Drove along a crick then turned west and crossed it. Kept going and crossed several more cricks. Now a town. "A town a-borning," Pa said. It was Kellogg on the new railroad survey. Through some heavy timber then we watered the horses and had a little to eat. Is real warm.

Early afternoon into Newton. Went on west and crossed the Skunk River. Not so small. It looked bigger than a crick. On we go and we are in Colfax. Stopped at a store and was told, "a mile or so on west is Squaw crick and a good camping place." They acted as if, or so it seemed to us, that they were afraid we might camp here. We did not think they were very friendly as most folks are. They get tired of emigrants too maybe although emigrants are good cash customers.

Crossed a crick. There is a vacant log house close. Pa and Charley went over to look at it. The inside had been used to store grain in. The sky is covered with rainy looking clouds. Uncle Charley had commented on there being quite a few vacant log houses we had passed. Pa thought we better stick to the covered wagon and our rabbit foot luck but the rest of us stuck with Uncle Charley. Pa lost as we thought sleeping in a log cabin house would be fine.

Pa, Ann, and the baby stuck to the covered wagon. Pa said, "I don't need any practice sleeping in a log cabin. I was born in one back in Ohio." Swept it out real good and brought in our bedding. Let it rain.

We were in for a big surprise. A pair of Skunks had decided on a home under the slab floor. When they heard our noise above they decided to come out and see what was going on. Ann was sitting in the surrey and spied them first. She called to Pa, "see the striped kitties." He looked and called to us, "come out quick. There are polecat arround." We looked and then moved fast. The kitties just looked. Luckey for us they did and were not between us and the covered wagon. We made it and decided no more vacant log cabins for us. For once Uncle Charley had nothing much to say except, "never smelled a thing. They must have just moved in."

There was a house close by. Likely it was the owner of the log cabin we had decided not to bed down in. Pa went to the house and asked if we could have permission to park off the State Road just in their barnyard and if it rained if the men could use the barn to sleep in. Of course we were not turned down. The woman said Ann and the baby could have a bed in the house. It was nice of her but Pa said that "he, Ann, and the baby would sleep in the wagon and the rest of us in the barn where there was plenty of hay for a soft bed." It onley showered a little after all.

What an experience. Pa told the man about trying the log house and how the skunks gave us a scare. He got a big laugh out of it and said, "there are so many skunks in this county that is why the Skunk River is named that and it has not changed much in skunk population in twenty years."

So we had a night in the barn for some of us. Even the horses were inside. These folks not only fed our horses but refused any pay. The lady came out and said, "don't you dare leave untill you have had breakfast with us. Not so long ago we were pioneers traveling just as you are now." Nice to expect flapjacks and bacon we told them. The man remarked, "just trying to repay some of the nice things that were done for us."

We know where we will eat in the morning. So night. Pleasant dreams.

Wednesday, June 4. Four weeks ago we were just leaving on the beginning of this trip. Now about a week or so to go.

We are up early but so are the folks in the house. The lady came out and almost demanded we come in and tidy up. "We know how you feel, not presentable. We came here in the early forty's by covered wagon and you are eating breakfast with us. Don't you remember?" and she laughed. Of course we had buckwheat cakes, fresh side pork and coffee. You could eat your fill with no smokey taste. Words are no good in cases like this. We did not get away so early. Pa told them we were headed for Carroll County and had been out and arranged for the farm last fall.

So we are on our way headed for Carroll County. Cricks and hills. Crossed a crick on a new bridge and stopped for our noon meal. It was the old smokey kind we are used too but good any way. Short rest and on we go. We are in Polk County. Annother crick. Roads are not so bad, considering. Stopped for camp on Four Mile crick. Sky is clear so we are thankfull for that. The counter showed under sixty miles the last two days but that's not so bad. We remember the striped kitties and the inside breakfast. Pa said, "it is less than fifteen miles to Des Moines, the Ioway Capital." We did not see much of it but some of us will later.

We will cross the Des Moines River tomorrow on a new bridge and our last big stream to cross. I am sleeping in the covered wagon tonight. Just don't feel too good. Camp life is getting me maybe?

Thursday, June 5. Pulled out for Des Moines early. I am going to ride in the covered wagon today. Don't feel so good yet but better. Must been two hours or so we crossed the river on the big bridge which looked new. Pa is driveing the team and Uncle Charley is rideing my horse, the first time for any length of time.

Did not see very much in this part of the new Capitol City. It looked like it was not very grown up. We followed what we were told was the old Mormon trail of 1856 for quite a while. Is the northbound mail and stage routes. Then we turned north along Walnut crick I believe it was for quite a while. Then we are in Dallas County stopping for a rest and something to eat. Watered the horses from our wagon supply for the third time on the trip. Moved on for several hours. Weather is warm but nice. In fact it feels just about right and so do I.

Here we are in the town of Adel. Crossed the north Racoon River on a bridge. This will be the same river that our new home— the log house—is on. Pa said, "the cabin is too close to the 'coon,' but that is where the spring is at."

Told that we were still on the old Mormon trail for some time yet. Crossed Panther crick and turned north. After an hour or so we made camp on the west bank then the road turns west. Anyway, while I did not see much I feel that the saddle is for me tomorrow. The counter showed thirty miles today. Not so bad. Pa remarked, "some of us will be back and see Des Moines soon." Night, rolling in.

Friday, June 6. Left Panther crick after an early breakfast. Four hours later we saw the Greenville Post Office then Mosquito crick. Crossed and watered the horses. We've gone fifteen miles. Not so long and we are in Guthrie County. Here is Ross crick. Watered the nags, rested a bit, then on into Panora. Camped on Middle Coon

River south-west of town. Guess it is not much over twenty miles to-day.

This is a good place to rest. The horses are doing all right. Uncle Chet said, "especially after so long a trip—over seven hundred miles from Hiram's figures and more to go." This is our fifth week.

Is early yet so Charles and me walk down to the river to fish. Uncle Chet showed up as he said, "to help carry the load of fish we were going to hook." Big joke. Anyway we fooled him and ourselves because we caught some real nice ones. The drawback is to clean the messy things. Back to camp and fish for supper.

Saturday, June 7. We are up early eating breakfast. Sun up high and bright. Its almost four-thirty. We're not late except for Sunday's, for forced rests, for repairs or some needed attention for the horses, or for rain. Been luckey so far. Few rainey days with lost time. Does not look like rain today. Pa said he hoped to be in Carrollton soon so Sunday would be at our own log house.

But now we must spend annother day at Panora because one horse on the covered wagon had a bad shoe. Nothing to do but wait our turn. Horse-shoer had work ahead of us. Our turn came and we are in. Is well after dinner before our horse has his shoes reset. Hiram decided there was no reason to move tonight as we are all ready set here. So we are here for the night. Pa suggested more fishing so to have fish for dinner tomorrow.

Is a good day's travel to Carrollton so no Sunday rest. We will be up and going with the sun. Pa haveing been to Carrollton last year knows where to camp unless a lot of changing since then. So we are unsaddled for the night. See you in the morning.

Sunday, June 8. Up extra early. Why the rush? Anyway breakfast is over and we are off for the north. Last leg before the County Seat. Crossed a crick and headed for the river. Has good gravel bottom to ford. Road wanders west then south then west. Wonder why? Then north through some timber. Crossed the "Coon" on a bridge or at least that is what we thought. Unkey says, "it just likes to look like one." Anyway it kept us out of the water. Moffit's Grove then a rest. On through timber. Crossed a crick and watered the horses. Then to Willow crick. Saw a sign "Dodge Post Office" and soon are there. Kept moveing through some timber and settlements. Turned towards the river and had to ford.

North a bit and we are in Carroll County at last. A rest stop then go up along the river to some log buildings. A sign said "Niles." We stopped and talked to the man. He said "it was six or seven miles to Carrollton and we better camp." It was not late but would be when we hit the County Seat. Pa decided to camp although he did not like to give up the idea of being there tonight.

Niles, believe it was, told the men he was trying to get a dam built and a mill on the river and hoped the Supervisors would help finance it as a public necessity. He must have quite a parsel of land here. So we are here for the night. Tomorrow Carrollton for sure.

Monday, June 9. Off as soon as we could see the so-called roads. Niles advised going west and north to cross the river on the Galloway bridge. He said "there were more hills if we went on the other side of the river." So we kept moveing. Here we are in Carrollton about three hours after sun up.

Pa located about the same spot for camping that he looked over last year when he was here. So while we arranged for camping Pa went over to what they called the Court House and found the Judge or whatever he was called. He did not have the time available to finish up on legal matters today so Pa has to go back at seven o'clock in the morning. So Charles, me, and Uncle Charley looked over the town which is the new Court House being built.

Unkey had to enjoy annother joke. He asked a man, "just where is Carrollton or Carrollton City?" The man, looking suprised or pretended to be, said, "you are right in the middle of it, the coming metropolis, of not only Carroll County but this part of the State of Ioway." I wondered if Unkey thanked him for this information. So here we are all back in camp. Pa is rather disgusted after all the hurrying to get here and have to wait untill tomorrow.

What a relief to get Archie and Howard into their quilts. They just were everywhere they were not supposed to be. So Charles and me go under the covered wagon for last night before the log cabin or so we hope.

Tuesday, June 10. Up but not so early as the date with the Judge is not untill after seven o'clock at his office. Pa told Charles and me that we and him and Mother Ann were to go to the Judge's office today. He told us that last night. Pa said, "some of the money left to your mother from her father's estate was now Charles and mine and was being used to pay a share of the farm costs and now we would be landowners."

Well, here we are at the man's office. The papers are ready to sign. Some have all ready been signed and fixed up. Things are sure slow. What a suprise when Pa pulled a canvas sack from somewhere. It must have been in his shirt. He counted out one thousand dollars in gold to pay for the land and some more to pay the Judge for legal fees. So Mother Ann, Charles, and me have our names on the deed. About noon Pa went back after he had dinner to get some more papers. Something about an abstract he called it. He was back to camp late afternoon.

I kept the kids while the adults went buying supplies so they would not have to come back to Carrollton very soon as it is eighteen miles each way. Uncle Charley pretended to be insulted that he had to be kid-keeper some of the time when the rest of us had to go the Court House. Where Pa kept his sack of gold all the way from Ohio is a mystery to some of us except Mother Ann who tells no secrets. She just gave a big smile when we asked her.

Lake City up in Calhoun County will be the closest town six or seven miles north of our farm. So likely we'll go more often to Lake City than here. It is a County Seat too. Being rather late to start for our log cabin home we decided we better stay here and pull out early in the morning. So our last camping night before we will be at our future home for a long time. We thought last night would be our last camp.

Wednesday, June 11. We are up early. All are anxious to get to our log cabin home on the new farm up on the "Coon" which we hope will be home for most of us for a long time. Our wheels have bent the grass towards the west for quite a spell. Not that our wheels were the first and neither will they be the last to cause the grass to lean towards the west.

We have found out that the man Uncle Charley had kidded about Carrollton was one of our near neighbors. Of course he knew who we were so the joke is really on Uncle Chet after all. So we are off early. Pa had been over this route last year so knows how to go. They are really trails or little more than wheel tracks from one high spot to annother. This prarie grass has never seen a plow. It is State Road No. 4 from the map and is marked. It wanders from one high spot to annother to keep out of the sloughs. It was not suveyed that way of course.

In a couple of hours we turned off to the left and north again. We are on State Road No. 11 which is worse than No. 4 if that could be.[6] The ruts are deeper if nothing else. In two hours we crossed Buck Run crick. Soon annother crick then here we are at the North RaCoon (coon) to cross over a nice looking gravel-bottomed ford. But how soft if may be out in the middle we will soon find out. Pa took my horse and went accross first. The Uncle Charley drove the carriage with Mother Ann and the baby. He let them out and came back and picked up Archie and Howard. I guess they were afraid they might fall out of the covered wagon into the river.

Uncle Charley rode Nancy back to our side and told me to follow him after the covered wagon on Nancy. Charles had a rope on his saddle and they gave me one. He said, "if the wagon gets stuck in the river ford we were both to use the hooks on one end of the ropes of hooking them into the iron ring on the other end of the tongue." He would get out of the wagon and see we got hooked in the tongue loop all right. He would get his knees wet but that would be fine. Then we should get back into the wagon. Hiram would be on the north bank and tell us what to do. But nothing happened. The team pulled right through and accross the river without stopping with the covered wagon. Really Charles and me wanted to see some excitement.

This was the second time we had used the loops on the wagon tongue. We had used it at the hill west of the Spoon River back in Illinois. Any streams we had forded before never needed help and this one did not either as it had a good solid gravel bottom at the ford. Here we are accross and loaded for the last leg. We turned east along the north bank of the river and crossed a small stream. Hiram and Ann in the surrey had hurried on ahead. Pa wanted Ann to be the first to see our new home.

There is the surrey. Now we see the log house and all the log farm buildings. The house don't look very big for four adults and three kids. We just stopped and looked. After thirty-six days on the move here we are. Was it really true and our travels over with for a spell.

Pa was the first to break the silence. "Well, here we are. We better get busy. We have to eat and will sleep here tonight with no one

to bother us." Then he pointed to the spring bubbling away as it had
likely done for centuries. It was not so far away. Then Hiram said,
"we will have to camp tonight as we have been doing. Might be a
couple of nights yet." Anyway we have our log house and no striped
kitties.

We walked over to the cabin door. Mother Ann was at the door
when Pa pushed it open. The floor was dirt. It does not look much
like home right now but no one said a word. The permanent spring
was one thing that sold Pa on the farm. We know it will be a few days
in getting things cleaned-up so we can move in to the house. The
spring water is real cold and tastes fine with a little iron.

You could see that some of the cracks between the logs had
been just recently worked on. We know the neighbors must have
done this. Inside the cabin some of the worst cracks have been
rechinked and there was new iron hinges on the door. Pa said, "I
know the old hinges were leather—what was left of them. I brought
new iron hinges but we can use them someplace else. We just won't
tell them."

We just prepared camp and started supper. No fooling with the
house tonight. It was not very long untill a neighbor from the west
came over. Pa had met him last fall. His name was Martman Sals-
burry and it was through him that Pa had arranged for some wheat
planting and also for some corn if we did not make it by June first.
He said "all been done, but not much sod busted yet."

We were reminded not to forget there were neighbors and to do
some hollering if they were needed. As he left Ann said, "well, that
is really repayment for some of the things we tried to do for others.
Anyway we like to feel like we are at home even if there is a lot to
do." Pa said, "we will get a slab floor in that building just as soon as
we can find the slabs." Then he said to me, "I will figure up what the
counter machine says tomorrow and we will know how many miles
we have traveled."

There was a pile of hay that looked like it had not been there
very long. Likely the neighbors' doings. In fact we are sure of it. We
spread some of the hay out and put our quilts on it and it was really
a soft bed. Hiram, Ann, and the three kids will sleep in the covered
wagon. Supper is over and we are at home.

Uncle Charley is camp watching tonight just in case he is
needed. He is to get Charles up if he needs him. We have a nice
campfire going to keep wild animals away—mostly the small kind.

They won't come very close to the fire. Nearest neighbor is nearly half a mile away.

Anyway we have a lot of weary miles behind us. Glad to have done it but would not care to do it over again or very soon anyway. Will try to write a few words about the house tomorrow when I have the time. Don't expect too much. We will all be busy as bees for a long time. See you in the morning.

Thursday, June 12. Was a busy day. We cleaned out the inside of the cabin. The men measured the inside for the slab floor. They are to go over to Oxenford's mill in a few days so we will have to use it as it is for a few days. Heard the men say the house was twenty-four by sixteen feet. There is a pull-up ladder inside. Charles, Archie, and Howard will sleep up there.

Ann says, "we will build a lean-to for me to sleep in since there are three of us besides the baby to sleep downstairs and we will be crowded." Uncle Charley will sleep in the covered wagon. I asked Pa about the miles. He said, "just say over eight hundred miles and thirty-six days. I will figure it out later."[7] So all for now. It was a nice trip.

So we will call this the end of the trip to Ioway. Bye for good.

NOTES

1. This appeared in Glenda Riley (ed.), "Pioneer Migration: The Diary of Mary Alice Shutes," Part I, *The Annals of Iowa* 43 (Winter 1977): 487–514 and Part II (Spring 1977): 567–92.

2. The ferry that carried the Shutes family across the river was probably the Decalion, a steam ferry in service on the Mississippi during the early 1860s.

3. Mary Alice obviously had Amana people confused with the Amish. The latter were located not too far from there at Kalona, but according to the route taken by the Shutes family through Coralville, Tiffin, and Malcolm, it had to be the Amana people, or the Community of True Inspiration, that they visited in Homestead.

4. This stop was probably near the Westfield stage stop in Jasper County near the Poweshiek County line. Rock Island Railroad maps from that time indicate some rails laid in the area. They were, however, used for construction and emergency service rather than regular passenger and freight service, which developed late in the 1860s.

5. Archie did not suffer permanent injury from his accident. Years later he married and became the father of LeRoy L. Shutes, the donor of this manuscript.

6. An 1861 Carroll County map, possibly the same one Hiram used, shows marked state roads. He carried several maps which he had carefully acquired before the trip. Hiram, an Ohio Wesleyan student in 1854–55 and a student of history, was known for his methodical accuracy as well as his desire to understand the larger meaning of his endeavors.

7. Mary Alice never recorded the final mileage. It was later recorded in an account written by Hiram, which was unfortunately either lost or destroyed. The mile counter hung in the Shutes's cabin for several years but was destroyed by fire in 1872 when an uncontrolled prairie first jumped the "Coon" River.

PART TWO
Daily Life and Family Cares

THE terms "housework" and "housewife" are now fraught with negative connotations. In nineteenth-century Iowa, however, both housework and housewives were crucial to a family's endurance and eventual success. Women could not turn to grocery, department, or discount stores for the goods their families needed; they had to make them at home.

Typically, men produced raw materials in fields, by stock raising or by hunting and fishing, and women translated them into finished products which spelled survival for a family—notably food, but also clothing, candles, soap, bedding, and medicines. Almanacs of the era especially recognized women's economic importance. Although we often speak of the "farmer's" almanac, these popular guidebooks came in many versions—domestic or household almanacs included large sections of recipes and instructions for such tasks as dyeing fabrics, making candlewicks, cleaning silk and other materials, washing clothing and featherbeds, and making soap and whitewash.[1]

At the same time, women bore and raised the children, who constituted their domestic workforce. Women supervised and trained young boys and girls of all ages. Moreover, women went into the chicken houses, milking barns, dairies, and, when needed, even the fields. They also learned such skilled trades as dressmaking, tailoring, millinery, and shoemaking, which they practiced on their families' behalf.[2]

In addition, women's domestic duties remained demanding and their equipment rudimentary well into the twentieth century. Because the first priority continued to be the fields or family business, it was not unusual for threshers to use the latest equipment, while women cooked threshers' meals on old-fashioned wood-burning stoves. Similarly, candles gave way to kerosene or oil lamps, but women had to clean, refill, and trim wicks daily. Canning also provided an innovative way of preserving foods, yet it involved hours of peeling, coring, cutting, cooking, washing, and sealing. And, when washing machines replaced tubs and boards, women frequently had to haul water and heat it on the stove, fill the machine, and carry away the dirty water. Such problems were magnified in areas that did not get rural electrification until the 1920s and 1930s.

Besides their domestic production, women stood at the core of families in other ways as well. Women not only bore and raised children, but they perpetuated cultural and religious values, cared for the ill and discouraged, celebrated holidays, and did much of the work of keeping in contact with kin. Today, numerous women hold paid employment outside their homes and thus forego such family duties. As holiday celebrations and kin networks weaken, we recognize the importance of such tasks.

Another twentieth-century change is single-person households and a lack of reliance on family structures. While a man or woman occasionally lived alone in nineteenth-century Iowa, it was unusual. A single man or woman usually lived with parents, a brother's or sister's family, or other relatives. They depended upon the women of their families for domestic goods and, perhaps even more importantly, for succor and comfort.

The women's writings that appear here indicate the repetitive nature of women's work, its critical nature to a household, and its lack of revolutionary change. They also show the time and energy women spent on family concerns, as well as the importance of family and community to nineteenth-century and early twentieth-century life.

NOTES

1. An example is *Housekeepers Almanac for the Year 1866* (Wheeling, WV: George K. Wheat, 1866).

2. A telling description of women's supervisory abilities and own work is found in, "An Iowa Settler's Homestead," *The Annals of Iowa* 6 (October 1903): 210. Skilled trades are discussed in Sarah Gillespie Huftalen, "School Days of the Seventies," *The Palimpsest* 28 (April 1947); 122–24.

PIONEERING AT BONAPARTE AND NEAR PELLA

Sarah Welch Nossaman and Mary Nossaman Todd

T HE FOLLOWING is a combined memoir. One of Iowa's first white women settlers, Sarah Welch Nossaman, contributed the first section; her daughter, Mary, added a shorter second part. Sarah wrote her portion when she was nearly seventy years old. She wanted, in her words, to leave her children "a record of some of my 'ups and downs' in life that may be of interest for them to look over after I have crossed over to the other shore."

Sarah was born in Wilkes County, North Carolina, on February 26, 1825. When she was six years old, her father emigrated to Richmond, Indiana. The family stayed in Richmond about a year. In 1831, when the Black Hawk Purchase was about to open in Illinois, the Nossamans hitched their team and headed west. Sarah remembered their arrival on the Mackinaw River, however, as less than joyous: "When we got to the new purchase, the land of milk and honey, we were disappointed and homesick, but we were there and had to make the best of it."

Sarah related that her father and mother "went to work with a will" to get crops in and to survive the first year, which included attacks of fever, rapidly diminishing food supplies, and the happy relief of such game as a wild pig and a deer. Besides these basic concerns, the Nossamans worried about living through the turmoil surrounding them, in which Sac and Fox Indians repudiated a treaty that had gone unfulfilled. Food, fever, and Indians continued to bedevil the Nossamans through future moves, which took them to Iowa.

Sarah added that neighbors could cause trouble as well, and that is where Mary picked up the story. She explained that climate, additional moves, and starting new businesses brought more burdens to the family. Still, the family held together throughout. In

Mary's words it appeared uncomplicated: "Here," she wrote, "we made another home."

The memoir first appeared in *The Annals of Iowa* in 1922. It is used here by permission of the State Historical Society of Iowa.[1]

ON the following April the Black Hawk War [April 6 to August 2, 1832] broke out, and some of our neighbors were killed near us, but we were providentially spared. While the war was raging at its hottest my mother urged my father to go to Jacksonville, the county seat of Morgan County, Illinois, and get his brother, which is old Uncle Johnny Welch of this place, to come and take us down to Jacksonville where he lived. We lived near Jacksonville one year, and after that we moved to Alton, Illinois.

In 1835 my father moved to what is now Iowa, but at that time it was part of Wisconsin Territory. We settled one mile below where Bonaparte now is, in Van Buren County. We had but few neighbors, among them being old Uncle Sammy Reed and his brother Isaac, and an Indian trader by the name of Jordan. I think Uncle Jimmy Jordan was known to most of the old settlers of the eastern part of this state. He was my father's nearest neighbor. It was here we had for neighbors Black Hawk, Keokuk, Wapello, Hard Fish, Kishkakosh, Naseaskuk and a score of others of the Sac and Fox Indians.

Here we had hard times and often went hungry. We lived there five years, one mile above where Bonaparte now is. The town of New Lexington[2] was laid out, so we had a post office, but if a letter had come for us we could not have taken it out of the office. Letters were not prepaid with a two-cent stamp as they are now, but the one that received the letter had to pay twenty-five cents before he could take it out of the office. While we lived there Black Hawk and his son were frequent visitors and often partook of my father's hospitality.

In 1837 or 1838,[3] I don't remember which, Black Hawk died of malaria fever. One of our neighbors, Dr. James Turner, thought if he could only steal Black Hawk's head he could make a fortune out of it by taking it east and putting it on exhibition. After two weeks' watching he succeeded in getting it. Black Hawk's burial place was near old Iowaville, on the north side of the Des Moines River, under a big sugar tree.

It was there Dr. Turner severed the head from the body. At the time it was done I was taking care of his sick sister-in-law, Mrs. William Turner. The doctor made his home with his brother. We knew the evening he went to steal the head and sat up to await his coming. He got in with it at four o'clock in the morning and hid it till the afternoon of the same day, when he cooked the flesh off the skull. So I can say that I am the only one now living that witnessed that sight, for it was surely a sight for me. If the rest of Black Hawk's bones were ever removed it was a good many years after his head was stolen.

The second morning after their ruler's head was stolen ten of the best Indian warriors came to William Turner's and asked for his brother, the Doctor. They were painted war style. He told them he did not know where his brother was. They told him they would give him ten days to find his brother, and if he did not find him in that time he would pay the penalty for his brother's crime. But he knew where his brother was. He was at the home of a neighbor named Robb, Uncle Tommy Robb as he was called by everyone, on the south side of the Des Moines River. But he did not want to find his brother and sent a boy to tell him to fly for Missouri, which he did.

The Indians returned to Iowaville to hold council and conclude what to do, and while they were holding council William Turner and his wife made their escape in a canoe down the river. William Turner kept a little store in New Lexington. He got his neighbors to pack and send his goods after him.

But the Indians demanded their ruler's head, and for three weeks we expected an outbreak every day, but through the influence of their agent and the citizens together they gave up hostilities for a time. The whites told them they would bring Turner to justice if he could be found. The sheriff chased Turner around for awhile, which only gave him the more time to get out of the way. The Turner family finally all went to St. Louis where the Doctor was found again, and to keep the Indians quiet the sheriff went to St. Louis in search of him, but he did not find him. He did not want to find him. But Turner got frightened and took Black Hawk's skull to Quincy, Illinois, and put it in the care of a doctor there for safe-keeping (I forgot the doctor's name) till the Indians would get settled down, and then he intended to take it east. But when he got ready to go east with it the doctor in Quincy refused to give it up, and he did not dare to go to law about it, so after all his trouble and excitement he lost Black Hawk's skull, and not only made Turners endless trouble, but put the lives of all settlers in jeopardy for months.

We lived principally on excitement and that was a poor living. But they finally got over it till all was peace and then we were happy. The doctor that had the head took it to Burlington and sold it to a museum and the museum was burned down, so Black Hawk's skull is not now in existence. The Turner family were warm friends of my father's family. They stayed in St. Louis two or three years, I don't remember just how long, and they all three died with the cholera. So I am left alone to tell the story.

My father was a potter by trade. He built the first pottery in the territory, I suppose, in the year 1836, but there were but few to buy his ware, so we had it hard for most of the five years of our stay in Van Buren County. But in 1837 Judge Meek of Michigan came to New Lexington to locate a mill. After looking around for a few days he bought Robert Moffatt out. His claim was on the land where Bonaparte now is. So then we had one neighbor with money. Where Bonaparte now stands was at that time what was called a heavy sugar orchard. Mr. Meek gave my father the privilege of making sugar on his claim till it was all cleared off and put in town lots. I do not mean we made sugar all the time, for there is but four or five weeks you can make sugar in the year, and that is in early spring. But it was three years or more before all of the sugar trees were cut off of the town site of Bonaparte. But when Meek started work that made a little money in circulation. It gave both men and girls a chance to get themselves what was called store clothes, for we all wore homemade cloth then.

I for one worked for Meek's family for the first year of their building their mills. I worked for seventy-five cents a week, which was the best wages that had ever been paid in the country at that time. Robert Meek's wife and I cooked for forty-two men, so you may know we did not have much spare time, and that was before days of cook stoves. We cooked by the fireplaces.

You will say goods were surely cheap in those days when wages were so low. I will give you the price of some of them—calico, 25 to

50 cents a yard; sheeting, such as we have now for 7 or 8 cents, was 25 to 30 cents a yard, and all other goods in proportion.

In 1841 my father sold his claim and pottery shop and moved two miles east of Fairfield, Jefferson County, this state. There we took a claim and began anew. There we had it pretty hard again but not as hard as in Van Buren County. It was there I married [to Wellington Nossaman] March 17, 1842. I will now leave my father's house and tell you of your father's and my own hardships.

We rented a farm near Fairfield the first year we were married. We raised a good crop and had plenty to live on. In 1843 the new purchase being opened for settlement, your Uncle Levi and Aunt Caroline, your father and myself with our babies then three months old, started to the new purchase. On May 17, 1843, we got to this part of God's footstool. We took a claim four miles south of where Pella now is. But when we got to our stopping place our feelings can be better imagined than described, for there was not a neighbor for fifty miles, no house, no nothing you might say but wild beasts and Indians. But we thought it was the only way we could get a home.

We went to work and built a shanty made of poles and covered it with elm bark, not slippery elm, but what we called white elm, but the sun curled it so badly we had to have a new cover every few days, and then it was but little better than no roof. After we had been at our new home a few days your Aunt Caroline and I went strolling out in the woods, and when we had gone about a mile from our shanty we heard the sound of an ax. We got back to the shanty as soon as we could to tell the good news to your uncle and father that there was surely white people not far away. We knew from the sound of the ax it was not an Indian. To our great joy we soon found it to be a camp of white men, but no women with them. We were not long getting acquainted and have remained warm friends ever since.

But there are but three of us left to tell the tale of our hardships, and they are Robert Hamilton, Green Clark, and myself. The rest have gone to their reward, except George Hamilton who is in Australia. They were Dr. Warren, Robert Hamilton, J.B. Hamilton, George Hamilton, Elbert Warren, Henry Miller, Henry McPherson, and his father. In the latter part of May and first part of June others began to come in and settle from two to five miles from us, and then we thought we had close neighbors. Among them was John Gillespie and his brother George, who made his home at our house or shanty, for we did not have a house built till in September, and David

Durham and family, George Harrison, Uncle Ben Lansberry, and wife, John Majors and family, Wilson Stanley and family, Caton and wife, Mowery and wife, Francis A. Barker and family, James Tong and family, and Uncle Ikey Wise and family. That many had settled in from two to ten miles around, and in the fall John B. Hamilton was married to Miss Ann Wilson of Lee County, Iowa. The following year R.G. Hamilton was married to Miss Rebecca Given of Lee County, also Green Clark was married to Miss Nancy Zeilson of Lee County, so we began to have nearer neighbors.

I will try to tell you of our first summer's stay up in this part of the wilderness. As I have told you we built a shanty in the thick timber four miles south of where Pella now stands, where we lived for five years, but not in the shanty, as we built a log cabin in the fall. When living in the shanty we had no door nor fireplace, so we could neither cook, nor shut out the skunks nor snakes, and they were both plentiful. We treated skunks very kindly until they were out of the shanty, but the snakes did not fare so well. It was not an uncommon thing to get up in the morning and kill from one to three snakes, they were of garter snake variety, but we would rather they had stayed out if it had suited them as well. At night it was hard to sleep for the howling of the wolves and the screeching of the owls, and I can't tell you how lonely it made us feel, but God was watching over us in our lonely shanty and kept us from harm, and during the day the Indians were our companions, so you see we were not entirely deprived of company.

As I have told you we got to our claim May 17. I also told you we raised a good crop close to Fairfield. When we started up here we put in our wagon what we could bring in the way of household goods, and provisions, and that was not much for we had to make our roads most of the way as we came, and on the evening of July 3 we found ourselves with only half of a dodger of corn bread and that was baked with the bran in it. That and red [indecipherable word] tea was our supper.

So we started by team to Fairfield, Jefferson County, next day for breakfast, but we did not get there the first day. About one o'clock the day we started, which was July 4, 1843, we stopped to let our horses take their dinners on grass. We stopped near where the new courthouse now stands in Oskaloosa, Mahaska County. All there was of Oskaloosa at that time was three men, a dog, a jug of whisky, an ax, maul, and a load of stakes for staking off lots. Your father said to them, "What are you doing here?" They said they were laying out a county seat. Your father said, "You had better wait till the county is laid off." Canfield, for that was the name of one of the men, made reply, "We are going to lay off the county seat and survey the county around it." But we thought but little of what he said.

After our horses had eaten their dinners on grass, we started on to my father's at Fairfield. We traveled till the sun went down and found ourselves at what was known as Waugh's Point, which is now Batavia. There we stopped for the night, clogged [shackled] our horses and turned them out to eat grass, but we were hungry and tired. We had some blankets with us. We laid them down under the wagon to keep the dew off and laid down on them for the night, but we were too hungry to sleep much. We thought we would get up about three o'clock and start on, but when we got up to start on our horses were gone. Your father started in search and tracked them by the dragging of the clogs through the grass. About ten o'clock he found them several miles from the wagon, so it was after twelve o'clock when he got back to the wagon.

It was a long hungry day for me. We started on as soon as we could get ready and at six o'clock in the evening we got to Father Welch's, as we thought almost starved to death, but we were not as nearly starved as we thought, but we were hungry enough. You will say, "How was it you were so long getting to Fairfield? We can easily drive it in one day now." But we had to make our own roads. Winding around and hunting out places to cross the streams took much time.

We stayed at my father's three or four days. We got several sacks of meal ground, and we had some bacon we had left down there. We put in the wagon what we could of our household goods we had left down there, and our bacon and meal, and started for our home in the wilderness again. We were three days getting back. On our return we stayed all night where Oskaloosa now is. During our stay at Fairfield, Oskaloosa had made a big improvement. Canfield had built a log cabin and had it covered with clapboards, but did not have the door sawed out. Your father helped him saw out one log so we could creep in and be under a roof, and that was my first night in Oskaloosa.

We reached home the day after our first stay in Oskaloosa and found our shanty about as we had left it, but Oh, the mosquitoes, and no way to shut them out. The only way we got any sleep was to cover up head and ears with a thick, heavy cover, and the weather hot enough to almost cook eggs. So you see pioneer life is not all sunshine. It has a great many black clouds.

In August and September we had several new neighbors come in, so we had a post office. A man by the name of Wilson Stanley was our postmaster. The post office was a mile west of our house, for we had a cabin built in September, and then we began to feel more at home. We had a floor to walk on and a fireplace to cook by and a clapboard door to shut. We did not think of such a thing as plank for floors. Your father split puncheons and hewed them and made a floor of them. When we lived in the shanty and it rained we did not eat for I had to cook by a log fire, as it was before the days of cook stoves. It was days of johnycake boards, dutch ovens, skillets and lids.

But you may ask how can you bake bread on a board. I will try to tell you. Take a board eighteen inches long and eight inches wide, round the corners off and make the edges thinner than the middle, spread it with well-made corn dough, set it on edge before a hot fire in a fireplace, and it will bake nice and brown, then turn and bake the other side the same way, then you have corn bread that no one will refuse. Set your johnycake board in front of something that will keep it on the edge.

I will stop giving receipts and talk of something else. After we got our house built and new neighbors began to come in we began to feel like we could entertain all Iowa. Oh, how contented we were! But the fall of 1844 found us with wheat and corn raised on our new home place, ripe and ready to grind, but our nearest mill was at Bonaparte, Van Buren County, one hundred miles away, and we had to go to mill there. But after awhile we got tired of that, so my father and your father put up what they called a stump mill. I have forgotten just the plan of the mill, it has been so long ago, but the whole thing went round by a six-ox power. It would grind three pecks of corn an hour. They ran it day and night. They did not grind wheat.

Often there would be from fifteen to twenty men waiting their turn to get a bushel of meal to take to their hungry families. But it was hard for me for I baked for all of them, and most of the time some of the men that came to mill would go hunting and kill some game, so that would make me more work to cook it. But I did not think it hard. Your father used to say we could keep as many as there were puncheons in the floor, and I sometimes thought there were two to a puncheon. But we had not run our mill but a few months till Cempstalk built a mill north of Oskaloosa on Skunk River that ground wheat as well as corn, and also Dunkin and Dr. Warren started mills on the same river. But Oh, the flour they made! Most of it was a dark gray, for they tramped their wheat out with horses on a dirt floor and had no way of getting the dirt out only to fan it out with sheets or blankets. So you see we ate our peck of dirt more than once. But we were much healthier then than we are now.

To say pioneer life is without its troubles even among neighbors is a mistake, for we had one neighbor that will never be forgotten by the old settlers. His name was John Majors. He broke over all rules and sent to Illinois and borrowed money and when the land came in market he entered three or four of his best neighbors' homes from them, which caused what is termed the Majors War, and for more than two years we had trouble. They caught Jake Majors, the oldest son, and gave him a coat of tar and feathers and made him deed his neighbors' homes back to them, but they sent off east and borrowed money and paid him what he had paid out for their homes, but he lost the interest for none of his neighbors wanted him to go to so much trouble for them. So Majors all sold out and left here and went to Missouri, so quiet was ours again.

• • •

Here my mother's narrative ends, much to our regret, and I will try to supply a few more reminiscences. I was quite a little girl at the time of the Majors War, but remember distinctly one night my father lay in the "loft," as we called it, with the scythe by his side saying he would "mow" the heads off of any who dared try to capture him, but no one came. Well do I remember the terror of my mother who sat up all night.

We remained on the farm until I was ten or thereabout, then in 1853 my father traded his farm for what was then known as the Franklin House, a long low structure standing at the southeast corner of the square in Pella. There we resided a number of years keeping hotel and did quite well, and the immigration was then at its height, but my father unfortunately conceived the idea of being a merchant, went to Keokuk and bought goods, loaded them on the *Badger State* and started home. She ran on a snag and sank, consequently the goods were much damaged. As he had them insured he was advised to throw them on the Insurance Company's hands and, unfortunately for him, did so. The company promptly suspended payment, so my father was left with nothing.

He came home and sold forty acres of land to pay the debt, for he was strictly honest, often telling us children to always pay an honest debt, "even though it takes the shirt from your back." We still had a piece of land on the Des Moines River whither we moved and began again. He build a lime-kiln and did a thriving business, as that was the only kiln in the country. People came from Des Moines and Montezuma and all surrounding towns. I have known as many as six or eight teams there at once when the men stayed all night waiting for lime. Of course we had to board all of them, and as we received no pay it took considerable of the profits and much work.

In connection with the lime-kiln he ran a steam sawmill, and as that was before the day of railroads, he found ready sale for all the lumber he could manufacture. He also cleared up a farm and in a few years made up all losses. He remained there until he accumulated considerable money when he again moved to Pella, in 1855, and engaged in the mercantile business, keeping store just south of the Square.

In 1853 the college, in which he took a lively interest, was founded, and he furnished timber, lime, and money to the amount of $1,000. He remained in Pella until he spent most of his earnings of former years, as he trusted all who came with a pitiful story, consequently he was soon left without means, and most of the money is uncollected even at this writing. While in Pella E.R. Cassatt and Jesse Hampson boarded with them and attended college.

About 1860 or 1861 he again removed to the bottom and commenced anew. He lived down on the bottom lands and during the spring of 1862 or 1863 the water came and deluged the land. We stayed in the house thinking it would soon abate. We had a canoe tied in the door and, like Thompson's colt, had to "swim the river to get a drink." We remained until it was almost knee deep in the house, then put all we could up stairs. They had to bore holes through the upper floor and swing the piano up to the joists, then the water was half way up the legs. We went into a cabin on the hill, fourteen of us in one little room, and had the floor covered with beds at night.

There we lived until the water went down and, my mother flatly refusing ever to return, neighbors came, took down the house and removed it to the hill, where we remained until 1868, then we moved about one and one-half miles north where father ran a brick kiln and also burned lime. Here we made another home, set out trees and cleared up another small farm. In 1871 he again moved to Pella, north of the Depot, and kept boarders. In 1876 he built the Depot Hotel where he resided, except two or three years while living in Colorado, until his death, October 23, 1893.

NOTES

1. Sarah Welch Nossaman, "Pioneering at Bonaparte and Near Pella," *The Annals of Iowa* 113 (October 1922): 441–53.

2. New Lexington was about two miles north of Bonaparte, but it disappeared when Bonaparte flourished.

3. Black Hawk died at his home near Iowaville, the site of his old town, on the Des Moines River in Davis County on October 3, 1838.

MEMOIR OF
Margaret Archer Murray

THREE WEEKS after she reached the age of eighty-seven, Margaret E. Archer Murray, another of Iowa's early settlers, wrote this account of pioneer life and daily concerns for her grandson, Murray Work of Des Moines. On April 27, 1938, she set pencil to paper to record events from her own memory and "from what my mother told me years ago." She asked her grandson's tolerance for her errors in grammar and spelling. "I am," she wrote, "quite deficient in education."

She related that her father, William Archer, was born on January 25, 1811, and her mother, Elizabeth Bushong, on May 15, 1817, both of Ohio farming families. William and Elizabeth married on September 15, 1837; five years later they took their four children, the youngest of whom was only a year old, and headed for Iowa. Using a team and covered wagon, they crossed the Mississippi River on July 4, 1846, and went to where the city of Waterloo is now situated. In a year's time, they relocated in Jones County, south of Anamosa.

There the struggle to establish home and family began. Margaret's mother bore seven more children, two of whom died in childhood and twins who died at birth. In the first part of her memoir, Margaret narrated her memories of her mother's life and of her own childhood. She demonstrated that two things were ever-present in women's lives: the struggle to produce food, as well as the birthing of, and caring for, children. She also noted that households were primitive—rag lamps, pickled rather than canned foods, and homemade clothing.

In the second section of her memoir, Margaret turned to her own adult life, describing her husband's background, their first home, and their children. Although the railroad, store-bought clothing, and a cookstove lightened her domestic cares, Margaret, like her mother, engaged in the daily struggle to feed a growing family. Later in life, however, after her husband's death in 1915, Margaret enjoyed an active widowhood traveling and visiting her children. True to her nature, she added a postscript: "I am Enjoying Life to the full."

Murray's account appears here by permission of Murray
Work and the State Historical Society of Iowa.[1] The punctuation,
spelling, and capitalization remain unchanged to give an idea of
the challenge less-educated women faced in recording their family's early histories and to preserve the flavor of the original document.

HER PARENTS' LIFE

1846. Built a log house that fall not able to get a door they fastened a quilt in the opening to keep out the snow & as much cold
wind as possable, the wolves came right up & howeld around the
cabin at night, all the protection mother had when Father was away
was an ax & the dog. as Father always took the gun with him for protection & to kill what game he might find while chopping fire wood
in timber they only stayed there one year as timer was sarce & the
winter bitter cold. So they picked up & moved farther East & South
to Jones Co & took up or bought 160 achers of land about 4 miles
South of anamosa & I think about 50 miles west of Davenport where
there was plenty of timber along the wapsapincian [Wapsipinicon]
River which was about 3 miles East of us Davenport was their nearest market & it took 2 days with a team to go & 2 to return there they
started their permenant home in the west

Built & log house from memory I think it was about 20 feet
each way had a door in South & window in North about 3 feet square
on the East side were the beds 2 big beds and & 2 trundle beds pulled
out at night & under in day time with a curtain around the 4 poster
then on west side was a huge fire place made of rock & rock chimney & chinged [chinked] with wet clay as was the whole house clay
chinking between the logs

fire place was real wide with crain built in chimney so as to
hang the cooking vessels they were all iron with iron lids iron teaket-
tel & for baking bread had a large iron bake oven with lid always had
big back log & smaller one in front had andirons in front to keep

wood from rolling out when bake day came had a nice bed of coles
to rake out of stone herth then set the oven on them with bread raised
& ready to put hot coals on top & we ate a lot of corn bread too but
I dont think she could bake pie or cake & for supper we often had
mush & milk, of course a part of our kitchen things were tin & that
had to be scoured evry saturday or at least it was when I got big
enough to do the scouring.

I can't remember if the house had a punceon [puncheon or split-
log] floor was either that or boards the roof was coverd with clap-
bords. for light at first we had grease lamps we had a shallow dish
first took a soft rad [rag] twisted it then dipped one end in melted lard
layed that end up on side of dish pored the melted lard over that then
it was ready to light

mother did all her sewing & knitting by that & the light from
the fire place & she sure had a lot of it to do as the 2 oldest children
died in 49 a girl & boy just 5 days apart & sister Rebecca was only
1 year old all 5 children had Scarlet fever in that one room house

mother made all our cloths by hand knit all our stockigs & mittens by lamp light but later she made candles 6 at a time Set them
aside & when they were cold enough to draw she would mold 6 more

they raised sheep & in the Spring after the shearing was done
she washed the fleeces then hand picked the wool to get out the burs
& the like often had wool picking invite a few women for the day.
after that the wool was sent to the carding machine & made into rolls
then mother had to spin it into yarn then have that woven into cloth
some for jeans for mens cloths & flannel for us children a part of the
yarn for kniting then she did all the coloring

used madder[2] to color red Indigo to color Blue peach tree leaves
for green don't remember what she used to color yellow we had a
few black sheep & their wool was left in its natural color for mitens
but for our Peticots & stockings we always had white yarn I never
wore colored stockings till after I was married. Sometime they would
trade the wool for jeans Father & the boys cloths which mother cut
& made I can remember Father had a store suit for sunday only I
have often wonderd how many years it lasted him. in the summer
time the men wore white toe [tow] linen pants & blue & white stripe
hickery shurting shurts now all these things had to have button holes
worked think of the stitches she took in those days and only had
hooks & eyes & buttons for fastening our cloths no saftey pins or
snapfasteners or zippers of cours that is a late thing. we used comon

pins even the little babies had their three cornerd pants pinned on with comon pins.

Murray I think of so many things to tell you I am likley to get some of them mixed in the telling Since I began this writing things came to mind I hadent thot of for the last 100 years.

we always had plenty of clothing to keep us comfortable & Plenty to eat we always had a great variety of meat for Father loved to hunt & in winter had time & at that time there was plenty of wild game such as Deer wild turkeys Prarie chickens quailes & rabbits & in summer squirls & Buffalos was plenty but he never killed one he always used a kifle [rifle] in hunting & our Pork barrel was never empty of pickeled meat with smoked beans and shoulders for summer use. we had a lot of cattle & sheep but never killed any for meat always used a lot chickens any time we wanted then as they only brought $2.00 per doz. Even when mother dressed them in winter & sent them to market & only 10c for roosters when they were over a year old

late in the fall at butchering time they butcherd our next years meat & all the fat hogs we had to sell & Father took them to Davenport & sold them & layed in a big supply of groceries & things we needed in the way of material for making cloths it would take him 4 or 5 days to make round trip with team & all dirt roads & coudent go faster than a walk all day but about every 25 miles there would be a hostelry [inn] & tavern had large barns & big feed lots where one could drive in to feed & water or stay the night of course we had small towns with Post office Store BlackSmith Shop & like, mother sold Butter Eggs & Beeswax & any thing we could spare off the farm in the summer & fall we gatherd Black berries wild grapes & any thing we raised on the farm that would bring money or exchange for groceries.

She dident know a bout canning fruit or vegatables dried the fruit & berried the cabbage turnips beet & potatoes made sourkraut by the barrell put up our own pickles in salt and freshened them as we wanted to use them I think when I was real young we grew tomatoes as anarnament [ornament] not to eat as for spreads for our bread always the year around we honey renderd & in the comb & maple syerip pumpkin butter & dried pumpkin for pies. we never had many pies till we got a cook stove

well speaking of wild things to eat we children began to roam the woods as soon as things began to ripen first was wild cherries

choke cherries plumbs wild crabs black berries & after frost came
black haws were ready to eat but remember we never had a whole
day off for play not even ½ day for we girls had to knit so many
rounds on a stocking before we were alowed to go out that had to be
done each day as soon as we learned to knit & we learned pretty
young

some things I can remember that happened to me when I was
about 7 or 8 years old one was a Forest fire we lived about 3 miles
west of the wapsiepinecan river and it was between us & the river
Father & 2 boys were gone most of the time for about 4 days and
nights fighting fire the smoke came up to our house till it almost
chocked us at times & at night the sky was red as far as we could see
men came to the house at any time to get a drink of water or milk &
mother kept hot coffee & meat boiled & bread baked so they could
have something to eat & some times they would lie down in the yard
& sleep an hour

do you know I can remember just how some of the men looked
cloths toren into rags & faces & hands black from smoke & dirt

So much of the timbr had been cut for wood & to make rails &
the brush left in the timber till it was a dry mass of brush & dry
leaves but no lives were lost as I remember & another thing happened at about the same time or a year later was a tornado I may have
been 9 or 10 years old at that time this was a tornado the folks had
gone to church on a sunday afternoon the church was about ¼ mile
from our house built on one corner of the farm as they came out of
church saw the storm coming at a rapid pace we were then living in
the 2 story frame house & they closed all the windows & doors but
the house shook so we could feel it shake a man came with them &
the men braced their shoulders against the doors & the windows

the worst part of the storm was 3 miles south of us & the worst
part of damage done was about 4 miles long & from 1 to 1½ miles
wide in that era [area] not a house barn or building of any kind was
left standing. all the stock killed but not so many people as it being
sunday alot were away from home. great beams from houses were
driven in the ground 3 & 4 feet you know those times we dident have
cyclones or twisters as we call them these days and we always expected our storms & floods in the month of June

I have digressed a little from the way we farmed our crops were
corn & wheat a large meaddow for hay just wheat enough to bread
the family & pay take to have it ground as it took so much work to

get it ready for bread the crop had to be cut by hand with a cradle that was real hard work swinging a cradle all day the sheaves were bound by hand. you picked up a hand full of the cut straws for a binder & if the wheat wasent tall enough had to make a double band then it was shocked when all was in shock it was hauled to the slacking ground near the stable & the thrasing floor was made ready for thrashing a big round ring was scraped with hoes till the ground was clean & hard then the wheat was layed around that with the heads laping & the buttes of the sheave out 2 such rings side by side was layed when tramped out with horses going round & round till all the wheat was tramped out

I cand discribe a thrashing floor so you will understand but some day I can show you just how it was done but the horse on the in side had a bridle & the other one a halter with lead strap well I couldent of been more than 6 or 7 years old when I was elected for the job of riding on the thrashing floor rode the in side horse and led the other one poor little me I rode and cryed & cryed & rode but to no avale had to do my share of what I was able to do that was supposed to be an easy job well I some times droped a sleep & slid off or the boys to hurry the horses would punch a horse with the fork handle he would jump & off I would flap they would take me by one arm and leg up I would go again we all did our share of work big & little they used a pitch fork to turn the wheat over as it thrased out and take the straw away by hand then it was ready to take to mill & made in to bread stuff flour not bolted [sifted] & middlings [coarsely ground] or shorts [by-product of milling] we used that for mush & brand for cow feed always had spring wheat

Now in raising corn first plowed the ground then borrowed it then marked the rows with single shouble [shoulder] plow one way across the field then across the other way then it was ready for planting Father marked the roaws & us children that was old enough to cary a gallon bucket of corn followed and droped from 3 to 5 grains in the cross & one of the boys followed with a hoe & coverd it then in time it was cultivated with single shoudel [shoulder] then it the fall it was cut & shocked later hauled to the stable & husked out as needed corn for horses & fodder for cattle. ...

My folks lived in these surroundings till 1859 or 60 then father built 2 story house had 5 rooms 3 down & 2 up we had plenty of room & a cellar size of house rock foundation starting at bottom of cellar rock floor in cellar rock chimney & big fire place in front room but mother got a cook stove at that time than we got pie to eat & a lot of things we werent used to the fire place had to heat that big room could freese ones back while you got warm in front then father only lived 3 or 4 years to injoy his hard earned new house died at the age of 52 years cause of his death was typhoid fever

You can readly see why children of that time were deprived of an education we only had school 3 months in winter & 3 in summer for the small children that couldent wade deep snow in winter time. I must of been 10 or 11 years old before I got to go to winter school then I wore a pair of boys boots with red tops & copper toes oh I was proud of them our flannell dresses were made to come to our ankle it was 2½ miles north west to our log school house with punceon [puncheon] benches to sit on no backs to them no desks in front had a table up where the teacher sat there we went once a day to write in our coppy books our studies were reading writing spelling & a little arithmatic

we always [had] in winter time spelling school one night a week at the school house old & young went & all took part it was fun for the children to spell down their perants we always stood in line and when one missed a word had to go to the foot of the class

we had a log school house with sod heated stove & had to carry drinking water from a farm well about ¼ mile wooden water bucket & one tin cup to drink from teacher called for some one to pass the water & every hand went up & teacher can I She would name some one then what water was left in the cup a little more water was aded & the next child drank it was counted quite a privelage to be called on to pass the water. ...

in Dec. 24, 61 my oldest Brother John was married & went on a wedding trip to western part of State then mother & us girls had all the farm chores to look after as Brother Ike was only 7 years old each day we drove the cattle to a creek & cut holes in the Ice for them to drink we got water from the well with Bucket & wind less [cylinder with rope wound around it] an all day job to carry water to sheep Hogs & chickens but we were used to it so dident mind the work.

that winter there were 400 Indians camped on the wapsie River about 3 miles from our House & they depended a lot on what people gave them for a living as the Snow was so deep & game scarce but they were verry friendly & did not steal some men wrote out what they needed most & they took these papers with them in their begging trips was feed for their ponies & meat corn meal or checkens for

themselves they mostly went in 4 2 men & 2 squas & road in single
file could see them most any day along the roads & &

oh how our dog hated them he could smell them ¼ mile out on
our East road & were they afraid of him they ran like toe heads from
the gate to the house they never sat on a chair Either stood or squated
on their junkers they always amused them selves by useing the tongs
at the fire place they never stayed after we gave them some thing always wanted the chicken killed & always seemed so great full for
what you gave them as soon as they could they moved on to ware
there was better hunting they used bow & arrow

& right here I want to say I always felt sorry for the Indians (&
do yet) being driven by white people yes they are mean & so would
you be if driven like they were

now in the spring of 65 mother & her sister and brother in law
who lived about ½ mile from us desided they would sell their farms
& go farther South where it was warmer in winter where they could
have fruit so they put out the crop and began to get ready & by mid
Summer had both farms sold & made Sales of stock farm implements household furniture our one team of horses was the one they
brought from Ohio. Old Rock & Fly were their names Some horse
buyers from cedar Rapids came & bought them & when they went to
lead them away oh how us children did cry & put our arms around
their necks. mother said the men turned their backs & mother cried
too the dear old horses had worked so hard & toiled to raise us children & then had to go among strangers to die I think us children must
of felt like they were almost Human we had been so happy to think
we were going to move & then that sad day mother had to insist that
we hush to think we cried all that day

well they bought young horses John got a team of beautifull
black horses & they rigged up 4 coverd wagons us 2 & uncle 2 he a
aunt mary had 9 children 2 up in the 20s & the youngest 2 years old
John & wife drove one team & mother & aunt Sophie the other she
was mothers youngest sister not married but came to live with us after Fathers Death then us 4 children which made 19 in all with 8
horses & 2 dogs to buy feed for on the way all we took was our cloths
& some bedding dishes to eat from & pots & pans to cook and bake
bread along the way we started Aug 25 dident stop to look at land till
we crossed the mosuri River at Arrock [Arrow Rock] Mo.

Just same year the civle war ended & you can emagin the condition of the country that far South the population seemed to be

mostly colord people they were verry friendly & kind to us they
brought peaches & other fruit to our camp in the evenings & wanted
to know about conditions in the North well there wasent any land to
be had at any price So all we could do was to turn back the colord
folks were so excitid and dident know what to do had always been
under the white in a masters hand & there were so much stealing going on some one had to sit up every night they drove the wagons in
a cirkle tied the horsses on the in side made a fire in the center & one
man & one women sat up all night

Brother Johns black match team seemed to be a temptation as 2
men kape on our trail for 2 days at first asked to buy the team & they
accused Bro of stealing them he at last threatened them that he would
put the Sherrif on their trail that was the last we saw or heard of them
we crossed the Mo [Missouri] river again at glassgal [Glasgow]
forded it both times then we headed for Illinoise crossed the Missippi
at Hanibal Mo & went out in Ill as far as Sterling Brown Co but they
had war prices on land out there then they decided to come back to
all Iowa but locate father South in the State so we crossed the Missippi again at Keokuk & came about 20 miles out in Lee Co to a little town named Primrose

a Family lived that they had knowen for years he had moved
from Lynn Co to Lee Co & had bought a farm mother rented rooms
in a hotel in town & this man went with her & John to find a place
we landed the 8 of Oct. She Bought a small Farm & we got settled
in Nov uncle Thomas & his Family stayed in Ill till the next spring
then came over to us he rented a farm & stayed one year then went
Hasting neb & took up all the land he & his oldest son could &
bought other land with a big stone housse on it & became quite well
off

The farm mother bought had a large apple orchard the fall of 66
2 men came & bought the apple crop paid her $15.00 & picked &
barreled the apples right in the orchard

We also had quite a lot of peach trees & a nice vineyard Bro
John & aunt Sophie Built a Brick dry kiln & we dried a large amount
of peaches and she sold dollars worth that winter up to that time we
dident know much about canning fruit our first jars were Earthen
were & had to use sealing wax to seal lids then we got tin cans with
big open tops these were also sealed with wax later came the mason
jars & rubber rings & was that an improvement & we could have

fresh apples all winter long John stayed on mothers farm till Sept 69 then moved to the western part of the state

& I was married Oct. 14, 69 & Sister Rebecca was marrie may 9, 70 & Sister Manda was marrie Dec. 31, 74 So mother was on the Farm alone with 2 boys as Will had came in that time after 9 years wandering She & them stayed on the Farm till Nov. 76 then she rented the Farm & made a sale & she & Bro J F came to live with us in milton but Bro worked in the Farm in Summer & stayed with us in winter to go to school in town as their country school only had about 10 to 15 scholars in the district he wasent married till Sept 2 82. ...

HER ADULT LIFE

[William Murray] began coming to our House in June 68 & on Feb 14 we became Engaged & on Feb 16 he left Primrose & went to Milton van Buren Co. & started in business for him selfe [as a shoe-maker] then on October 14 69 we were married at the metropolitan Hotel in Ft madison by Presbyerian minister name of W B Nobel was married at 11 a m then after we bought a cook stove & a few other things for housekeeping & had them shiped to Farmington where we could pick them up later went back home to mothers that was a 20 mile drive Stayed there a week then hired a Farmer with farm wagon to take us & my few belongings to milton our future Home. distance from Farmington to milton was about 39 miles took us full day to get there that was Oct 21 stayed at his Boarding place till 23 then went to House Keeping 2nd floor in 2 rooms

now Murray I am going to tell you as near as I can just what our Furniture was in our large room had small no 7 cook stove & that did for heating as well for 2 winters then had a fall leaf table & 3 chairs a Preferoated tin door safe for dishes & food then turned on Side & wooden box with calico curtain in front for pots & pans on top was my work table & wooden water bucket in that room we cooked ate & sat it had 2 windows & 3 doors one opened in a Hall one to our bed room & the other to bed room of our land lady so I dident have much wall space than in our small room had bed Small stand one trunk my trunk was small & it was pushed under the bed had a mearor which hung above the stand this room had 2 windows, carried our water from a well in back yard & washed down stairs in land ladies kitchen same day she did they had no children & they were verry verry good to us in more ways than one the man spoke verry broken French & she spoke broken Scotch I never know a man than I had more confidence in than good old Freshman old Presley Marsan

we lived there 17 months on March 71 we Bought an old 4 room House 2 lots with a Barn at Back we lived there 6 years there in that time William Built a double shop out in front on corner one Side he used & the other rented for Harness Shop

Our first Baby was born there in July & mother & Bro J F came to live with us in Nov same year we all lived practly in one room as kitchen was to cold the north Sill had roted & lift a hole that one could throw a cat out through (maybe not quite that big).

Our first Rail Road was built through milton in fall of 72 it was the B C & Q then later Will moved his Shop Building over in new part of town & in may 77 he bought a new 6 room House was built in 75 & is still standing we got that & 2 lots for $600.00 no improvement at all but as we got able bought 2 more lots built 2 more Rooms to the House made some improvement evry years Set out all kinds of fruit till we had at one time the nicest places in milton

when we were married he had only saved $300.00 that had to buy tools leather to work with buy what little Furniture we got Pay House rent Shop rent & our grocery bill we made a rule not to go in debt & we dident things werent So Expensive at that time but I never had carpets rugs or curtains at my windows till we moved to the new House dident Even have a rocking chair till I was married more than 7 years but most of my neighbors were almost as poor as we were we had no high up middle class or poor

Milton only had a Population of about 300 when we first went there after the Rail Road came we soon had a Population of 1300 or more & now after 50 or 60 years it has a Population of about 900 well we lived there from 1869 to 1919 that is I kept the Property but your grand Father lived there 1915 all that time he Pegged away when I say Pegged I mean that at first he used wooden pegs & wooden lasts & used linen thread with hog bristles twisted in the end & sewing awl to make a hole to sew through & used a pegging awl to make a hole to put in the Pegs how I wish now I had saved some of these old tools to give you

he never took but 2 real vacations the first was in aug 78 he with 4 other men rigged up a coverd wagon & took a trip out in Kansas took blankets & slept out at night he sure enjoyed it for a time but got tired of slow travel & came back by tran & again in 81 he went to Ohio when he came Home said he dident enjoy visiting

but he did a lot of hunting when we were first married game was more plentifull wild turkeys quails & rabbits in winter time wild pidgeons & Squirls in Sumer time in Summer children went bare foot Shoe work was slack

after years & years of coaxing the children & I got him persuaded to apply for a Pension for servis in the [Civil] war $12.00 per month was the amount but was increased till at the time of his Death he was getting $50.00 per month if he had lived 6 more years would of gotten 75 when he was about 65 he sold the Shop & most of the tools & stock of leather for $1100 with that & what we had saved & the 50 a month he & I could live verry nicely as both girls were married & gene was away doing for him self Soldiers were exempted of property tax

then not long after that every thing changed your grand Father passed away in may 1915 & there I was alone not a relative or child near but a host of Friends

then what was I going to do well I kept the place 4 years but there only through the Summer months So I gave it up after living there 45½ years Some of Happiness Some of Sorrow & at the last a few of discontent. ...

I left milton in Dec 1915 went to Des moines where both girls lived at that time & on the first of Jan 1916 went to Pensicola Florida Spent 4 months that is a Port for Ships navy yard Fort where Soldiers were stationed Station where there were 8 diferant modles of air plaines made & tried out daily Old Forts to explore of old Spanish wars & we could get a ticket at any time to visit Fort Pickens on a government Boat they werent alowed to take pay. ...

I spent a lovely 3½ months there then I spent parts of 2 winters in chicago with your Father & mother in July 1918 I decided to take a trip west went to cody wyoming & in august went by auto to yellow stone Park camped out up there a week did our own cooking had taken along 2 tepees to sleep in Snowed just a short ½ hour as we were going throu the golden gate but it soon melted & we spent a wonderfull week sight seeing went back to cody rested 3 days then Started on another trip to Seattle then up the Sound about 65 miles to arlington wash & from there 7 miles out in the interior in the mountains where the tall trees grow & the mountain streams flow. ...

then left Seattle for Colo Springs where your Folks had moved in the mean time arrived there about sept 15 my First Sight of the Dear old Rockies in Colorado. ...

Well to continue I stayed with your Folks till 30th of Dec mon at noon & it had begun to Snow just a little bit & till we got to goodland it was a Blizard but we kept on going & got as far as colby Kan the train stalled in a snow drift & there we stayed 50 long hours & how the wind howled & the snow drifted after the Dinamo ran down the lights went out in the cars after that we only had one candle to a coach but all Passengers with Paid tickets got their meals free I was one of that number in our car we kept watch meeting new years Eve Sang Songs told Stories & made Speaches we had one Pullman & one Dining car on wed night at 10 P m a Snow Plow reached us with a Freight train behind that & our train right behind the Freight & at that we lost 4 hours in reaching Kans City where I was going & oh was I tired & dirty for we dident have any hot water on the train to clean up with Wayne lived there at the time So I stayed there till last of Feb then went back to milton Sold my property

Divided all my Bedding Dishes & any thing the girls wanted then made a sale of all the rest of Furniture & Every thing loose that Spring of 1919 then I went to Des moines & on July 9 went again to Colorado Springs where I stayed till last of June 1920 then went back to D M my next trip I made in november. Same year went to St PetersBurg Florida on thanksgiving day was gliding down the Tennesee River a Beautifull stream of water reached chattanooga about 4 P m not far from there is Lookout mountain & on the side way up toard the top is the word IOWA for somp thing the Iowa Soldiers did in time of civil war from Jacksonville on the East coast we went across to St PetersBurg on the west coast a town at that time of about 1600 mostly all of northerners dident amount to much in summer time Stayed there 5 months where there took a trip to Bradentown. ...

my next trip was in June 1923 went to wyoming again last of august went to mont [Montana] Spent a month on a Ranch oh how I did Enjoy that month out of doors all day in the big open spaces got back to D M that time on the 12 of oct took little trips here & there till 31 went to calif in aug & returned last of oct

Out of the 48 states I have been in 21 of them have been as far East as Evansville Indana & as far South as St PetersBurg Florida as far west as Southern california & as far North as northern Iowa

& now I am getting old dont know how much good I have done

or otherwise but would love to think when I have Passed to the beyond that the world has been better for my having lived in it

    margaret E murray, june 28–38

NOTES

1. This first appeared as Margaret E. Archer Murray, "Memoir of the William
Archer Family," *The Annals of Iowa* 39 (Summer 1968): 357–71.

2. Madder is a vine with small yellow flowers and berries that yield medicines
and dyes. From its red roots comes red dye.

MY EARLY DAYS IN IOWA
Abbie Mott Benedict

ABBIE MOTT'S family line was a long and complicated one. Shortly after the American Revolution, her great-grandfather settled near Temple Mills, Maine. One of his sons and Abbie's paternal grandfather, Adam Mott, married Rachel Davis and lived on a farm west of Farmington, Maine. One of their four children was Abbie's father, Joseph Mott. On the other side of the family, her maternal grandfather was James Bean, who married Hannah Roberts and lived in Belknap County, New Hampshire, for many years. One of their nine children was Anna Alma, Abbie's mother.

In 1855, when Abbie was eleven, Joseph and Anna Mott relocated in Iowa—along with many members of their respective families. As Quakers they abhorred slavery and believed they would escape its bounds west of the Mississippi River. An article in the *Friends' Review* lured them by describing a Friends' settlement in Iowa at Hesper and Springwater, north of Decorah in Winneshiek County. They took the railroad as far as the Mississippi River; after that, they used a variety of transportation and arrived in Springwater in October of 1855.

Abbie's recollections expose an unusual woman, one who moved twenty-one times in the first twenty years of marriage; always reestablished a home for her family, seemingly without complaint; and kept track of an incredibly intricate family network. Besides performing the usual domestic work and bearing children, Abbie enforced Quaker worship and such beliefs as no alcohol consumption and abolition of slavery within her household.

Abbie wrote her memoir in 1921; it first appeared in *The Annals of Iowa* in 1930. It appears here in slightly abridged form with permission of the State Historical Society of Iowa.[1]

WHEN he first arrived in Iowa, and before his family came, my father got a quarter section of prairie land six miles north of Springwater. However, Ansel Rogers persuaded him to get nearer "town" and helped him to trade this land for one hundred and sixty acres located on Canoe Creek three-quarters of a mile west of the sawmill, also twenty acres more of timber land on the south side of Canoe Creek. It was on this land at the intersection of five roads [in Canoe Township northeast of Decorah] on the north side of Canoe Creek near a small pond that my father built his house after we came in October, 1855. He used green lumber just as it came from the sawmill. There was frost on the wall behind the bed in the kitchen all winter until next spring. It was years before he had shingles split and shaved to cover the roof. For nearly five years we used a ladder to climb to the chamber above.

Father made some four-legged stools. Then he laid some boards on the two stools for bedsteads. We had three of those beds. Mother made a good supply of bedding, blankets and a number of feather beds. We tacked up a sheet behind the kitchen bed and hung sheets in front for curtains, and hung a valence all around underneath the bed. My father bought a small cookstove and several chairs from Aaron Street to furnish his new house, as about this time Aaron Street and his family sold out and went down the Mississippi River to Louisiana to chop wood for supplying the steamboats with fuel. His daughter, Mary Street, got so she could chop a cord of wood per day. They soon returned to Springwater, however.

Before we came to Iowa Ezra King had married Eunice Street, a daughter of Aaron Street, and was living in a log house he had built near a spring on the side of a hill about a quarter of a mile to the northeast of where my father build his house. I stayed some at Ezra King's to tend the baby in the fall of 1855 before we got into our new home. Many years later, on account of my mother's health not being good on the low ground near Canoe Creek, my father moved into the old house built by Ezra King on the south side of the hill. Here he lived for many years with his second wife and daughter Annis. Here he died. The site of the of Ezra King log house is the present home (1922) of my half-sister, Annis Mott Ellingson, the sole survivor of Springwater still living in the vicinity. The little Quaker community of Springwater of early days has now entirely disappeared from the map.

As a small girl I got much happiness out of the twenty acres of woods belonging to my father on the south side of Canoe Creek. Here I gathered flowers, gooseberries, plums and wild crab apples. It was also in this woods that my father got out saw logs and sold the timber in Decorah. Our old desk, still in my possession, is made of cherry lumber that my father sold Charles Goltz, a cabinetmaker in Decorah in early days. We bought the desk in 1875 at the time we moved from Bluffton to the Blackmarr house on Mechanic Street in Decorah.

The old community of Springwater largely centered around the sawmill of early days. This had been built on Canoe Creek by Beard & Cutler in 1850 or 1852. Ansel Rogers, who first lived in Hesper, later bought the Springwater sawmill and moved his family there. In 1855, the year we came to Iowa, he built a gristmill on the west side of the dam. My mother helped to make the gauze bolt for sifting the flour after she came in October. Ansel Rogers was a leader among the Quakers who were settled in and around Springwater, and his home, a short distance southeast of the mill, was a center of activity in these early days. Friends' meeting was held in the front room of their log house. We went to meetings there twice a week, and to Sunday school on Sunday. ...

On August 31, 1856, Albert Aden Benedict arrived in Springwater. He came by team with his brother-in-law, Lorenzo D. Blackmarr, who had married his sister, Ann E. Benedict, in Ohio. They brought their daughter, Rose Blackmarr, with them. Another man with a second team came with them. Henry N. Chapel had married Matilda Benedict in Ohio and they also came to Iowa to live, and went on a farm north of Hesper.

In the spring of 1857 Lorenzo Blackmarr bought the gristmill at Springwater and some land near by, and he and Albert Benedict ran the mill. In the fall of 1857 Blackmarr rented the gristmill to Aaron Street, who had returned from Louisiana. Blackmarr then went back to Ohio on a visit.

In 1857 my brother, Clement Mott, was born at Springwater.

In February, 1858, the Springwater gristmill burned down, and when Blackmarr came back from Ohio he traded the lot and house to Henry Chappel for the land half a mile north of Hesper and went there to live. Chappel moved his family to Springwater. At the same time Blackmarr sold forty acres of land to Albert A. Benedict, who later bought ten acres more on the west of Ansel Rogers at $9.00 per acre. This land extended somewhat over the creek into the timber to the south of the creek.

In 1858 Aunt Lucretia Bean came to Iowa to live. She was a well educated woman, and taught school for some years in Iowa. In 1859 Russell Tabor, assisted by Albert Benedict, built a steam gristmill in Hesper. After this Albert Benedict was engaged in carpenter work and milling, but I do not know where. He lived with his sister, Ann Blackmarr, at Hesper, where he also attended school. The first time I ever saw him was one time when he came down from Lorenzo Blackmarr's at Hesper to visit with his sister, Cynthia Rogers, at Springwater, where we were attending meetings held in Ansel Rogers' house. I remember going with a bobsled load of "unattached" young people to a school exhibition half a mile east of Hesper. I do not know if Albert Benedict was in this crowd of young people or not. This may have been the winter before he came to Iowa. ...

In 1859 I attended school for six weeks at Hesper, where I boarded at Lorenzo Blackmarr's. I stayed there and went to school with their daughter, Rose Blackmarr, for company. George Holoway was the teacher. When Albert Benedict came home to Blackmarr's to go to school I returned to my home in Springwater.

The first Quaker Meetinghouse in Springwater was built about 1859 or 1860 on the north side of Canoe Creek on the north side of the road about half a mile northwest of the mill and about the same distance east of my father's house. My aunt, Lucretia Bean, taught school here for a while. I went to school to her. It was a tuition school. She was not teacher here, however, when the church burned down in 1862. ...

I remember there was lots of singing in the homes of those early days, although there was no singing in "meeting." There was no choir. My mother was one of the best singers in Springwater. My father did not sing any, but he loved to hear my mother. She sang hymns mostly. Many antislavery songs were sung at social gatherings. Charlie Gordon was one of the leaders in this. He also had a geography class which I attended.

Early in the spring of 1860 Albert Benedict built a house on his land at Springwater. He got out saw logs from the timber south of Canoe Creek. He intended this to be the finest house in Springwater. This house stood on the south side of the road and was between my father's house on the west and the old Quaker meetinghouse on the east. The prospective marriage of Albert Aden Benedict and Abbie Anna Mott was announced at a monthly meeting at Hesper. A committee was appointed to see that the rules of the Society of Friends were properly observed. I do not remember who was on that committee. There was no license law in those days, and the only record that was kept was that kept by the church.

Albert Aden Benedict and I were married in Quaker style on Wednesday, July 4, 1860, in the old Friends' Meetinghouse at Springwater. It was new then. Ours was the third wedding to take place in it. My wedding dress was of white calico with a purple figure in it. The hoop skirt was fashionable in those days and I probably wore one.

Albert was dressed in a dark coat, white linen pantaloons and black boots. He wore the large kerchief tie that was the vogue at that time. I have an old daguerreotype of us both which was taken only a few days before our marriage. I was only sixteen years old and Albert about twenty-five. Albert and I stood up together on the first step of the raised platform, and each in turn repeated the words that had been adopted by the Society of Friends for the solemnization ceremony. This had been committed to memory previous to the wedding. After this ceremony was over the witnesses who were present signed our certificate of marriage and the committee later made their report at the next monthly meeting at Hesper. Our marriage certificate is framed and hangs on my wall as I write. ...

My sister, Rachel Mott, who had attended school at Providence, Rhode Island, was sixteen when we came to Iowa. She got a position teaching school south of Looking Glass Prairie and boarded around at the homes of the pupils. George Benedict's boys went to this school and she became acquainted with Edwin Benedict. They were determined to get married before we did. Edwin Benedict and Rachel Mott were married July first, 1860 (the Sunday before we were) by Justice of Peace Tilden, west of Springwater. This was quite a surprise. They went to live on a homestead in Freeborn County, Minnesota. They came back to spend the winter of 1860–61 with their parents in Iowa. Edwin hauled wood and lumber to Decorah to keep busy.

One time Albert Benedict and James Mott went to visit Ed Benedict and wife at the home in Minnesota. There was but one room in their house, and when Uncle Ed wanted to change his clothes he took them in the evening and retired "out of doors" to do it. Forever after the boys referred to "out of doors" as "Uncle Ed's bedroom." Calico curtains were sometimes expensive and very toney for pioneers, so "outside" was like Prof. Breckenridge's corn meal mush that he furnished his pupils—"Good, wholesome and *very clean*"—quite an inducement for young Norwegians to come to attend his school from the country.

I shall not take the time to describe the exciting political campaign of 1860 that resulted in the election of Abraham Lincoln and the breaking out of the terrible Civil War in 1861. The sequel will show also that I had many "little things" to think about during those years.

On Tuesday, October 15, 1861, Oscar Clinton Benedict, our first child, was born at Springwater in the new house that Albert had built for us. Our first move to Decorah (for one week) was the week Oscar was a year old (1862). We lived on Broadway just west of Lander's large brick residence. Harvey Benedict came from Ohio and took Albert's place in the Stone mill at Decorah, so we moved back to Springwater to run the Springwater mill. ...

Sometime during the next month (March, 1862) the Quaker Meetinghouse at Springwater burned down. We had been at Mother's with the baby (Oscar) till the evening, and about ten we were awakened by a bright light from the east and all was ablaze. The building was being used as a school and a schoolboy had put ashes in a nail keg and left it in the entry. Nathan Rogers was the teacher at the time. A public school building was put up soon after some distance to the north where Friends held meeting until the new Meetinghouse was built at Springwater the following year (1863) by Harvey Benedict. The new Meetinghouse was built across the road to the east and north of the old Ezra King house afterwards occupied by my father. A cemetery was laid out adjoining.

Early in 1863 Harvey Benedict and family went to Ohio to dispose of some land, and when they returned to Iowa Sarah Hole (Sarah Gidley Benedict Hole) came with them. She was the mother of Harvey and Albert Benedict. Sarah Hole had lost her first husband, Aden S. Benedict, about 1842 and had married again to Jonah Hole, a Quaker preacher, who had been killed in 1862 by his being thrown from a buggy. Harvey Benedict's brother, Asa Benedict, and Susan Benedict, an adopted daughter of Harvey and Lovina Benedict, also came with them. Asa Benedict went to live with his brother-in-law, Henry Chappel. Harvey Benedict must have built the new Meetinghouse after he came back from Ohio.

On Sunday, September 6, 1863, Allard Eugene Benedict was born at Springwater. ...

In December, 1864, we moved to Bluffton where Albert worked in the mill there for Lyman Morse. We lived there until the following spring. On Tuesday, February 14, 1865 (Valentine Day), Florence Anne Benedict was born. She was my little valentine. In March, 1865, when Florence was three weeks old, we drove from Bluffton to Springwater in a sleigh to visit my folks. The following week Lorenzo and Ann Blackmarr came down from Hesper and took home their daughter, Rose Blackmarr, who had been helping me when Florence was born.

Soon came the big flood and ice run on the river [Upper Iowa River]. It surrounded the Morse house where we lived in the north addition. We grabbed the babies, Oscar, Allard and Florence, and a loaf of bread and went up the stairs through the log part of the house where Philip and Hannah Morse lived, tearing away the sheet she had tacked over the stair door. The floor of the lean-to which we occupied was a step lower down than the log part of the house. When the water had wet about half way across our carpet it floated a big cake of ice into the yard about a rod from our door. That proved to be the high point of the flood, however, and it soon passed on.

As soon as the roads got settled in early April (1865) Henry Chappel came and moved us from Bluffton to Springwater, where we lived only one month. In April I went to see Uncle Henry D. Earle, who was very low. It was while I was here that I heard of the assassination of President Abraham Lincoln [April 14, 1865]. Uncle Henry Earle died April 19, 1865, and was the first to be laid away in the new cemetery by the new Meetinghouse. I heard of Hannah Roberts Bean (my grandmother) and Sarah Hole (Albert Benedict's mother) walking near the grave, and in a year or two they were both lying near. Grandmother Hannah Roberts Bean died in October, 1865, and my mother, Anna Alma Mott, about six weeks afterwards, December 19, 1866. Sarah Hole and Henry Chappel's eldest daughter died not long after. My sister, Lucy Ellen Mott, died in October 1868, of typhoid fever. Aunt Eunice Bean Hardy came to Springwater at the time Grandmother Bean was ill, but arrived too late to see her. Aunt Eunice died soon after, in February, 1869. It seemed as though the funerals came very frequently during this time.

In May, 1865, we rented the Stone mill at Decorah for one year. Then we made our second move to Decorah. We lived in a one-story, three-room cottage between the Ammon-Scott machine shop and the Dayton store. This house was torn down when the Tremont Hotel burned a year or two afterwards.

It was in 1865 that we bought the old Singer sewing machine from a young man by the name of Mr. A. Bradish, who was agent for it at that time. Bradish had been to California during the gold rush in 1849 and had injured his leg, and in fact was lame all his later life.

During the summer of 1865 Albert was taken sick and we moved back to Springwater. When he got better, in October, he got a team of colts and drove back and forth between Springwater and Decorah twice a week and boarded himself at the mill office, and I lived alone in Springwater with the children until the contract for the mill was up in April, 1866. We lived in Springwater and Albert ran the mill until 1869.

In the summer of 1868 Lindley Chase, John Chase and Albert Benedict took a three weeks' land seeking trip in a covered wagon, driving a team of mules. They drove in central and southwestern Iowa looking for the "Promised Land." Some places, especially one camping spot near where the town of Panora, Guthrie County, now stands, the mosquitoes nearly ate them up. The story goes that Lindley Chase started to mow some slough grass for the mules, but the mosquitoes came out so thick he had to drop his scythe and run for the camp, and never went back after his scythe, and for all they ever knew it may be lying there yet. When they got back to Fort Des Moines they took a free ride to Oskaloosa on the new railroad, riding on the construction train. They attended the Friends' Yearly Meeting there and saw the new Meetinghouse.

In the month of May, 1869, we sold our home of sixty acres in Springwater, and in August drove overland to Clay County, Iowa, where Joseph Brownell and John Chase had located on homesteads. My brother, James Mott, went with us. We drove a covered wagon and a team of oxen called "Bootlegs" and "Tom." This was a trip that will always be remembered by our children, Oscar, Allard, and Florence, although at one time it got so monotonous that little Allard teased his father to "drive where there was not so much grass and more sandhill cranes." At one of our camping places our oxen ate up our box of dried herrings during the night.

On account of every other section of the land being assigned to the railroad a man could homestead only eighty acres, so Joseph Brownell let us have half of his quarter section. Brother James Mott took his homestead to the north of us about half way between our place and the Spencer Post Office. The description of our homestead was east one-half of the northeast one-fourth of section twelve, township ninety-five, range thirty-seven west of the fifth principal meridian [Lincoln Township]. Our Clay County homestead was located about six miles south of Spencer Post Office and a mile northeast of Annieville Post Office and about five miles west of the big bend in the Little Sioux River.

When we arrived at our homestead Albert and James set off one of the covered wagon boxes on the ground and used the running gear of the wagon and the oxen to haul native lumber up from Sioux Rapids, about twelve miles to the south of us, to build the framework of our sod shanty, in which we spent the following winter. The wagon box with its cover was left on the ground all winter and was used as a store room. It was in here that the "half-of-beef" was frozen and kept that first winter that formed one of the elements of "sod house soup."

Our sod shanty was built fourteen feet by twenty feet square with about seven foot eaves. It stood east and west. A heavy post was set in the ground at each end with a fork at the top into which a heavy ridge pole was placed. Posts were set at each corner and along the sides. The sides and ends were then boarded up. There was but one door and that was at the east end near the south side. There was one window in the east end and one in the middle of the south side.

Then with a prairie sod breaking plow strips of the virgin prairie, sod were turned over around the building spot. This served a double purpose. The strips of sod were cut into lengths about two and a half feet long and carried to the new building, where they were laid up like brick around the outside, forming a thick wall. The roof was thatched over with long coarse slough hay. The hay was then completely covered over with a layer of sod to hold the hay thatching in place. The hay that hung down at the eaves was trimmed off even with the edge of the sod. Those who failed to do this suffered in the prairie fires that followed.

Albert made a box which extended up through the roof and on the top of this he nailed a large milk pan with a hole cut in it for the stovepipe to stick up through. This was done to keep the hay thatching away from the stovepipe and made a fairly waterproof job. The sod house had a board floor, a very unusual thing for sod houses in those early days. A hole was dug in the ground below the floor near the stove and fitted with a trap door in the floor. Here potatoes were kept during the winter, an important element that went into the famous "sod house soup." A short partition was built in the west end of the room. Our bed was on the south side of this partition, while brother James had his bed on the north side. Oscar slept with his uncle James, while the two smaller children, Allard and Florence, slept in a trundle bed that slid underneath "Uncle Jim's" bed when not in use during the day. Above the partition and over the beds was built a platform where a year's supply of flour was stored, which was bought and ground at Estherville.

Our sod house was built on a slight knoll, the ground sloping away to the north, south and west, while it was quite level away toward the east, with the Little Sioux River in the distance. Off to the westward was a big swale or slough of bog land. A barn was built just to the southwest of the house and a haystack was placed just northwest of the barn to help protect it from the winter storms. Around the entire place were the fire guards. The fire guard consisted of two strips of plowing in the shape of a square, one outside of the other a safe distance away. The grass between these two strips of plowing was kept burned off at all times whenever there was any danger of a prairie fire. It was in this desolate, wind swept prairie sod house that we lived during the fall and winter of 1869–70.

The men folks hired a man who had a mower to cut hay, and after the hay was stacked, the sod house and barns built and the fire guards plowed around them, Albert and James drove to Estherville, twenty-five miles away, to buy wheat. They had it ground into flour there for the winter. Albert tended the mill one night to grind it. While at Estherville they visited Henry Chappel who was now on a homestead near Estherville. Merrit Chappel, their son, was working in the mill and Cynthia Chappel, their daughter, was teaching school. While the men folks were gone to Estherville and I was alone with the three children, a Mr. Grant set fire to the prairie grass, which burned a streak east to the river a mile north of us. The wind changed in the night, which made a "head fire" of the whole strip. I saw the fire coming right toward us, a red hot glare a mile or two long, a most alarming sight. Without waiting to admire the beauty of the scene I took a kettle of live coals to the northwest corner of the fire guards to start a back fire, but hardly got it started before the main prairie fire came with a roar and passed by on both sides. It burned fiercely, following the tall dry grass of the slough towards Brownell's, but it did us no damage. Some years later Henry Chappel's sod house in Estherville was burned by just such a prairie fire that got into the hay in the roof.

The following spring, on March 14, 1870, we had a feathery snow coming straight down with no wind blowing. About eleven A.M. a blinding blizzard came from the northwest which lasted for two days and nights, or until about three P.M. on the 16th. It is almost impossible to describe the desolateness and bitter cold, with the howling wind and blinding snow, of a blizzard of early days. Modern young people never will be able to realize the terrifying aspect of such storms. I will not attempt it. A taste of such a storm is described by Hamlin Garland in *A Son of the Middle Border,* page 310.

A man about forty-five and a young fellow about sixteen and a boy of twelve had come over from Grant's to borrow our long sled which Albert and James had made from poles from the "back forty." They went after wood about five miles to the river, and all of them perished in the blizzard coming back. The boy was found next day after the blizzard, the older man in about four days, but the sixteen-year-old boy was not found until the following spring after the snow went off, some three weeks later. The older man had lived out in the mountains and must have tramped many miles in a circle before giving up. He was found east of the river, the tail of his coat only showing above the snow where he had fallen in a deep drift.

In 1870 Albert Benedict entered into partnership with a Garrett Marcellus who was located on the Little Sioux River near a bridge, to build a gristmill. They contracted for hewed timbers for the mill of Peter Moore and his father at Gillett Grove. Albert bought a lot and built a board house just west of the proposed mill site. There was a "bee" to haul the timbers from Gillett Grove. Albert went to Dubuque and bought the machinery for the mill and shipped it to Newell, which was the nearest railroad station at that time, and hauled it on wagons from there. Harvey Benedict came back with Albert to help install the machinery in the mill. During the summer I went back to the sod house and stayed the necessary time on it to prove up on the claim.

On Thanksgiving day, Thursday, November 31, 1870, while skating on the mill pond, Willie Marcellus broke through the ice and was drowned. The funeral was held in the mill building. He was an only son.

In 1871 Uncle Ed and Rachel Benedict sold their farm in Minnesota and moved to Ida County, Iowa. They came to see us while we were still at Spencer. It was on that visit that we first heard of the drowning of their little son, Ralph, just before they moved from Minnesota. He had seen the older children playing in the edge of the lake and evidently had tried it himself. Rachel supposed he was away playing with the rest of the children, but when they came to look for him they could not find him until they saw his dress in the water. One of their children had lived only two weeks and another one was smothered in bed when only a few weeks old. Another son, Willis, was born on the Odebole (river) soon after they settled on the "forty" [acres] to pasture cattle they had invested in only a few years ago. Willis married and went to Canada and died soon after. Sister Rachel's married life ended when she died August 3, 1872. She left four of her seven children.

The partnership with Marcellus was not a pleasant one, and so our share was sold out, and in October, 1871, we again returned to Decorah. We went by stage from Spencer to Algona, which was the end of the railroad at that time. On our arrival at Algona we heard of the big fire that burned Chicago, starting on October 9, 1871. Until the following spring we lived in Decorah in a brick house that stood to the west of the old Chicago, Milwaukee & St. Paul Railroad depot. This was in the southern part of the town. In the spring of 1872 Albert formed a partnership with his brother-in-law, the firm going under the name of Blackmarr & Benedict. They bought the Bluffton mill located at Bluffton, Winneshiek County. Here we moved in 1872 and lived in a house near the mill for about three years. Here the children, Oscar, Allard and Florence, went to school and formed their childhood impressions, being eleven, nine and seven years old respectively when we moved there. Bluffton and its picturesque scenery will always retain a place in their memory.

In 1874 Lorenzo Blackmarr died, and Charlie Meader, who had married his daughter, Rose Blackmarr, took over the mill and we moved back to Decorah. At Decorah we lived in a house directly across from Dr. Bullis. On account of this house being later sold to a Dr. Smith it was known in later years as the "Smith house." It was a white frame house only a short distance to the north of Dry Run Creek. It was here that Frederic Estey Benedict was born on Saturday, June 5, 1875, and Grace May Benedict was born Thursday, September 14, 1876. While we lived here we bought the Estey organ which I still have in my home. It came about the same time as Fred, hence his middle name. The day Grace was born my brother, James Mott, started to attend the Centennial Exposition at Philadelphia, Pennsylvania.

In 1877 Albert formed a partnership with my brother, James Mott. The firm went under the name of "Benedict & Mott." They bought the stone flour mill southeast of Decorah known as the "Trout Run mill." My brother James Mott married Miss Bertha Christen, who was clerking in a dry goods store in Decorah, and they went to live in the little house on the hill just back of the mill. It was in this little house that Roy Mott was born and the twins, Walter and Wallie.

In the spring of 1878 we bought the property in Decorah on the west side of the Fair Grounds, where we built the "square house." We sold the house in the west part of Decorah to Dr. Smith, and while the square house was being built we lived in a frame house a block or two southwest of the public school building, which, on account of its peculiar color was afterward known to the family as the "pink house." On Thursday, October 10, 1878, Albert's brother, Harvey Benedict, while shingling on the east side of the roof of the square house, fell off on to the rough ground and was killed. The square house was completed and we moved into it in December, 1878. While we were living in the square house the children, Oscar, Allard and Florence, went to school in the old public school in Decorah, walking over Pleasant Hill west of our place to get there. Before we moved away they attended Slack's Business College and Florence also went to Breckenridge's Institute. Oscar also worked in a creamery at Waukon as bookkeeper.

On Monday, November 7, 1881, Wilber Garfield Benedict was born at the square house. We had his photograph taken when he was about five months old, just before we moved away. July 19, 1880, my aunt, Lucretia Bean Truman, died of consumption in West Decorah. She was buried in Friends' Cemetery at Hesper. Early in 1882 the square house was traded in towards a farm on Trout Run Creek which was owned by an Englishman by the name of Tibbits. This farm was afterwards known as the Trout Run farm and was run in connection with the mill property. It was about a mile up the Trout Run Creek to the southwest. We moved here from the square house early in April, 1882. Trout Run farm was a most beautiful place nestling in a valley and surrounded on nearly all sides by high hills, some of them steep, precipitous limestone cliffs. The place was particularly marked by a long row of magnificent white pine trees that grew along the east bank of Trout Run Creek commencing nearly opposite the house and extending southward to the high bluff a half mile south of the house.

Living at the Trout Run farm was pleasant although it meant much hard work for all. Allard and Oscar helped run the farm and Florence helped me with the housework. Miss Sophia Halsey taught school at the Trout Run schoolhouse and boarded with us. Fred and Grace attended there. Florence also taught this school a term or two before we moved away. The big woods to the south and east of our house were full of prairie wolves and they made a great deal of music with their howling nights. Albert shot one or two and Oscar trapped several of them and got the bounty on their scalps. Oscar also purchased a new Remington rifle with which Oscar, Allard, and even Florence had a great deal of sport shooting at a target, and they made life miserable for all the gophers and woodchucks in the pasture across the creek to the west and along the bluffs.

Oscar, Allard and Florence were the "young folks" and had considerable company come out to see them from Decorah. They also used to drive in to Decorah in the evenings to attend gatherings there. The "Rink" at Decorah was one of the popular attractions, and several masquerades were on the program, in which they took part.

These were the days of the famous Decorah Light Guards and the Decorah Drum Corps. Oscar and Allard joined the Decorah Light Guards, which was the crack company of the state militia, and they attended some of the encampments before we moved away. My brothers, James and Clement Mott, were both violin players and they would frequently come up to our house and have Florence play the accompaniment on the Estey organ.

In the summer of 1883 the Burlington, Cedar Rapids and Northern Railroad was built to Decorah. It ran diagonally across our farm from the southwest to the northeast and then turned across the creek and ran directly between the mill and the house of the mill property. In going between the house and the mill they had to blast out a deep cut in the solid limestone from twenty to thirty feet deep. This was a nerve-racking experience for the Motts who were living in the house at the time. One very large rock struck the east front of the house caving it in badly and breaking several windows. A small rock came down through the roof of the mill. Hardly a day went by but some damage was done by the blasting.

About six A.M. while it was still dark, on December 2, 1884, we were alarmed by a bright red glare in the sky down the valley to the northeast, and soon my brother Clem Mott came hurrying on horseback to let us know that the mill was on fire. Albert and the two boys, Oscar and Allard, hurried down to the mill to see if they could be of any help. There was nothing that could be done to save any part of it, and it burned down to the bottom, leaving only the four stone walls standing. It is presumed that sparks from the engine of an early freight train set the fire. An oil painting by Allard Benedict is hanging on my wall at Safeside, and is a very good picture of the old mill before it burned and before the railroad was built.

The burning of the mill brought on a crisis in our affairs. In the spring of 1885 the partnership of Benedict & Mott was dissolved and James Mott took over the Trout Run farm and moved his family into it while we again moved back to Decorah to live while Albert found a new location. We lived in the Barthell house in the southwest part of town just across the alley west of the Clark Goddard and the Caldwell residences. In the spring of 1885 Albert made several land-seeking trips into Iowa, Missouri, and Kansas. Oscar accompanied him on one or two trips. After considerable search Albert bought the Stone farm, which consisted of some two hundred and forty odd acres situated on a rolling upland about two and a half miles northeast of the town of Atlantic, Cass County, Iowa. Here we were destined to live for nine years.

On Thursday, June 4, 1885, we moved to Atlantic. Oscar and Allard with the horses and household goods went in a carload via the Chicago, Milwaukee and St. Paul Railway. The rest of the family, Albert and I, Florence, Fred, Grace and Wilber, went by the Burlington, Cedar Rapids and Northern passenger train. Before taking the train we stopped at Grove's for our meals. Many of our friends came to see us off, among them my brother, James Mott, who had been with us on our Clay County trip and had now been a partner of Albert's for so many years. This was the last time I saw him.

We went via Cedar Rapids, West Liberty and Des Moines, arriving in Atlantic very early in the morning of June 5, 1885, the day Fred was ten years old. We lived for six weeks in a rented house in Atlantic about one block west of the Courthouse, while the men folks, Albert, Oscar, and Allard, cleared away the forest and built a house into which we moved as soon as the roof and siding were on. All hands, including the children, helped to lath the house after we moved in, and it was plastered soon after. We had bought an extra large size wood-burning heater, which was too large to go through any ordinary door, so we placed the stove on the floor as soon as it was laid, before the studding was up, and then built the house up around the stove. This stove kept us warm all the time we were there, and stood there winter and summer, and was one of the things we were obliged to leave in the house when we moved away.

After the forest was cleared away a magnificent view of the town of Atlantic was disclosed from our front lawn. For this reason this farm was known as the Atlantic View Farm, and this name was painted on the rudder vane of the Halliday windmill we bought of D.P. Hawes and erected a year or so later. We lived on the Atlantic View Farm for nine years, from 1885 to 1894, the longest time we ever lived in any one place, up to that time. In the first twenty years of our married life we had moved twenty-one times, and we felt that we could now settle down and make a home. We set out many orchard trees and grapevines and made a large garden south of the house.

Life on the Atlantic View Farm was a pretty hard struggle. We were under heavy obligations, having bought too big a farm with too little money of our own. Albert felt that now the children were grown they could be of great help in creating an estate. Money was scarce in our little family and we did not have many luxuries. A large part of the woods and brush land had to be cleared off and this was done the following years. The wood was cut and sold in Atlantic, a stump puller was purchased, and the stumps pulled up and piled in the yard and helped to keep us warm, twice, once when cutting them up and again when they were burned. In the summer of 1885 Oscar married Miss Eva Couse at Decorah, and they came and lived with us until the renter's house became vacant the following year, then he moved there, where he lived all the rest of the time he worked on the farm. Here Flossie was born.

Wednesday, April 14, 1886, we witnessed what was known as Cass County and Audubon County cyclone. It was preceded by a terrific hail storm which stopped suddenly and it was followed by a ground fog which we noticed was traveling rapidly to the south. Going out on our front porch we first saw it coming towards us from the south in the form of a black, funnel-shaped cloud several miles distant. It gradually swung to the east and went directly through Grove City where we first saw the buildings, trees and wreckage flying through the air. The whole storm was in plain view of where we stood about two miles southeast of us on the opposite hill across the valley. It passed through the Troublesome Creek valley directly east of us tearing its way through the trees and demolishing houses, and disappeared to the northeast leaving a swath of destruction in its pathway that was marked for many years after.

On Wednesday, November 11, 1885, Florence was married to Joel David Hawes. The wedding took place in our new house on the Atlantic View Farm. Joe's father and mother came from Decorah for the wedding, and they all returned to Decorah together. Joe and Florence located on the Hawes farm, near Washington Prairie, fourteen miles east of Decorah. They lived here for several years and then moved to Decorah, where Joe entered the implement business there.

The Atlantic View Farm became quite a burden to us and also became associated with troublesome times, so it was decided, as Albert expressed it, to "put a period" to everything and make a new start in a new place. So the farm was sold late in the fall of 1893 to be delivered the following spring. We stayed on the farm during the following winter and had a public sale the following spring, selling off everything except the household goods. We moved to a rented house in Atlantic located two or three blocks west of the Courthouse, where we lived during the summer and winter of 1894 while Albert looked for a new location.

During the summer of 1894 Albert spent most of the time looking around for a farm. He was determined to take sufficient time to find a farm he liked and that he could handle without keeping his nose on the grindstone. Our family was now grown up, or nearly so, and in a few years our children would be leaving us to make homes of their own. It was, therefore, important that we have a good home, pleasantly located where we would not be bothered with old associations, and which we could handle without such a burden as the last one had been. We had followed what Hamlin Garland calls "The Middle Border" long enough.

After a great deal of search Albert finally bought the Jones farm located in the northwestern part of Thompson township in Guthrie County, Iowa. This farm consisted of about two hundred and forty acres and we bought it as such a rate that we could pay for the farm complete, and for the first time we were entirely free from debt. We were now so well situated that in honor of the event Albert in his characteristic way, named the farm "Safeside," feeling that we were now on the safe side of things in general.

We moved here from Atlantic early in the spring of 1895. Fred came home from Decorah in time to start putting in the oats on the north forty. During the summer of 1895 we built a new house on the site of the old one. Oscar came from Atlantic to help. Fred put in the crops that year and did most of the cultivation and harvesting while the house was being built.

After the new house was built we settled down to make our permanent home, so my "Early Days in Iowa" may be brought to a close. Let younger hands take up the story from here.

NOTE

1. Abbie Mott Benedict, "My Early Days in Iowa," *The Annals of Iowa* 17 (July 1930): 323–55.

THE MEMOIRS OF
Matilda Peitzke Paul

I N 1854, Ferdinand and Wilhelmina Kant Peitzke migrated from Germany to Wisconsin in hopes of providing a more comfortable life for their children. By the time Matilda, the last of the couple's nine children, was born in 1861 the Peitzke family had moved to Stacyville, Iowa. Four years later the family relocated again; in 1865 they purchased a farm near Riceville where Matilda's father planned to construct a brick home for the family.

Much of Matilda's early life revolved around the Riceville homestead. She played and worked on the farm, enthusiastically attended local schools, and after her father's death in 1870 spent six arduous years helping her family finish the brick house and farm the land. Her recollections chronicle the tremendous burden placed upon a wife by the death of her husband and economic partner.

Shortly after her mother abandoned the Riceville farm in 1876, Matilda became engaged to Ferdinand Charles Paul. When they married in 1880 they were able to recover the old Peitzke homestead which then became the Paul family home for many years.

Only eighteen years old at the time of her marriage, Matilda ably shouldered the duties of a wife and, within the first year of marriage, the responsibilities of a mother. All four of the Paul children (Mabel, Amy, Edna, and Alice) were born in the brick home. Here, Matilda sewed and washed clothes by hand, at the same time rocking the baby's cradle with her foot. Besides her domestic chores, Matilda also made and sold dairy products, took in boarders, and participated in outdoor labor. As her husband's health declined, she drove the harvester, husked corn, and picked potatoes, her youngest in a box nearby.

The Paul family lived a modest yet full life until 1931 when Ferdinand Paul died. Matilda and her daughter Mabel moved to Clear Lake where they experienced another personal tragedy when Matilda's fifty-year-old daughter Amy died within the following

year. It must have seemed like the end of an era for Matilda Paul,
yet she found other things to make her last years pleasurable: the
company of her three daughters and her grandchildren, the writing
of her memoirs, and the comforts of her new home. Her death in
1938 at age 77 concluded a long life which began in frontier Iowa
and ended in modern, twentieth-century Iowa.

Matilda Paul refused to believe that she was remarkable in
any way, yet she was the prototypal pioneer woman who worked
hard, made the best of life on the frontier, and as her youngest
daughter Alice Paul Butz recalled, relied on humor and religion to
cushion the rough spots in her active and demanding life. In 1935,
Matilda Peitzke Paul's granddaughter, Mabel Ruth Haas, urged
her to record her recollections of pioneer life in Iowa for her family.

When Matilda Paul completed her recollections in 1936, Mabel Haas transcribed them into a typed document which she later
deposited in the Manuscript Collection of the State Historical Society of Iowa, Iowa City. Portions of the original have been
deleted, and some minor changes made in grammar and punctuation for ease of reading. The excerpt presented here appears with
the generous permission and assistance of two of Matilda Paul's
children, Edna Paul Hammond and Alice Paul Butz of Clear Lake,
Iowa, and the State Historical Society of Iowa.[1]

MY memory takes me back to the summer of
1865 when I was four years old. I lived with my parents on a farm
near Stacyville. My father cut all the wheat with a cradle and the hay
with a scythe at that time. My next oldest brother bound all the grain
and raked up all the hay with a homemade hand rake. He also helped
do the stacking. He was less than 16 years.

One afternoon in the summer of 1865 the stage driver stopped
at our door bringing a pale and sick-looking passenger. It was my
oldest brother who was returning from the Civil War. He was sick
most of the time while in the South and on duty as a soldier, unable

to march or take an active part, and finally was dismissed and brought home sick and unable to sit up. My mother and father were writing to him when be arrived not knowing he was on his way home. You can hardly imagine with what joy he was greeted. He was very weak and slept most of the time for a long time after coming home. He was too young to be drafted to go to war, but was hired as a substitute by a man who had been drafted.[2] My parents knew nothing about his plans until after he had gone as he was working away from home. [He] was very young, only a few months past 17 years old when he returned home in the summer of 1865.

In the summer of 1865 father bought a farm in Howard County, two miles north of Riceville just across the line from Mitchell County. There was an old log house and a straw shed on it. The house was about 12 × 18 all in one room, with one door and one window. There was a low upstairs all in one room without a window. Had to climb a ladder to get up to it to go to bed. The roof on the house was very poor, and the snow often drifted onto our beds at night while we slept. In the summer when it rained we used all our pans and pails to catch the water trying to keep the beds dry. A shallow hole under our house answered for a cellar, and when we needed potatoes we lifted up one of the wide floor boards to get down in.

Had no well on the place when we moved there. Had to carry all the water up a long steep hill from a little stream. There was not much land cleared nor broke when we moved there so there was plenty of hard work ahead.

The day we left our home at Stacyville, we loaded what little furniture we had, consisting of three chairs, cook stove, home made table and cupboard, two benches we used in place of chairs, and two large wooden chests that were brought from Germany, some beds and bedding.

The first winter, there was no school in our neighborhood but the next four summers had a few months of school in the old Still House. It was built of logs. For seats there were long benches placed on three sides of the room. Had no desks or table to write on, instead had a slanting shelf across one side of the room attached to the wall. When occasion came to use a desk, we turned and faced the wall while writing or working arithmetic.

We got our drinking water for the school from a spring about a quarter of a mile away. It was considered a favor to go after water;

consequently we changed off. When the water came our teacher would let us pass it, first to teacher then to pupils, all drinking out of the same longhandled tin dipper.

Farmers in pioneer days had no pastures. The cattle roamed at large. The grain fields were fenced with rails. The farmers cut down trees and split them up in strips which they used for building fences. We turned the cattle out of the cow yard in the morning to go in any direction they pleased. Towards evening we children had to hunt for the cows until we found them. The leading cow wore a bell which was fastened to her neck with a strap buckled around her neck. Often we had a hard time locating our cows as it was nothing uncommon to find them several miles from home. All bells had different sounds; I now have the one we used when I was a child and its ring still sounds familiar.

We as well as children of other families were required to herd our cattle certain times of the year, and sometimes when the weather was sunny and not too cold we really enjoyed it, but often when it was cloudy and chilly it was very tiresome and plenty hard enough to keep them from getting into the corn fields.

I must also tell a little about the way milk was taken care of. While we lived on our farm there were no creameries nor cheese factories, the milk was put in pans to cool and left long enough for the cream to come to the top which was about 24 hours, then the cream was skimmed off with this kind of skimmer and kept in a cool place if there was one, until there was enough cream to make several pounds of butter in a dash churn.

I remember how I used to dread to have mother call me and tell me to help with the churning. It seemed as if the butter never would come; sometimes it did take hours to churn. There was no ice to be had to keep milk or cream cool; and it had to be kept in the cellar if there was one; and if there was no cellar, the next best thing had to be done; and it all made plenty of work.

I will tell a little more about our school days while living on our farm north of Riceville, nothing so thrilling but we learned a little and always had plenty of fun. Our teachers had very little education and schools were not graded. [We] usually started at the front of our book at the beginning of every term and went as far as we could, then start[ed] all over again at the beginning of next term. [We] stood up in a row when we spelled, and some teachers gave a prize to the one who [was] left.

We played many games at school, such as Pussy wants a Corner, Pull-Away, I am on Dickies Land, Ring around the Rosie, Needles Eye, Drop Handkerchief, Poison, and other games. It still thrills me when I think of it. Often in the winter we slid on frozen ponds and slid down hill and snow balled each other.

I must mention flies and mosquitoes which tormented pioneers. There were no screened doors nor windows and flies were so thick in the houses and all over everything, we used a little limb, thick with leaves, to keep them off food while we ate. That is too terrible to dwell on. Later on had window and door screens made of mosquito netting. Every morning the flies had to be chased out of doors, with branches covered with leaves. Mosquitoes were so plentiful one could hardly endure their bites before the day of screens; we gathered up very fine chips at wood pile and made a smudge and kept it going to keep mosquitoes from tormenting us.

Then there were many kinds of snakes. The little green snake, garter snake, hoop snake, spotted water snake, and worst of all the poisonous rattle snake which sometimes killed people. I was bitten by one when I was around 12 years old, but was doctored up right away by placing my foot in mud and keeping it in fresh mud for about six hours, and it left no ill effect. They also gave me a little whisky. Thus one poison offset another.

My father was a brick-maker by trade, and we had been living in our old log house for nearly four years. By the spring of 1869 he had gotten things in shape to begin making brick and build a new house, but his health failed and he had to give up the work before he burned the brick. He then had very poor health until his death on January 25, 1870. My brother William had to go ahead with the farm work that summer; father did stack the grain by having someone hand each bundle to him. After father got too weak to do any outside work, he spun yarn for stockings, and when spinning got too hard he knit woolen stockings for the family. In pioneer days no one in a small town kept ready-made coffins, but [they] were made by a carpenter when needed. [Father's] funeral was held at the Baptist church in Riceville and he was buried in the Riceville cemetery.

In the spring of 1870 we went ahead finishing up the brick for the new house and hired a couple of men to lay the brick and got the new brick house all done ready to move in by fall.

For the next three years William, who was then 20 years old, had to go ahead and do the farm work with the help of the younger children. Herman, the next oldest boy at home, was 10 1/2 years old the first summer after father died. We all helped what we could in the field. In the spring we younger children dropped the corn in the rows in planting time and the older ones covered it up with a hoe (there were no corn planters in pioneer days), also dropped potatoes. When the corn first came up we had to stay out in the field and chase the black-birds to keep them from digging and eating the corn as fast as it came up. It was our work in spring to pull weeds for the hogs for feed. We often had to watch our cattle to keep them out of other people's as well as out of our own fields. I think we had a reaper in the early '70s for cutting grain, but it had to all be bound by hand. Before I was old enough to bind grain I helped carry bundles in piles, ready to be shocked up.

In March 1876 Mother sold the farm to my sister Emma and her husband. Mother and I moved our furniture down to my sister Bertha's June 1, 1876, a week before I was 15 years old. Bertha let us have one room 15 feet square in her house to live till mother built a cottage right nearby for us to live in. I continued going to school the same as before; when there was no school I sometimes helped the neighbors some with house work, and I often did sewing for other people. We could buy no ready made garments but had to make all underwear, dresses, and most of the ladies' and children's coats were homemade. Often the men's and boys' pants and jackets were homemade, so there was plenty of that kind of work to be had.

I drove horses on reaper for a neighbor one harvest while we lived there; he paid me pretty well I thought. And the next year I drove harvester for Mr. George Smith who lived about two miles southwest of us. I got good pay there too. I think 50 cents a day and board. I got some money for clothes that way.

I met Grandpa [Ferdinand Paul] for the first time the fore part of March 1877—when be came to hire out to Fred Stark. I was nearly 16 years old. Little did I think then that he would be my life companion. He started to work the twentieth of March and worked there eight months. He presented me with a little beaded purse on my birthday the seventh day of June. He often came over to see us in the evening after his work was done. In July he asked me to be his wife, and after thinking it over from all angles, I promised him I would be his true wife as long as I lived.

On the thirteenth day of January 1880 Grandpa and I were married. I had a wine colored wedding dress made with a polonaise,[3] and the skirt was trimmed with several rows of pleating and the polonaise with one row of pleating and a bias strip of velvet of the same color on top of the pleating. I had white ruching in the neck of the dress and pleating round the sleeves at the wrists and a nice white silk tie with little stripes of coloring of different designs across the ends. I had a velvet hat trimmed with white, a new black coat, and a cape trimmed with white ribbon. The cape was cut in a circular style and reached to my shoe tops. I had gloves and high shoes which laced up on the side. I certainly felt that I was well dressed.

My sister Amelia was a dressmaker by trade, and she made my dress; I learned much of the art of sewing from her. I was busy all that autumn of 1879 getting my sewing done ready for housekeeping. I made enough quilts, sheets, and pillow cases for two beds. Mother gave me one feather bed and four goose feather pillows, [and] I had four linen table cloths, plenty of towels, and dish towels. I had all of ten dresses or more and plenty of underwear, all tucked and trimmed with ruffled embroidery, and several fancy night gowns, and this all kept me quite busy sewing.

Grandpa and I were certainly proud of our baby girls and took the very best care of them that we knew how. I made all their clothes by hand and enjoyed it. I really took pride and pleasure in the work, which I did mostly at night, after we rocked them to sleep. I did all the washing by hand, rubbing every garment, and often stood on one foot while rubbing and rocking the baby's cradle with the other foot to keep her from waking up.

We had considerable timber on our farm, [and] Grandpa sold wood. One time when taking a load of wood to town one of our colts was following its mother and ran into the pole wood which penetrated its lungs and killed it. This was a big loss to us financially; also a big loss because we had love for the colt.

During the years we lived there we often fed tramps. One morning four different ones begged their breakfast there, we fed them. One summer evening after dark, two men stopped for bread and milk to eat [and] said they would pay us. They said they traveled nights and slept day times. They paid us each 10c. We thought they were escaped convicts and were very much afraid of them. Their hair was cut close to their head.

Nearly every fall I made several gallons of apple pickles, canned plums, [and] mince meat. [The] several gallons of sauerkraut added to the cucumber pickles, [which] I had packed in brine, and the green tomato pickles gave us considerable things to eat. We always had our own meat and potatoes and wheat for flour. [We] also raised buckwheat to be ground into flour for pancakes. Some years we raised sugar cane for sorghum [a kind of molasses], gathered wild crab apples for sauce.

Together with all my sewing and knitting I made a hooked stair carpet and a number of hooked rugs, rag carpets, and so forth. It took 1 1/4 pounds of rags for a yard of carpet. I think I had my first rag carpet woven in 1888; I was so pleased with it and appreciated it more than you can imagine. It was made with bright stripes and "hit and miss" and certainly looked beautiful to me.

We still went on with our farming the best we could. Grandpa's health was poor, but he did what he could and I helped with the work, such as driving harvester, mower, and hay rake. In the fall I helped husk corn [and] picked up the potatoes. We usually raised around seventy-five bushel. Mabel and Amy [M.P.'s daughters] went to school, [and] we took Edna [a daughter] to the field and put her in a large box where she could play while I picked up potatoes. We built a new barn in the summer of 1887 or 1888; also a hen house. We had carpenters to do most of the work, but I helped Grandpa finish up.

Charlie VanAuken stayed with us several weeks during the winter of 1890. There were seven to do the work for. I did all the washing, on [a tin wash] board often standing on one foot operating cradle with other foot at same time. For the next year I had very little time to help Grandpa, but as he couldn't stand it to ride on the mower, he took care of Alice while I run that and the hay rake. I helped him do the milking. The girls took care of Alice. At that time we sold our cream which saved me lots of work. In the summer of 1891 we milked 12 cows; we had some of Mr. Biddle's cows and paid him for the use of them. That was the only time we ever milked so many cows.

We helped Grandpa considerable with the farm work. I quite often did a good share of the plowing, when we had a riding plow; also raked hay in haying time. Then the girls and I helped him pick up potatoes, and when it came time in the fall to husk corn the girls and I helped Grandpa with that, and it saved him hiring help. We enjoyed husking corn when the weather wasn't too cold, but sometimes it was altogether too cold for comfort, when there was even danger of freezing hands or feet.

Now I want to conclude my Memoirs. To me, what I have told

doesn't seem worth while at all, for I cannot express myself as I should or would like to do. I must now tell about Grandpa's failing health. I noticed it very decidedly by 1928, and often I sat and looked at him, knowing he was failing fast. He also realized this and tried to get help by doctoring which gave some relief but nothing permanent. He not only tried Osteopathy, Electric machine, Chiropractic treatments, but several different kinds of medical doctors, sparing neither time nor means. At last he went to a hospital for medical treatment, but everything he tried failed, and about two weeks after his return from the hospital his sickness proved fatal, and on April 9th, 1931, he breathed his last. Then everything was so different for me. I hardly knew what to do.

We rented our farm by the last of May, had our sale the latter part of October, and moved to our present home November 9. Then, we had so many callers every day. Our old friends and neighbors certainly remembered us. I am glad too to have Edna and Alice living so close by, and am thankful for many other blessings I have. Now, Mabel and I are comfortably settled; we have gas heat, which makes it very convenient for us.

NOTES

1. This appeared as Glenda Riley (ed.), "The Memoirs of Matilda Peitzke Paul," *The Palimpsest* 57 (March/April 1976): 54–62.

2. The practice of hiring a substitute was common during the Civil War and often involved young men who were underage for the draft or volunteer service.

3. Originally worn by Polish women, a polonaise was a dress with the top skirt divided in front and worn pulled back over an elaborate underskirt.

Pioneer Life in Palo Alto County
THE MEMOIRS OF
E. May Lacey Crowder

ALVIN VOSBERG LACEY, born July 3, 1832, at Mason, Michigan, and Sarah Eveline Carr, born on November 13, 1836, at Ellensville, New York, married on November 23, 1857. Because they had little more than their clothing and his trade as a carpenter, they at first lived in the home of Alvin's married sister, Harriet Lacey Tressler. They had their first child, Fred, on September 6, 1858. Nineteen months later, on March 31, 1840, Frank made his appearance. At that time, the Crowders lived in White Rock, Illinois, where rising prices prohibited them from taking up their own land. Consequently, they decided to move farther west where, May later recounted, "Land was to be had almost for the taking." May added, "Iowa, with its broad prairies and fertile lands, was beckoning."

Alvin and Sarah migrated to Iowa late in the fall of 1860. They traveled by covered wagon and camped out every night with their two young children. When they reached Howard County, they found it more crowded than they had anticipated. They took up residence in an abandoned corn crib and set to housekeeping. They soon moved to a log cabin where May was born on November 2, 1861. Her childhood memories include the additional strain put on her mother when, in late summer of 1862, her father enlisted in the Thirty-eighth Iowa Infantry.

May's mother adapted to her new circumstances by becoming a dairy entrepreneur. When May's father returned from the war, he brought a newly freed African-American man with him as a farm worker and also promptly sold May's mother's nine cows, perhaps because he preferred to be the "breadwinner" in the family.

In 1869, the Crowders moved again; Alvin Crowder claimed a homestead in Palo Alto County. In time, May's mother prevailed, for the family eventually turned to raising cows as its primary livelihood. May also made it very clear that the women of a fam-

169

ily often brought in the only "cash" money to be had and kept the
operation solvent during hard times. May also described the critical roles her mother played as doctor, teacher, religious influence,
and frequent hostess to friends, travelers, and schoolteachers.

Because of her wonderful memory for detail, May also gave
a vivid picture of family life and work during the 1860s, 1870s,
and 1880s. These reminiscences were written between 1930 and
1932 and were edited by Mrs. Crowder's daughter, Mrs. Walker
Moore Alderton. The manuscript has been shortened and much
personal material omitted. It first appeared in the *Iowa Journal of
History and Politics* in 1948 and is presented here with the permission of the State Historical Society of Iowa.[1]

A FTER they finally arrived at their destination, in
Howard County, there was not a vacant house to be had, but they located an empty corn crib, a pretty cold-looking place even to camp
in. It had a roof, however, and mother, being accustomed to making
the best of things, made it fairly livable by tacking blankets and spare
bedding to the slats. They soon afterward decided upon an eighty-
acre farm, which they bought. On it was a small log cabin, consisting of one room and a loft, in which they made themselves comfortable for the winter. The farm was at the edge of the woods and fuel
was plentiful.

One of the neighbors mentioned a wagon-load of potatoes intended for the market, which had been frozen during the night. Father looked them over and offered a dollar for them. His offer was
accepted and he started home with his purchase. As he drove he
sorted the potatoes, throwing out the frozen ones. He found that there
were enough good potatoes to last the family through the winter.
With a little more judicious buying the family was provided with the
necessities by the time winter set in.

Father, in the meantime, had obtained work at carpentering. His
first work was several miles from home. Mother, with her two ba-

bies, was timid, so he used to walk home at night and back again the next morning. Father was a small man, five feet six inches in height, but he was strong and wiry, and nothing seemed to tire him.

I was born in the little log cabin near Chester, Howard County, Iowa, about one mile from the Minnesota line on November 2, 1861. The Civil War had begun the previous spring and my father, like most young men of the time, wished to be in the thick of it, but under the circumstances he delayed enlistment, ran the little farm, at odd moments hauled and cut wood, and in other ways prepared for army service later on.

At last, when I was not quite a year old, mother consented for father to go and on August 14, 1862, he joined Company I of the Thirty-eighth Iowa Infantry. The newness of Iowa and the fluidity of its population in 1862 is indicated by the fact that not one of the 104 men of Company I had been born in either Minnesota or Iowa, the states in which the company had been recruited. One-fifth of the company had been born outside the United States, seventeen of them being of British origin.

While the men were on the way to the front there was an epidemic of measles among them. Many of these recruits were neighbors and friends and father took upon himself the duty of nursing them. All recovered. In the army, nurses were very scarce and when it was learned that father was adapted to that work, he was immediately given hospital duty, much to his disgust. Being active by nature, he much preferred the infantry. In fact, several times he left the hospital and made his way to the fighting troops, but each time he was returned to hospital duty, in which he spent the remainder of the war years.

While father was in hospital work he was naturally exposed to all sorts of contagion. Sanitary conditions were bad and there were few conveniences. As for antiseptics, about the only things available were soap and water, not always the best soap or the cleanest water. Smallpox was prevalent in its worst form, but father had been vaccinated twice and physicians said he probably would never have it. For one whole summer he nursed the victims of that disease, feeling no anxiety on his own account. But the following summer, when he had not seen a case for several months, he was suddenly stricken with the dreaded disease.

He had a very severe attack, but he was in the hands of two nurses as competent as any who were available. His skin was kept

constantly oiled and, as an additional precaution against disfigura-
tion, his hands were tied. Although he recovered without the pits or
scars often left by the eruption, his eyes were permanently affected
and he later completely lost the sight of one of them. His early death
on February 1, 1885, at the age of fifty-two was attributed to the af-
ter-effects of this attack of smallpox.[2]

When peace finally came, the men from our section of the country were brought up the Mississippi River by boat and disembarked
at Davenport. No longer under orders and free to do as they wished,
they threw their knapsacks down in a pile on the shore and proceeded
uptown to celebrate their freedom. When they returned several hours
later, a large, very black Negro was sitting there watching their
things. "What are you doing there, Snowball," said father. "Well, dey
didn't seem to be anybody taking care of dese, so I thought I would,"
was the answer. That was the beginning of the acquaintance and, as
a result, "Nigger Jim" came home with father and remained for about
a year and a half. He was honest and faithful and idolized the whole
family. I was between four and five years old at the time and was a
great favorite with Jim, whose admiration I reciprocated. ...

Father considered the farm a home rather than a moneymaking
enterprise. A good team of horses, one cow to supply us with butter
and milk, a pig or two for meat, chickens enough to supply the table
with eggs and a chicken to eat now and then were all he wanted. He
expected to earn money by working at his trade. Mother had different ideas. During his absence she had accumulated nine cows. Butter sold for sixty cents a pound so she was able to support the family
nicely even though she paid sixty cents a yard for her calico. But
milking cows did not appeal to father; one week from the time he returned there was only one left.

There was no herd law in Iowa at the time and the farmers
turned their cattle out in the morning to graze wherever they would
during the day. A bell was strapped on the neck of one of the herd to
make it easy to keep track of their wanderings. One evening when
Fred was seven and a half and Frank not yet six, they were sent to
bring the cattle home. It was one of those delusively pleasant days in
April and the little boys started without their jackets, wearing only
their pants and calico waists [shirts], expecting to be gone only a little while. But the cattle were farther away than father thought and
when the boys found them, the animals refused to go in the direction
Fred thought home should be.

A cold north wind sprang up and the cattle went better, quite willing to follow the course of the wind. Fred finally decided that he did not know where he was and the boys abandoned the cattle and tried to find their way home without them. By that time it had grown quite dark. The boys were too tired to go any farther and lay down in the woods, where they spent the night. As time passed and the boys did not come, father started out to find them. Fred heard his shouts and answered, but his childish voice did not carry so far. The neighbors were notified and all responded except one, a very unpopular man that night. The search was kept up all night without results.

As soon as it began to grow light, the boys arose and started on. They soon came upon a road which they followed until they reached a house where they stopped to inquire the way. They were weak from hunger and shivering with cold so they could hardly stand or speak. Fred explained that they were lost, had been out all night, and wanted to know the way home. The man, evidently in a bad humor, told them to follow the road they were on and it would take them to the school section. Then he added, with an oath, "Be off, you little devils." The boys did not know what "school section" meant, and, as the road was a very dim one, when they came to another which looked better to them Frank insisted on following it.

Finally they came to the house of Bill Nye. He had been a comrade of fathers in the army and the boys were not afraid of him. They were taken in, each one was given a big cup of hot ginger tea, and they were fed and warmed. Mr. Nye then took them on horseback and started home with them. On the way they met father who transferred them to his own horse and brought them home. The neighbors were called in from the search by shooting and blowing horns.

When I was seven my parents decided to remove to Storm Lake, Iowa, that location seeming to have more promise for the future than Howard County where we were living. Our few belongings were loaded into a couple of covered wagons and we started on the first of May, 1869. It was a wonderful trip for us children. One wagon was drawn by a team of horses and the other by mules. The country was still very new and there were few bridges over the streams and little or no grading done on the roads. The spring had been rainy and we sometimes found ourselves stuck in the mud. Then it became necessary to use both teams on one wagon. At times a long chain was attached to the wagon tongue and the horses and mules were hitched to that, in order to give them solid footing.

Mother had packed a big barrel of provisions and we camped wherever night overtook us. We stopped for an hour at noon and took a cold lunch out of the barrel. At night our simple cooking was done over a camp fire. There was always tea for father and mother and meat or eggs and a warm vegetable for all, as well as pie or cake. While mother prepared the evening meal we children raced and romped enjoying our relief from the long hours in the wagons.

Our one cow was tied at the rear of one of the wagons and her calf, which had been left unweaned in anticipation of the journey, was permitted to run free. At night the calf was tied up and the cow was turned loose, for we well knew that she would not go far without her calf. One evening, after things had been arranged for the night, the calf broke loose. He immediately started at top speed to make the most of his liberty and the cow followed the calf. The tie rope was dragging and we children finally got hold of it, but it took our combined strength to hold his calfship and guide him back to camp.

At the end of two weeks we arrived at Fort Dodge, then a little town, on the Des Moines River in Webster County. There father met Mr. Xenophon Loomis, an old neighbor and a Civil War veteran, whom he had known in Howard County. With his wife and baby daughter Loomis was living in a little shack at the junction of the Des Moines with a smaller stream called the Lizard, about a mile from Fort Dodge.

That part of the State was then settling up very rapidly and Mr. Loomis proposed that we spend the summer with them and that he and father pool their resources and break prairie together. As father had most of the equipment necessary and needed the money, he decided to do this, and we moved into the little shack with the Loomis family. Mother was to go with the men to do the cooking, for the breaking crew boarded themselves. Father used both horses and mules. Mr. Loomis had oxen. The summer was very wet; much of the time the water followed the plow. That made the pulling easier for the animals but was rather hard on the man who held the plow. Fred rode one of the lead horses but Frank and I remained at home with Mrs. Loomis.

One Saturday there had been a very heavy rainfall and both the Des Moines and the Lizard were rising rapidly. The breaking crew arrived on the opposite side of the Lizard and found the water too deep to cross at the ford as they usually did. I well remember standing on the river bank and looking across at the party and their teams gathered on the other side. That muddy water carrying all sorts of debris looked completely hopeless to me. But a rowboat was procured and they were rowed across, the teams swimming part of the way. All sorts of strange things were coming down on the water. A young man tied a wagon box to a tree and launched it into the stream. He had a spear tied to a long slender rope with which he salvaged whatever he could that looked worth saving. Between times he bailed out the water that was constantly pouring into his improvised boat. When he got tired, he called to the men who were standing about watching the rising river to haul him in.

A branch of the Illinois Central Railroad, then known as the Dubuque and Sioux City, was in process of construction that summer and the bridge crossing the Des Moines River just above its junction with the Lizard was partially completed when the flood came. All morning men were swarming over the big timbers trying to strengthen the structure so the water would not carry it away, but toward noon an ominous cracking was heard and the men ran for their lives. All had reached safety when, with a tremendous crash, half of the structure went out. One man had left his coat on the bridge and ran back after it as the timbers of the wrecked section went floating downstream. He retrieved the coat but just as he sprang from the bridge there was a second crash and the rest of the bridge went out. He must have needed that coat, for he took a fearful risk. For the next two weeks the weather was too wet even for breaking and mother and the men remained at home.

According to the Homestead Act of 1862 any citizen of the United States over twenty-one years of age could acquire 160 acres of land priced at $1.25 an acre or 80 acres of land on which the government price was $2.50 an acre if he lived on the homestead for five years and complied with other requirements. A later amendment provided that time spent in the military service of the United States was to be deducted from the five years required in ordinary cases, but the veteran still had to take up residence on his homestead and improve it. Father and Mr. Loomis decided to take up homesteads.

Father's first plan had been to take a Homestead near Storm Lake in Buena Vista County, but when the breaking season was over he was influenced to change to Palo Alto County where a good many people he knew were now going. Father and Mr. Loomis went to the government land office at Fort Dodge and filed for their claims. Our

new location was in Township 94 north, Range 33 west of the Fifth
Principal Meridian.

The two men started across country to inspect their property,
taking with them lumber for a little shanty to be built on Mr.
Loomis's homestead. It took one day for them to erect the little
shack, just a frame of two-by-fours at top and bottom, with boards
running perpendicularly nailed to them, a roof sloping one way, a
door, and two windows. Later a neighbor described it as a "lean-to
without anything to lean to."

When the men returned, the wagons were again loaded and we
started on the last lap of the journey to our new home in Palo Alto
County. After the many rains of the summer, every pond and slough
[marsh] was brimming full. There were no roads, only trails. In some
places, where there were not even trails, we drove by compass. We
now had two teams of mules. When we approached a slough the only
thing we could do was to drive in and trust to luck or Providence to
get out on the other side. One night we camped only three miles from
our stopping place of the night before. In five days of constant effort
we drove the fifty miles.

The "shanty" looked small, indeed, standing alone in the midst
of those endless miles of prairie—not a tree or shrub to relieve the
monotony. Mother said she was sure we had nearly reached the end
of the world and that just a few miles farther on we should come to
the "jumping-off place," but we moved in and were happy to think
that at last we were going to be settled.

Grass there was in plenty and the men began at once to build
shelters for the stock for the winter. We still had our cow and calf,
now a husky six-months-old steer. A stable was built on our homestead with a framework of timbers brought from the Des Moines
River, six miles distant. The walls and roof were of the long, coarse
slough grass. It made a very warm, comfortable shelter for stock and
for several years no other barn was built. When these sheds had been
built on both homesteads the men turned their attention to getting up
hay. In a few days more hay had cut and stacked enough for the
months of winter.

While the hay was being put up, mother and the two boys dug
the cellar for our house. At a depth of about five or six feet, as I remember it, they came upon what seemed to be wood ashes. There
was much speculation as to when and how those ashes came to be
there. We had arrived in September, 1869, but it was the first of No-

vember by the time father was ready to commence work on our house. Lumber and other materials had to be hauled from Fort Dodge, a distance of some fifty miles, with no roads except the trails father and Mr. Loomis had made.

While father and Mr. Loomis were away on one of these trips, we had our first experience with a prairie fire. Mother had insisted that the men burn firebreaks before leaving, so they broke a couple of furrows a few rods apart to completely surround the buildings and the hay stacks and then burned off the grass between them. Just before noon after the men had gone, I noticed that the sunshine on the floor looked very yellow. "What makes the sunshine look so funny?" I asked. Mother looked around. "It's a prairie fire," she exclaimed.

Soon the flames became visible. The fire was coming with racehorse speed, for the grass was long and heavy and a prairie fire always creates a strong wind. Great sheets of flame seemed to break off and go sailing through the air directly over the house and stables, but nothing inside the firebreaks was ignited and soon the danger was past. The burned-over prairie, however, was drearier than before.

A short distance from the house there was a stretch of bottom land with an outlet on the opposite side, called Beaver Creek. Muskrats had been very plentiful there and the creek was dotted with their cone-shaped houses, built of the grass stems, and weeds. These made fine fuel for the approaching fire and many of these houses smouldered for hours after the fire had passed. We hoped that the muskrats had escaped, as seemed possible since they always have one entrance to their house below the water line, for muskrat hides brought about ten cents apiece.

Construction was begun on our house at once. It was on a very pretentious scale for that locality, for it measured sixteen-feet wide by eighteen-feet long and was a story-and-a-half high. Downstairs there was a living and general purpose room with a pantry and bedroom partitioned off one end. These two smaller rooms were separated by a stairway to the second floor. A door from the pantry opened into the cellar way which consisted of steps cut into the dirt wall. The cellar was used for our winter's supply of vegetables as well as for milk and butter. The upstairs was all in one room but was divided by curtains. This served as sleeping quarters for us children and for anyone else who chanced to pass by when night was approaching.

On the tenth of November, 1869, six months after leaving

Howard County, we moved into our new house, although there were as yet neither doors nor windows. Father's work bench was set up in the second story where I used to enjoy watching the curling shavings as he planed the lumber for the doors and window frames. Inside, the house was lined throughout with tarred paper; and on the outside it was banked with earth a foot or two above the bottom of the walls to prevent freezing in the cellar. About four feet on the house father laid a low wall of rocks so abundantly found on the prairies and the space between this and the house was filled with earth, forming a terrace.

Towns were far apart then and everyone's home was open to any traveler. This was particularly true of our place. People drove for miles to "get to Lacey's" to spend the night. Occasionally a stranger passing through would offer to pay for his accommodation, but by far the greater number were entertained as guests. Father would put the team in the barn and give them feed. The traveler was sent to the house for his meal which mother always seemed glad to get no matter what the hour.

This house stood for about ten years before it was torn down and replaced by one somewhat larger and much better built. The new house contained three rooms upstairs and all the rooms downstairs were larger. An additional closet under the stairs was an improvement, too. The house was very much on the same plan as the old one excepting that the stairs were partitioned off from one side of the living room and could be reached from an outside door as well as from the living room.

When we moved into our first house we had very little furniture. A couple of chairs, one Boston rocker (the best chair to rest in that has yet been made), a few dishes, and some cooking utensils were about all we had. Father built a couple of benches to eke out our supply of seats. Later more chairs were bought. Father built three bedsteads of lumber. The one for himself and mother was strung with cord which took the place of the modern springs of which we had never heard. Those for the children were supplied with slats on which "ticks" were placed. These ticks were made at home and filled with fresh clean straw to serve as mattresses. The two bedsteads upstairs were made very high to permit storage underneath them of seed corn, small tools, and even parts of harness for which there was no suitable place in the sheds. Mother had comfortable pillows and a good feather bed which her mother had given her when she was married.

When father bought our cookstove in Fort Dodge he was very careful in selecting it. He knew that a large firebox in a stove took less fuel than a small one. Also he wanted to be able to see the fire so he took a chair and sat down before the stove to see whether the fire would show. His judgment was good; that stove was the best for all purposes of any for miles around. Our fuel was wood from the timber along the Des Moines River six miles distant and father and the boys made many trips for wood during the winter that followed. We were quite comfortable in spite of the fact that our house with its board walls lined, with a single layer of building paper stood on the open prairie with no shelter of any sort.

The winter of 1869–1870 was severe; storm followed storm. There was a great deal of snow and every little breeze lifted the snow in the air. Sometimes a slight thaw would melt the snow a little, but it would freeze again during the night so a thin crust of ice was formed, but the next high wind started it blowing again.

Later in the winter, father made one of his trips to Fort Dodge for much needed supplies. As soon as his business was transacted he started on the return trip, expecting to stop at the house of a friend overnight and reach home the following day. During the night a furious storm arose and when he looked out in the morning he saw that the air was full of snow. Had there been any road they would have been obliterated. It looked like a desperate undertaking but he decided to push on. He soon learned that he had no idea as to where he was going and he concluded that it was better to leave the direction entirely to the mules. Holding the lines loose in his hands he let them go where they would.

I well remember that day. Often mother went to the window, though it was impossible to see farther than ten feet on the lee side of the house. It was like looking at a wall of snow. Once I heard her say, "Oh, if he is out in this storm he will surely perish." About two in the afternoon, as she was looking out, she saw the tips of the mules' ears emerging from the flying snow. They had brought the wagon home across miles and miles of trackless prairie directly to the house. What guided them? I still wonder.

Enough snow had sifted into the stable to make it very uncomfortable for the stock. Father, a Mr. Bernard, who was a transient guest in our home, and the two boys started to shovel it out. The cow and the yearling were taken out and left on the sheltered side of the stable. The yearling passed around the corner of the stable out of sight of the cow but remained in the shelter of the shed. As soon as the cow missed him she started out to find him, following the course of the wind. When the men discovered that the cow was gone they tried to find her. They went as far as they dared, following her tracks until these were covered by the blowing snow. Knowing it was not safe to go farther they turned back. Next day they started out again and found the cow just barely alive in a drift of snow, but she lived only a few minutes. The two best mules and a horse father had acquired had died from a contagious disease, so our small amount of stock was reduced by more than half. For years afterward this blizzard was referred to as "the March storm." Fortunately it was the last bad storm of that winter.

During these early years, as I have said, wood was our only fuel and had to be cut and hauled from the Des Moines River six miles away. Sometimes we were very short of fuel indeed. One evening mother was trying to get supper with so little fuel that it seemed impossible. Retta Richards, the teacher who was boarding with us, brought in some hay twisted into bundles about the size of a stick of stove wood and in a few minutes the fire was burning merrily and we soon had supper on the table.

This was our first experience in burning hay, but it became our standby for fuel for the next three years. We learned that the tall, tough slough grass made the best fuel and many homesteaders put up that kind for the winter's supply. We were fortunate in having a cookstove with a large firebox so we got along nicely with it. Those with stoves having small fireboxes did not succeed so well. In the coldest weather a big armful of hay was brought into the house and there converted into bundles. The floor was pretty well littered in the process but it was "clean dirt" and was easily swept up with a broom.

About this time someone invented a cookstove for burning hay. This stove had a very large firebox into which the hay was stuffed. It was then held down by a weight which could be raised or lowered as necessary, forcing the hay to burn slowly with a steady flame. I believe these stoves were rather successful though we never tried one. In homes where these stoves were used there was always a pile of hay in one corner of the room which made a very comfortable lounging place for the boys of the family in the long winter evenings.

Mother had brought seeds which she had raised in Howard County. We children were all very much interested and to stimulate our industry and ambition, mother measured off a little patch of ground for each of us and told us we could raise anything we wanted in our individual gardens. One day mother, Frank, and I went to the edge of our farm and planted a row of sunflowers. Mother said they would shut off the view and relieve the monotony a little.

The planting of trees was began early that first spring (1870). We took slips or cuttings from growing trees and stuck them in the ground, leaving a few buds at the tip to form leaves. They soon formed roots and in a few weeks the little switches began to grow. About the only trees available were willows and Lombardy poplars. Later we gathered maple seeds and planted them. The willows were used for hedges at the boundaries of the farms. Wild gooseberry and currant bushes and wild plum and crab trees were brought from the river banks and set out.

Once I complained to mother that those trees would never be like the trees I had been accustomed to in our home in Howard County. "But these will be all in nice straight rows," she told me. But those sedate, straight rows of trees did not look right to me; they were too artificial. Though many years have passed and I have seen many beautiful parks planned and completed by the hand of man, I still think natural planting cannot be improved upon.

That first fall we took pails, sacks, tubs, everything that would answer the purpose and went to the river to gather wild grapes and plums. We took lunch along and made a picnic of it. Sometimes several neighbors' families went together and made the trip a real affair. The fruit was dried, canned, or preserved to add to our winter's supplies. For several years the settlers depended on gathering the wild fruits. Even though grapes, plums, and crabapples grew well along the river where they were protected by natural timber, many of the early settlers declared that fruit could never be raised in that locality. Later we were to learn that all fruits suited to that latitude would do well. We planted our orchard the second season on a sunny slope where it was protected from the cold winds by the willow hedges but it was many years before we had fruit from it.

Some of the wild plants were also used for food. Occasionally sheep sorrel was used for pies until rhubarb was grown. Lamb's quarter, dandelion, and red-root were used for greens.

Wild game, particularly wild fowl, was very plentiful. Whenever we went anywhere in the big lumber wagon the gun was taken along. Many meals were rounded out with the game brought in. The first winter in Palo Alto County more than forty wild ducks in addition to wild geese, brants [small, dark geese], cranes, prairie chicken, and other wild fowl fell victims to our need for fresh meat. The whole country was a perfect wild birds' paradise and equally good hunting. After the ground was broken and crops put in the wild game used to feed on the ripening grain and corn. Some of the men and boys, my brothers among them, used to set traps to catch them. ...

Planting and sowing in those early days were done in very primitive ways. When the sod had been broken the farmer, or his wife, followed a furrow and cut through the turned sod with an axe. The corn was dropped in and the ground pressed down by stepping on the hill. One of our neighbors had a hand planter which he had made. Two sharpened blades at the bottom were plunged into the turned sod and the corn dropped in at the same time. A little later father bought a couple of corn planters that were also carried by hand.

Small grain was sowed by hand. The farmer carried a sack suspended from a strap which passed over the right shoulder and under the left arm. As he walked across the field he scooped up handfuls of grain and scattered it before him with a swinging motion of the right arm. The birds, which were numerous, followed, picking up their share. For this reason the harrow followed as quickly as possible; then came the roller to crush the clods of soil and pack it around the seed. ...

When the grain was ripe it was cut with a "cradle," which consisted of a scythe with a sort of rack attached. The forward swing of the cradle caused the grain to fall into the rack as it was cut and with the backward swing it was dumped out in a nice, neat pile, if the cradler was sufficiently skillful. A man followed to bind the grain into bundles, making a band from a handful of grain. The bundles were then placed upright forming the shocks. ...

Neighbors exchanged work during harvesting and threshing. Often it was made the occasion of a big dinner, the farmers' wives going along to help with the cooking. On the whole those neighborhood gatherings were very enjoyable affairs. They gave the farmer's wife an opportunity to exchange ideas with her neighbors, gave her a change of surroundings and scenes and an opportunity to form lifelong friendships. When life consisted of work and work and more work every day in the week, even a slight change was welcome. ...

In the old days the farmer and his wife arose at four in the morning and several hours were spent in taking care of the stock and milking the cows. Then came breakfast and the day's work in the field for the men and, sometimes, for the women, too. The children had their work to do as soon as it was possible for them to work. Brother Fred took a man's place from the time he was ten years old and Frank followed suit though he did have a little better chance for schooling since he attended a few spring terms.

The summer of 1874 brought the first visit we had from the grasshoppers. One day during the afternoon recess at school, we remarked on how many grasshoppers there were. It was the beginning of a scourge that lasted intermittently for several years. In the fall the grasshoppers deposited their eggs in holes which they bored in the ground. In many places the ground was thickly perforated with holes a little smaller than a lead pencil, each one containing many tiny eggs. There was a warm spell late one fall and the eggs began to hatch. People rejoiced, thinking that the winter would kill the grasshoppers. One of the neighbor boys caught several grasshoppers and shut them up in a bottle which he put out of doors during a freezing night. In the morning the grasshoppers were apparently frozen and rattled like grains of sand when the bottle was shaken, but when they thawed out they hopped about as lively as ever. One ingenious American invented a machine which could be run over the field to scare them up and catch them, much as one catches the clipped grass behind a lawnmower. They were then burned and in this way some of them were destroyed, but the full-grown ones came in veritable clouds that destroyed the crops.

Two years later the grasshoppers came again. They had come to within a few miles of us when a strong south wind halted them for a time. Since the grain was headed out and the corn in silk, the farmers waited in great anxiety, knowing well that the wind would probably change within a few days. For just a week the 'hoppers were held back. Then on Sunday a north wind brought them to us. The next morning we saw Fred looking across at the cornfield. I can see that field now, so green and thrifty looking. "That field is not worth a dollar," he said. It was true; the 'hoppers had cut the silk from the undeveloped ears and that fall we had a fine crop of cobs. They had also cut off the heads of the grain so all we had was straw.

We had eight shoats [young hogs] to get through that winter in some way. Since there was no feed, the hogs were turned out to shift for themselves. In the haystacks they found some dry weeds which they chewed and seemed to get some nourishment. Four had vitality enough to get through till spring; the other four died of starvation and cold. In the spring as soon as vegetation started and the fields were being cultivated the survivors were shut up and it became my duty to pull weeds for them. In this way they were kept alive until there was corn for them again.

When mother's brother, John, thought it was best to buy out the other heirs to grandfather's little farm in Illinois, father went back and bargained with him for $230 as mother's share. Mother took that money and put it into milch cows. From that time for several years she made butter for market. Butter was packed in one hundred pound firkins (wooden crock) or smaller tubs and kept in the cellar until fall when it was hauled to Algona, the nearest market, thirty miles away, a three-day trip. Usually the money was used for winter clothing and supplies. Hogs were acquired to use the surplus milk and thus stock-raising became our principal farming industry. My parents planned to keep enough stock to use up the grain which the farm produced.

At that time people turned the stock out on the unfenced prairies, only watching them out of their own fields, so there was no lack of pasturage. Later a herd law was passed requiring owners to keep their stock off other people's property. Then the farmers combined and hired a herd boy jointly, each man paying him according to the number of head of stock he had in the herd. Cattle were then herded on public land or on uncultivated land owned by speculators.

Wheat was raised for flour for the family. It was taken thirty or forty miles to a mill, usually to Sioux Rapids. Corn was ground at the same place. Grain was for feeding rather than a cash crop as there was generally more money in stock. The principal crops were corn, oats, and some barley. As a general thing money from a farm was put into machinery, which, in many cases, was left to rust out right where it had been used last.[3]

During those early days most clothing was made at home and by hand. There were very few sewing machines in that locality. In fact, the first few years there was none in our neighborhood. Aunt Harriet Tressler obtained the agency for the Florence machine and sold a few and also got one for herself. At that time a clean calico dress was plenty good enough for church or Sunday school and a gingham or calico sunbonnet frequently took the place of a hat. I once heard a young lady remark that her mother had spent sixteen dollars on her one Saturday. That was worth boasting about.

Everyday wear for men usually consisted of a pair of overalls and a "wamus" or "roundabout." This was a short jacket gathered into a belt at the bottom and finished at the neck with a close fitting, straight or turn-over collar. The sleeves were gathered into a cuff which buttoned tightly around the wrist. When these garments or any everyday clothing were bought ready-made the sewing was usually so poorly done that it must be done over at home.

One of the neighbors, whose wife was a victim of tuberculosis, thought to make the work easier for her and bought a pair of ready-made overalls. Next morning when he put them on and started to build the fire, he stooped over and the new overalls began to rip in the seams. The next day mother went to see this neighbor and found her sitting up in bed sewing on the overalls and wishing her thoughtful husband had bought the goods and let her make them out-right.

...

Wreaths of hair flowers, worsted flowers, and even seeds were made by the girls and women who had a taste for that sort of work. Mother had a very beautiful wreath made of different kinds of seeds, which she bought from the woman who made it. The frame for the wreath was covered with pine cones with a border at the inner edge of large kernels of corn and an outer edge of peach stones. Hair flower wreaths were made from the hair of the members of the family and of friends. I made one of these once on which I spent many hours that might better have been spent in improving my mind, but one had to have some recreation and there were no movies to attend!

Among the industries practiced at home in the early days was the making of straw hats. Not every one knew how to do this but mother was one who did. Before the first crops were raised hats were made front blue joint, a wild grass which then grew rather tall on the uplands and had a stem very much like that of wheat. It was stiff and hard to work with and as soon as possible wheat or oat straw was used. The straw was first plaited [braided], four or more strands together, then sewn into shape. The hats were fitted to the heads as they were sewn, so the boys had to come into the house often to try them on. The hat was begun at the center of the crown, the brad sewed around and around until the required size was reached. Then it was turned by drawing the braid tighter and the crown was continued until the required height was reached. It was then turned again by sewing the braid more loosely and the brim was formed.

Knitting, which was done by most of the women, was usually confined to the necessities—socks, stockings, mittens, mufflers, and wristlets. A few did fancy knitting, such as lace edgings, chair tidies,[4] and even bedspreads. These bedspreads were usually made from carpet warp, though I have seen a few that were made from the finer cottons. Crocheting was more popular for the tidies and laces, for it could be done more rapidly. Ordinary sewing thread was often used, usually in white. Crocheted edgings were used on underwear, pillow slips, aprons, and especially on children's clothes.

The day of the spinning wheel had about passed at that time, though I have seen a few women spinning. The yarn for knitted hosiery and mittens was bought at the stores. Many knit their cotton stockings also. Some of these were very elaborate, being knit in "featherwork," "shellwork," or "oak leaf" patterns. When we wore those stocking showing the pattern which was continued over the instep, we thought we were very much dressed up.

Frequently enough, while the men were learning to farm, the women and children actually supported the families. They raised chickens and eggs for the table, raised the vegetables and fruits, and made butter to sell in exchange for things not produced at home. The women were not unaware of this fact and were quite capable of scoring a point on occasion when masculine attitudes became too bumptious. One of the farmers sold his hogs for what he considered a very good price. He came home and told of the deal with a great show of self-satisfaction. With a swagger he picked up the pail to carry the feed out to the pigs. His wife stopped him right there. "You don't need to feed those pigs tonight. I've done it every time so far. They are to be fed just once more and I'm going to do it."

A chronicle of my recollections of those early days would be incomplete without some mention of the griefs and disappointments. The first death in the community was that of one of the Bernard family, a "blue baby"[5] that lived to be over a year old. Father made the casket and the neighbors formed a procession and carried the little body out for burial on the farm.

Within three years after one of the families located in our neighborhood, a shocking tragedy occurred in their family. Two brothers of about fourteen and sixteen were out in the cornfield at work. They got into a dispute and the older boy struck his brother with a cornstalk. The younger boy ran to the wagon, picked up the gun brought along to shoot game, and shot his brother in the back of the head, killing him instantly.

But life had a lighter side. Evenings and rainy days we sometimes had a game of checkers at home. There were a few families in the neighborhood who played cards but this was frowned upon by my mother. Father would say, "Come, let's have a game of checkers. I think you can beat me this time." That was just what happened. Then perhaps he would say, "Now I think I am going to beat you." And it turned out that way. Father was an expert but he had little chance to really enjoy the game at home for none of us ever learned to be more than indifferent players. We also played "Authors" and some kind of history game which was fun for those who were good in history.

Father had a strong, true, and melodious voice and quite often he sat before the fire in the evening and sang for his own amusement. If company came different ones would contribute to the entertainment by singing. Stephen C. Foster's songs were popular then. Those I best remember hearing are: " Nellie Was a Lady," " Old Folks at Home," "My Old Kentucky Home," "Massa's in de Cold, Cold Ground," and "Oh Susanna." "Dixie" was sung a great deal as were "The Red River Valley" and "The Little Mohee." Hymns that everybody knew were sung by the whole group. I also remember hearing my father sing, "I've Told Thee How Fair the Roses Are," "The Dying Californian," "The Soldier of the Rhine," and a great many war songs and comic songs of which he knew an inexhaustible number.

At that time doctors were few and far between. Every family had a "doctor book" which advised a treatment for every ill and injury to man and beast. Many wild plants were used as medicines, most of them steeped and drunk as tea. Among these were "Culver's root" taken "for the liver." The dandelion, both as extract and as wine, was used for the same purpose. Tonics were made from the butterfly weed, sweet flag root, sassafras bark, and boneset. Of course sulphur and molasses were taken nearly every spring. For colds, pennyroyal, prairie balm, and horse mint were popular remedies. Mullen was used externally for pleurisy. Mullen seeds were among those mother had brought with her from Howard County. Smartweed was used externally for boils. Cubeb berries were smoked for catarrh. Castile soap was used to cleanse wounds on stock as well as for hand and shaving soap. Dry baking soda was also applied to barbed wire cuts on the stock.

Mother's father had been a doctor and she had learned a great deal about caring for the sick. Within two years the whole neighborhood had come to depend on her and she was called upon in cases of sickness for more than thirty years. In the cases of childbirth the neighbors would just drive by and tell her when they wanted her, always taking it for granted that she would be there—and she always was. There was no charge; such service was merely one part of being a good neighbor. But her assistance was not unappreciated. I have a silver cream ladle which was given her by Mrs. Alexander, a Scotch woman who lived near Ayrshire, Iowa, and on one occasion a neighbor gave her a calico dress.

During the second winter in Palo Alto County (1870–1871), father and mother began to think of school for the children. There were enough children in the neighborhood to draw public money. In the spring father and Mr. Sanford led in organizing the school township, an area six miles square. There was no building but it was decided to use the upper half story of our house for school purposes. A Mrs. Wilson, a widow, was chosen as the teacher. With her came her little boy and a crippled sister. They brought provisions and lived in our house. Teacher and pupils entered and passed through the living room and climbed the steep stairs to the upper room where there were already two beds besides anything that needed storage space. Father made a long bench and desk for the pupils and space was made at one side of the room under the sloping roof. The regular attendants were the three Bernard children, Cousin Kate, my two brothers (when not busy in the fields), and myself. Fred, oftener than Frank, had to be at work, but I was seldom asked, or permitted, to lose a day of school. It was hard for mother to have the children trooping through her living room, which was also dining room and kitchen, eight times a day, for we had recess both forenoon and afternoon as well as the noon hour. But she was willing to put up with any inconvenience for the sake of her children.

The following winter it was decided that school should be conducted in the Sanford home. Like us, the Sanfords were of the very few who had an upstairs room. Cousin Kate, Fred, Frank, and I were to take our provisions and bedding and stay there during the five school days, returning home for the weekends. The Sanfords had a large family of their own and we found this plan very uncomfortable in winter. Before long mother decided to teach us herself and we studied at home through the long winter evenings, sometimes by the light of the fire from the cookstove.

The next autumn we had another teacher, Maggie Martin, one of a family of teachers who devoted their summers and winters to teaching the children of the early settlers. Maggie conducted the second school which was held at our house. The following spring a little schoolhouse was erected and we had the same teacher again. We now had a few "real school desks" and a chair for the teacher in addition to the old desk and bench we had used before. The teacher "boarded around." ...

At the close of this term of school the little schoolhouse was hauled away to another district and we were again without a building for six months. The following spring (1874), school was again conducted in our house. Our teacher this time was Retta Richards, another of the well-known pioneer teachers. Retta boarded with us and thus avoided the exposure some of those early teachers were obliged to endure. I presume she paid a dollar or a dollar and a half a week, though I do not remember. Even in summer weather there was much danger of a soaking in a sudden shower and in the morning the long grass which met over the narrow road was always drenched with dew. It was impossible to walk abroad before ten in the morning and escape wet feet. Dresses were long and skirts were almost invariably wet to the knees. Some cases of tuberculosis were thought to be traced to colds contracted while walking to the schoolhouse through those heavy dews.

During the summer of 1874 our first permanent schoolhouse was built. The interior was a simple oblong, wainscotted about three feet above the floor and plastered above that and overhead. The woodwork was finished in oak graining. The painter's idea of a good job was to imitate as many knots and imperfections in the wood as he could find room for. It was our school, much the best we had ever had, and we were very proud of it.

A partition near one end formed an entrance hall where we left our wraps and lunches. During recess and noon hour, when the weather was too cold to go outside, we used to play there. One of the favorite games was "Blind Man's Buff." There was a row of shelves at each end of the hall and one of the boys, Willie Young, a little, wiry fellow, used to go up those shelves like a monkey. He would then stand on the top shelf dancing and singing while the "blind man" sought him frantically. Another game was "Hot Buttered Blue Beans," also known as "Hide the Thimble."

On Friday afternoons following the recess there was usually a program of recitations and a spelling match to close the day. As the last "scholar" started for his seat someone struck up the song "I Shall Never Learn to Spell." Everybody joined in the singing, which started with the following stanza:

> Oh, dear! Oh, dear! I shall never learn to spell;
> I shall always be a dunce, I know very well.
> For the letters get mixed up in such a queer way
> That I never can tell what they mean to say.

In those days there was little or no insubordination in our school. Most of the year meant drudgery on the farms, and school was a relief from hard work. We were looking forward to the time when we could leave the farm and do something else, preferably in a town or city, so there was a good deal of speculation the first day of school as to how much help the teacher was likely to be as a stepping-stone to our ambition.

The last day of school there was always a sort of picnic. There was little or no studying or recitations and in the afternoon many of the parents came in and there were declamations and dialogues and sometimes an essay or two. The teacher read a report of the attendance, the work, and sometimes, the shortcomings of some whose work had not been up to the mark, for there were some of those, too. Then the teacher gave each pupil a picture card labeled "Reward of Merit." Usually there were prizes for the ones who had done the best work in certain branches. Some teachers gave an "Exhibition" at the close of the term. In one of the dialogues I was Miss Pickspiders, an old maid. In another I took the part of the Irish servant girl. As I look back now I can see that considerable talent was displayed in the acting, although we had never seen any plays and our stage properties consisted of sheets for curtains and furniture borrowed from the neighbors. Our own scanty wardrobes or borrowed clothes were the costumes. ...

The summer term began about the first of June and lasted from three to six months, according to local circumstances. The winter term began about the first of December and lasted three months, that being the time between the last of the corn-picking and the first of the spring plowing.

Mother's family were Baptists, in keeping with their Rhode Island origin. Grandfather's brother, Stutely Carr, was a Baptist clergyman at Greenfield Center, New York, and later at Springfield,

Pennsylvania. Father's family belonged to the Methodist Episcopal Church. Mother was very religious. The letters exchanged between her and her sister usually contained something which revealed religious feeling as a family spirit. A customary closing I remember was, "Yours in the Lord." ...

Mother read the Bible to her own family a great deal. One custom which she carried on from her father's practice was to have each member of the family circle open the Bible at random on New Year's morning and read aloud the chapter to which he chanced to turn. There was supposed to be some special guidance for the reader to follow in the new year.

In the Protestant communities all the younger people who had no place to go and wanted something to do attended prayer meetings with their elders. The first prayer meeting I can remember was held at the Sanford's at their invitation. There had been no religious services of any sort and I asked what a prayer meeting was. Mother explained that it was a gathering where everybody who wished to do so could take part by offering a prayer, making a talk, or singing a song as the spirit moved. When the question of attending this prayer meeting came up, at first father said we would not go. But when he went to the barn to do the chores mother followed him. When she came back she announced that we were going. "I knew I could persuade him" was all the explanation she gave. Later, the New Year was begun by a week of prayer meetings, the families gathering in a different house each day. For the rest of that year such meetings came to be held every Thursday evening.

Great Oak Township bordered ours, Rush Lake, on the north. It was settled almost entirely by Irish Catholic families while the eastern part of Rush Lake and the western part of Ellington, the township to the east of us, was settled by "Dutch" (German) Catholics. Not infrequently people from these settlements attended the prayer meetings and other services of the Protestants, and occasionally the Protestants attended the Catholic services. On one such occasion a farmer who had driven a long way to attend a service fell asleep and snored loudly enough to be heard all over the room. Father Smith stopped in the midst of his sermon to say, "If that is a Protestant, wake him up gently, but if he is a Catholic, cast him out!"

There were no church buildings in the vicinity at that time except the Catholic church in Emmetsburg. A Baptist congregation was organized at our house on May 23, 1873, and the charter members included father and mother and twenty other persons. Religious services were held in a schoolhouse, the Methodists and Baptists using it on alternate Sundays. It was several years after Curlew was established before there was a "meeting house" as my mother called it. ...

Probably through the connections of Elder Kettlewell of the Freewill Baptist Church, a library was donated to the Sunday school by a more prosperous church. Those books were a boon to us as to many others, for books were very rare. Novel reading was strictly forbidden in most of the families. I have since wondered where the line was drawn between those library books and the forbidden novels. One library book, which we all read, was *Claude Duval,* the story of the noted English highwayman and about as sensational as anything could be. But reading was scarce and we read everything we could get our hands on. Existence for us was pretty drab and I cannot see that a little excitement, even a stimulating book, harmed us at all.

Possibly as an outgrowth of the interest in this first small collection of books the time came when the people of the township decided that a public library would be a fine thing to have and some of the public money was set aside for that purpose. Aunt Harriet Tressler, father's sister, was a very intelligent woman and had good taste in literature, so she was chosen one of the committee to select the books. One of the good church members, Isaac Perry, objected strenuously to any novels, but Aunt Harriet used a little wholesome ridicule. She said she expected to find him behind the door reading novels himself. ...

Elder Kettlewell served the church without any stipulated salary but was paid by "donations" and an occasional contribution of money. The donation parties were held in the winter. An officer of the church would announce at a regular church service the time and place of the gathering. It was understood that everybody was to come. Some people came as far as ten miles. All brought pies, cakes, bread, cold meats, pickles, butter, cream—whatever they had or could make for a feast. For their donation to the preacher they brought sacks of grain and potatoes and whatever else they could spare from their farms. The older people and the small children came in the afternoon and had supper together. Usually a price of twenty-five cents was charged for the supper. The young people sometimes came later in the evening. A devoted young man might drive six miles to get his girl and then drive to the appointed place. Occasionally two or three boys would pick up a party of young people to come together in a bobsled.

The time was spent by the young people, particularly, with romping games such as "Volunteer" or "Weevily Wheat." "Volunteer" was the grand right and left figure of the square dance. The players stood in opposite rows facing each other instead of forming in sets as in the cotillion or quadrille. In this way all could take part. "Weevily Wheat" was sung to the tune of "Yankee Doodle." It was similar to "Volunteer" but had more changes. ...

Dancing was frowned upon by the religious members of the community but these play party games were approved by the faithful, though, perhaps, with the tongue in the check. Many and heated were the debates as to which was worse, dancing or the "kissing" games that were so often indulged in. There were also the old-fashioned games like "Drop the Handkerchief," "Post Office," "Needle's Eye," and others, as well as charades, magic music, and a few calling for mental gymnastics. ...

The first literary society or lyceum was organized when I was about eleven. The members were all farmers but some had been educated for the professions and were rather well-informed. There was always a debate in which most of the members took part. The president of the lyceum announced the subject of the debate and the leaders of the opposing teams a week in advance. Each leader chose the others for his team. Everybody present was supposed to be on one or the other team.

One or two members edited a lyceum paper which purported to give the news and usually did give something witty or otherwise regarding each one of the members. Sometimes someone contributed a series of alphabetical rhymes, using the names of the members with more or less realism. But the jokes were always good-natured and usually were understood that way. One or two members would be appointed to write essays and others recited selections from poets or prose writers. ...

In the winter of 1879 Fred organized a debating society. Most of the farmers, old and young, joined. The temperance question, the evil effects of tight [corset] lacing, which was common at the time, and many other questions of greater or less importance were discussed. A glee club provided music, and essays and recitations made up the usual program. For many years the debating societies were a feature of the winter months. Schuyler Cummings was one of the prominent debaters. He had been educated to be a lawyer but in some unexplained way he had drifted to an Iowa homestead. On the rostrum he was perfectly at ease, but on the farm he was the worst misfit imaginable. ...

Among the old settlers in Palo Alto County was a man named Williams who had a very good musical education, as did his wife also. Both were fine singers and Mrs. Williams played the organ very well. They thought the young people should have some education in music. Mr. Williams made it known that if the young people would meet with him at the schoolhouse in his school district every Sunday afternoon through the summer he would instruct them in vocal music free of charge. My brothers and I, as well as quite a number of the younger people, took advantage of the offer. That was my first music instruction.

The following winter Mr. Williams organized several classes, one in the Rush Lake School, one in the Center School, and a third in Silver Lake School. He announced that any member of one class would be welcomed at any of the others. Emmet Barringer, the teacher of our school, boarded with us and was a member of the class at the Center School. He sang tenor, Frank sang bass, and I soprano. We three used to practice at home and these evenings are among my most pleasant recollections. Some weeks we attended all three singing schools. We all enjoyed singing and the long rides in wagons or sleighs were no small inducement to our regular attendance. We had a homemade sleigh with two seats which we used when the crowd was not too large.

Two years later several of the neighbors, our family among them, bought organs and instrumental music was added to our accomplishments. Frank and I wished to become real musicians but teachers were few and far between and opportunities for practice not much better. A little music for my own pleasure and the entertainment of intimate friends was as far as I ever went. ...

On May 1, 1877, Fred and I began our careers as teachers. I was past fifteen at the time and Fred past eighteen. He taught the "home school" and I a school about eight miles distant, in the township of Ellington. ...

It was not until 1882 that the railroad was built through our part of the County. Many of the farmers sold out and took their profit at once. Father said he had waited fifteen years for that road and he was not going to leave just when it came. With the coming of the railroad, the founding of a town, the building of a grain elevator, and the establishment of the post office, the pioneer period in our part of Palo Alto County came to a close.

NOTES

1. E. May Lacey Crowder, "Pioneer Life in Palo Alto County," *Iowa Journal of History and Politics* 46 (April 1948): 156–98.

2. Sarah Eveline Carr Lacey died at Curlew, Iowa, on March 19, 1915.

3. Typically, money went into farm machinery because the fields were seen to provide the income of a farm. Because there was little understanding of the importance of domestic production done in the home, capital investments in the home workplace came infrequently. May seems to be disgruntled about this situation.

4. A tidy was a knitted or crocheted covering used on the back and arms of chairs and sofas to keep them clean.

5. A blue baby is one born with cyanosis or blue coloration of the skin. This is caused by a lack of oxygen in the blood due to a congenital heart lesion or under-expansion of its lungs.

Eighty-Six Years in Iowa
THE MEMORIES OF
Ada Mae Brown Brinton

DA MAE BROWN had a slightly different story to tell. Rather than making the trip and establishing a new life herself, Ada was born of Iowa pioneers. She grew up treasuring her heritage—and enjoying the fruits of an earlier generation's foresight. Her comments also demonstrated the continuity of women's work, concerns, and equipment over several generations.

Ada's engrossing story began in the late 1860s when her father, Thacher Brown, and her mother's family, the Farnum Hinksons, decided to relocate in Iowa. Thacher Brown was the first of the group to migrate to Iowa land in 1868. In 1869, Farnum and Sabra Ann Hinkson purchased native sod land across the road from Brown in Adair County, Iowa. The Hinkson's elder daughter, Rhoannah, had met and become engaged to Brown in Lawrence, Massachusetts, where she worked in the textile mills; as settlers in Iowa, Rhoannah and Thacher were married. In the years that followed, Thacher turned from farming to take up dairying and carpentry in Stuart, Iowa.

Ada was born in Stuart on May 5, 1891. In her early twenties Ada married Marion Brinton, the son of a local well-to-do farmer. Four children were born to Marion and Ada: Justine Eloise, born in 1916, died following an accident in 1918; Elaine Maxine born in 1920; Everett Brown born in 1924, died of intestinal flu in 1925; and Eloise Mae, born in 1927.

Through thrifty practices and industrious effort, Marion and Ada made a comfortable living on their farm. In the sixtieth year of their marriage, Marion died on April 28, 1974. Shortly after her husband's death, Ada Brinton moved from their farm home to an apartment in Stuart. During most of her long and active life, she had been an avid diary keeper. In 1977, Ada reviewed some of her large collection of diaries and searched her keen memory to produce a reminiscence her family could share.

The publication of the abridged version of her reminiscences which follows was made possible by her kindness and cooperation. The complete manuscript is available at the State Historical Society of Iowa. Special thanks also go to her daughter, Elaine Brinton Phair, for her help with the manuscript.[1]

M Y father, Thacher Brown ... purchased a farm south of Menlo, most of which was on well-laying ground. It did have a small creek and timber on the north end. Water and timber were considered very essential. ... Papa bought a team and necessary farming equipment with which he "broke" the southern part of the farm and planted crops that same spring. He built protection for his horses and then started to build a house.

In 1869, my maternal grandparents of Grafton County, near Canaan, New Hampshire, Farnum and Sabra Ann Hinkson, journeyed by train to Morrison, Illinois, with their children: My Mother, Rhoannah, 21; teenage Adda; and younger brother Fred Oscar. They stayed with the before mentioned Horace Hinkson, brother of Farnum. There a team, wagon and supplies were purchased, and with them my grandfather and his son, Fred, proceeded on to Adair County, Iowa, where my father was located. In due time my grandmother with the two girls traveled to Iowa by train.

Following are excerpts from a letter Mamma wrote May 30, 1870, to Aunt Ada Brown in Massachusetts:

> Having good weather, the prairie is green, grass quite tall so people are cutting it for their horses. The flowers that grow here are lovely bright colors that make a pretty bouquet. "T" [Thacher] is breaking sod, hard work so we did not go to church. The Methodist minister preached. (Apparently denominations took turns.) The house is generally filled. They go and carry their babies. Sometimes there are over a dozen little bits of things. They look as if they should be at home. People are not at all

proud. They do not stop for looks. They wear sunbonnets and big aprons to church. The men ride on a board put across the wagon if they are too poor to be able to have a spring seat, and the women sit down flat on the bottom of the wagon. That is the West! The people around here do not trouble themselves much to get acquainted with the Yankees, as they call us. ...

Earlier, during the time my father was in Lawrence, Massachusetts, my mother was working in one of the large textile mills there. My father and mother met in Lawrence while attending the same Baptist Church. After coming to Iowa, they were married on Christmas day, 1869. My mother, Rhoannah Hinkson, was 21 and my father, Thacher Brown, was 24 . ...

My father was a hard working man—was said to remark that he could outwork any team. However, he broke his health doing so and had to give up farming. He then bought the dairy farm just east of Stuart where I was born and he began doing carpenter work. He had learned the carpenter trade from his Uncle Elisha Merriam in Lawrence, Massachusetts, under whom he served his apprenticeship. ...

The dairy Papa operated was a type conforming to that date. Milk was carried in 5 and 10 gallon cans in a covered four-wheel wagon drawn by one horse. There were regular customers. When a hand bell was rung in front of a house, the customer would bring out containers and the milk was poured into either a pint or quart tin measure according to the amount desired. Milk tickets were sold in advance in $1.00 amounts—red printed tickets for quarts and green for pints.

The dairy farm was sold in 1893 or 1894. In '94 my parents, sister Luella and I went "back east" to visit relatives and attend a Brown family reunion. ...

After selling the dairy farm and the trip "back east" in 1894, my father built a nice cottage of 1 1/2 stories, plus a full basement. This was located out "on the hill" on Nassau Street, west of the business part of town. ... Those of us who lived out "on the hill," as it was called, were sort of set apart from the rest of the townspeople, for there were no houses connecting that area for many years. ... Upon moving out "on the hill" my father continued with a small dairy—he usually had three to four cows. It was my job to deliver the milk. We had a faithful driving horse by the name of "Fannie." She was hitched to an open buggy. Fannie knew the route as well as I did.

When in a block where there were three or four houses to which I was to deliver—I carried the bottles in a heavy wire container which held eight bottles and left the bottles of milk in exchange for empty ones with tickets—and as I proceeded down the block Fannie walked along the street without any instruction, ready to pick me up at the last house.

While this milk business continued it meant work for my mother to keep the bottles clean and filled. Due to the fact that my father always kept only Jersey or Guernsey cows, our customers were among the people who could afford and preferred this quality of milk. I came to know these families personally (many remained good friends the rest of their lives), as new people were seldom added to the list and the route was confined to a small area—three or four blocks in the central part of the town—as the quantity of milk was limited.

My parents attended church regularly and I was brought up to do so. In my teenage years this required five services a day on Sundays: Sunday School, Morning Service, Junior League in the afternoon as a teacher, Epworth League in the early evening followed by the Evening Church Service. Each year Evangelistic services were usually conducted for a week to ten days in the church by an outside evangelist and a "music leader." I accepted Christ during one of these meetings, was baptized and joined the Methodist Church on August 6, 1906.

As a young child I was "entertained" in various ways during church services. I remember lying in the pew with my head on my mother's knees so as to watch the glitter of many spangles on the beautiful chandelier which was hung from the center of the high ceiling of our church. I also listened to the ticking of my mother's watch when she would say, "Listen to the little boy chopping wood." In the summer she carried a fan which folded completely out of sight into the handle case. Upon pushing a slide button the fan would open out into a fluted circle with handle—that fascinated me. Another form of entertainment was provided by my mother's allowing me to try on her mitts—these were a form of gloves used in summer, made of knitted silk without fingers, open beyond the knuckles. ...

My parents were loyal church workers. My mother was President of the Ladies Aid Society for ten years. The Ladies Aid met every two weeks in homes and how they did work! They raised money by piecing quilt blocks and then quilting them, by tying comforters, tearing and sewing carpet rags, making aprons and sunbonnets and other wearing apparel. Mamma and Lue made all of the fancy sunbonnets which became very popular. They took special orders as to color, for the bonnets were white on the outside with a solid color underneath. The crown was machine stitched with rows of stitching about one-fourth inch apart. ...

The Ladies Aid Society at one time sold vanilla and lemon extract which came from a company in gallon jugs. The jugs were kept in our basement and Mamma transferred the extract into glass bottles and labeled them with proper stickers. I also remember about a large Scripture Cake being made one time in a new dish pan. The recipe was typed and given with the purchase of a piece of the cake. All of the ingredients of the cake had been mentioned in the Bible.

In our church there were two special programs each year in which youngsters took part and for which much preparation was made—Children's Day, the second Sunday of June, and the Christmas Program, always given on Christmas Eve. I served on committees for these programs in my teen years and know what a lot of patience and time is required as there were always some children who were hard to restrain. The programs were made up of Sunday School individuals and classes singing, speaking pieces, and performing drills. ...

For Christmas there was always a large evergreen tree decorated by tinsel and lights. At the close of the program Santa Claus would appear from the entrance to the auditorium causing great excitement by his costume and chatter. At the time of my earliest recollection presents also were hung on the tree. The packages were labeled for the smaller children (presumably from their parents). The names were called out by Santa and specified helpers delivered the packages. I well remember a large beautifully dressed doll hanging rather high on a branch. Naturally each little girl hoped the doll might be hers. This caused envy and disappointment to such a degree that these gifts were discontinued. Instead, cute little paper boxes filled with candy and nuts were given to each child from the teacher of each class. These classes of younger children were called forward, one at a time, and the boxes were handed out. Then the classes of older children were called and each child received an orange or a polished apple.

There were always evening church services in all of the churches in my day. A large tree grew on the outer edge of the sidewalk almost directly in front of the Methodist Church. Some of the young fellows congregated under the tree to wait for girls to come from the evening service. It must have been too handy as it was cut down eventually!

At four I started my school experiences as a first grader at Whittier School House (West School). The first and second grades were in the basement in a room which was halfway under ground with tall windows of eight panes. We entered the basement through a one-story wooden-type building at the center of the brick school. This covered the stairway leading down. Then to the east of this wooden structure was a wide cement outside stairway with banisters which led up to the double doors opening into a hallway. In good weather scholars lined up in two rows and at a signal given by the teacher in charge who was standing in the doorway we marched up the stairs. ...

There was a large playground to the south of the building and wooden walks led to two outhouses, one for girls and one for boys, and each divided into two separate compartments. There was a well with a pump in the northwest area of the front yard. Walks were across the north and west sides of the grounds with tall soft maple trees on these sides.

I went into High School at twelve years of age, which was too young. At that time there was an assembly room where Freshman, Sophomore, Junior and Senior year students did their studying and from which the students marched out to appointed classrooms as the piano was played. School began at nine o'clock with "chapel." At this time Scripture was read by faculty members, the Lord's Prayer was recited by faculty and students and then there was a singing session. The songs (not popular music) were openly requested by the students. On one occasion the Principal, a man greatly disliked, in the process of correcting one of the big boys in the assembly room, got into an awful scrap. The boy was knocked on the floor on his back and the Principal was choking him until he was getting blue in the face. Some girls cried and ran from the room, others screamed, whereupon some of the other boys pulled the Principal off.

I did not go to school beyond the middle of my junior year. My big handicap was algebra. I had gotten a poor start in the subject my Freshman year and was having to repeat second year algebra in my Junior year plus the regular Junior year studies. I was discouraged and at Christmas time I got a clerking job in the J. B. Grove Store and quit school. ... Later I regretted that I was allowed to quit, but it was not an uncommon thing to do at that time.

I did continue to clerk on Saturdays and on call until eventually I became a full-time clerk. I always liked it, learned a great deal and knew women from far and near. The store drew trade from other towns, many coming on passenger trains which were then available.

For a number of years "Bates Hall" was the location of all entertainment features [in Stuart]. That was in the second story of the building occupied by the George Ryan Dry Goods Store. The Reverend Billy Sunday conducted some meetings in Bates Hall. There were musicals and public gatherings of all kinds there. In observance of Lincoln's birthday a program was given in Bates Hall and I spoke the poem which was said to have been Lincoln's favorite, "Why Should the Spirit of Mortal Be Proud?" In addition I sang in an operetta there, sang a solo for a high school graduation, our Stuart Quartette (of which I was a member) participated in a musical there and I was in a play. The Country Club put on a dandy play at Bates Hall—the play was repeated because it was so well accepted. A traveling stock company appeared at Bates Hall, producing a different play every two weeks. A Lecture Course, consisting of varied high-class entertainment over a period of three or four weeks in the wintertime, was held at either Bates Hall or the High School Assembly Room.

There were some very cold winters. ... Everyone wore warm knit long-sleeved and long-legged underwear either plain cotton, fleece lined or wool. Feminine attire included long stockings, summer and winter, usually two petticoats which were starched and worn under lightweight dresses in the summer. (My mother knit fancy stitched underskirts for us for winter wear.) Remember, we rode in open conveyances and in summer there was no air conditioning. In the winter soapstones,[2] hot water in jugs, heavy horse blankets and buffalo robes were used extensively when riding. "Buffalo robes" were originally made from tanned hides of buffalo, later from hides of cattle or horses.

In my years at home with my parents we had feather beds on our beds in the winter months. These were ticking filled with soft feathers from duck or goose breasts. It was the most wonderful feeling to sink into them and keep warm. They were somewhat lumpy. When making the bed, my mother used a wooden yardstick to even the top so that it would be perfectly smooth.

The arrival and departure of passenger trains at depots was always a major event, not only of interested persons gathered to greet those arriving or to bid "adieu" to those leaving, but there was usually a news reporter on hand and there were idle bystanders on the platform. The interior of small town depots was much the same. In the center of the room was a tall pot-bellied stove. Wooden benches with curved backs and smooth seats were around the perimeter of the room. I can still hear the clatter of the telegraph keys as they ticked endlessly in the office. ...

In the early 1900s Stuart's streets were either dusty or muddy. There was no solid ground of any kind. Hitching rails were along Main Street. Flies in the stores were a pest, drawn largely from the sweat and manure from the horses.

I was young when I learned to ride horseback, having a nice sized riding horse, larger than a shetland pony, which I greatly enjoyed. ... father always got up at 4 a.m. to do chores and would bridle and saddle my horse in readiness for me. He continued to do this as long as I was home.

In the winter, with sufficient snow, sleighs and bobsleds were used extensively. Nothing can ever replace the pleasure of slipping smoothly over the snow. An added pleasure was to hear bells and chimes attached to the harness. My father had a long string of bells about the size of golf balls which were fastened around the body of the horse. Marion [her fiancé] had chimes the size of baseballs which were fastened on a leather piece. At times, of course, there were "spills" from the sleighs and bobsleds, either purposely or otherwise, but the falls were cushioned by snowdrifts.

In our church two special services were often the same Sunday: The School Baccalaureate in the evening and the Memorial in the morning. At the Memorial service the members of the "G.A.R."[3] followed by Veterans of the Spanish American War and their auxiliaries marched down the front aisle carrying flags and were seated in the center seats. It was an impressive sight as I recall to see the white-haired Civil War soldiers. Their auxiliary was called "Woman's Relief Corps."[4] There was a window in the Methodist Church carrying symbols of the two Civil War organizations.

On the 31st of May, Memorial Day, there used to be celebrations held at North Oak Grove Cemetery. The G.A.R. soldiers rode out from town while people walked. A band led the march. There was a small bandstand in the cemetery situated for the program. Usually the band played and a speaker gave a suitable address. One year our "Stuart Quartette" (I was one of the singers) sang a couple of songs as a part of the program.

The Fourth of July used to be really celebrated. I always had some firecrackers which were fun to set off. My father showed me how to place one under an empty tin can to make a big noise. Also, he put a couple of long nails in the end of a lightweight pole of some kind in which a firecracker was placed as soon as it was lighted and the pole raised in the air. It seemed a safe way to shoot off the larger firecrackers. ...

Our house was thoroughly cleaned each Spring and Fall. Carpets were taken outside and either thrown over the clothes line or put on the grass where a carpet beater was used to remove the dust. The dining room in my parents' home was covered by rag carpet. ... It was made from clothing discarded in our family. The clothing was washed and torn into strips which were sewed end to end, rolled into balls and sent to someone who had a loom on which to weave any length desired. It was fun to try to discover some former dress. The width of the woven strips was 36 inches, so the strips were sewed together for the width required for the room.

Marion and I were engaged in 1913. In the fall of 1914 preparations were made for the building of a house on the farm owned by Marion two miles west of Stuart up on a high spot from which the view of the countryside was wonderful in all directions. Marion bought books of houseplans and we discussed plans in them. Papa was consulted as well as Marion's father. Rock for the foundation was laid by Roy Morrison, a reliable mason. The floor of cement covered the entire basement under all of the house with a garage under the large front porch. Papa and a contractor in Stuart built the house. Somewhere Father Brinton had seen finishing casings used in framing doors and windows which were different from any used in our vicinity. They had a smooth curved exterior. He ordered the lumber from a Minnesota lumber company. I was most grateful in all future years when cleaning for this extra effort on his part, for other casements usually had ridges which were dirt catchers. White pine was used in the house. ...

Our wedding was in my parents' home on December 9, 1914. We invited only our immediate families. ... The wedding was at "high noon" followed by a very nice luncheon. The second course of the luncheon was a slice of brick ice cream with a lavender bell in the center ... and angel food cake plus fruit cake which had been made from a recipe used at weddings in Mamma's family. My wedding dress was silk crepe—dainty flowers on a deep purple background. I had a cream colored chiffon shoulder cape trimmed by deep cream lace on the sleeves. Marion wore a vested dark blue suit.

The weather was good but later snowflakes fell on us as Bert Chittick [Ada's brother-in-law] drove us in an open buggy to the railroad depot to take the train, which came shortly after two o'clock, to Des Moines. We stayed at the Savery Hotel. The great evangelist, Billy Sunday, was holding meetings not far from the hotel. We attended, and for the first time we heard the song "Brighten the Corner Where You Are" and never forgot the tune and the words. ...

In Omaha we looked for furniture and purchased a brown leather-covered large chair. ... Among other gifts, Father Brinton had slipped me a $100 bill. This was spent for the chair. We received very useful gifts, many of which were used all our lives. ...

Our years were busy happy ones. For years after moving to the country I still took part in various activities in town. I often drove to Lue's and to my parents' home. In fact I was away in the afternoon almost daily. Marion always inquired at noon if I had plans to go. If so, he harnessed a horse and left it hitched to the buggy all ready for me. After we had a car he made sure all was in readiness for me.

Marion had been a charter member of the Stuart Country Club.[5] I was initiated. This club was a most worthwhile organization and the leading one of the vicinity. Most of the time the members were farm couples within the neighborhood. We were active for 55 years. Our topics and discussions were based on those of leading issues concerning the betterment of our homes, of our country and naturally concerning farm improvement. We had many good times together, meeting once a month in our homes. At no time did we play cards. We often had prominent outside speakers. At one time Henry A. Wallace, who later became Secretary of Agriculture and then Vice President of the United States, was our speaker. ...

Corn picking was done by hand, throwing the husked ears into the wagon as a reliable team kept slowly walking ahead without interruption except to be turned at the end of the row. Marion picked 100 bushels a day, much above the average. At noon and at night the corn was shoveled by scoop into the corn crib. Marion was in the field by daybreak. That meant husking mittens getting soaked by the frost on the corn husks. Our kitchen range would have mittens laid

on the oven door to dry out during that season of the year. As time
went on Marion's third finger on his right hand became somewhat
curved which he always said was caused by his grabbing the ear of
corn off the stalk with a brass husking peg worn on his finger.

Sowing oats was accomplished by loading the seed into the
wagon box with a mechanism on the end which could be adjusted as
to the amount of seed allowed to go through and be evenly spread
over a certain area. This was the only farming operation in which I
helped. Marion drove the team (later, the tractor) while I rode in the
wagon box to see that enough grain was being pushed into the
spreader—not a hard job!

During the years when our family was growing up and we had
hired men I did a great deal of canning of fruit, vegetables and
meat—chicken, beef and pork which we raised. Thus we did not
have a problem of going to the butcher shop in town except when
large roasts were required to feed the twenty or more threshers, plus
the women who helped prepare the food. Breads, pies and cakes
were baked at home, of course. In reading my diary of 1935, I came
upon the following menu for threshers at our home that year: Mashed
potatoes, beef roast, gravy, ham loaf, baked kidney beans, creamed
corn, homemade cottage cheese, dill pickles, apples cooked with
lemons, plum jelly, fresh rolls and butter (both homemade), two
kinds of cake, homemade ice cream, iced tea, coffee and cream.

During my early days on the farm and during World War I,
everyone was making their own soap for laundry work. Of course on
the farm where home butchering was done it was an easy thing to
have the required grease. Tallow was melted along with hog fat—in
fact the tallow presumably made better soap, but it was not used
alone.[6] I am going to record a recipe which should produce good results: 5 lbs. grease, 5 qt. of cold *soft* water, 1 cup lye, 1/2 cup am-
monia, 1/2 cup Perfex can also be dissolved and added. Dissolve lye
in a little soft water. Mix with all ingredients. Stir until creamy and
it thickens. Pour mixture to set into enamel, stoneware, or a wooden
box lined with white cloth. (We used the latter.) Don't get the mixture on hands until in hard soap stage.

The job of washing clothes was quite different from nowadays!
In town my Mother used a copper boiler in which to boil white
clothes and to heat the wash water. At least she had good facilities for
those days. The pump was outside the door of the cement floored
room in the basement which opened up at ground level. We had a

stove down there, so water didn't have to be carried far. If the water was hard, some lye was put into the boiler of water which brought a thick foam up on the top. This foam was dipped off. Often some bluing was added. The washing machine was hand propelled. On the farm my machine was run by a small gasoline motor until we had electricity—I also had a double tub machine. Time was saved with that as one tub could be used for rinsing. Later I had an enamel lined electric machine and finally we had a modern washer and dryer installed on our back porch.

We always had soft water in our entire water system on the farm. Our large cistern filled from gutters around the roof of the house. Water was heated by pipes running through the cook stove and stored in a tank back of the stove.

For refrigeration, butter and sweet cream were placed in a bucket which was lowered on a rope down to the top of the water in the well. When our house was built, Marion had a hole, perhaps ten feet deep, made in the basement floor. The hole was cemented like a cistern. A dumb waiter with shelves was lowered and raised by a small chain on a pulley. This kept food reasonably cool.

The principal fuel for our cook stove during the summer was cobs, as they made a quick hot fire, though frequent refueling was necessary. It was a chore to keep enough cobs available. Many were picked up from hog feed lots. These had a distinctive odor not appreciated! The cattle feed bunks and the horse feed boxes in the barn provided the other cob sources. Wood, if available around the place, and coal were also used in the cook stove. In our early days there were two or three small spots north of town where coal was mined, but it was a poor grade (too much slate or too soft) and choked up the stove and pipes.

Stuart had Chautauqua for a number of years.[7] This was held in a large tent on the grounds of the West School for a week in August and provided entertainment for both afternoon and evening shows. This was well attended and people came from Menlo and Dexter, as well as the Stuart community, to enjoy the programs. The advent of radio spoiled the Chautauquas.

Saturday night was the time when farmers particularly "went to town." Chores and supper were hurried up as it was important to park one's car in a favorable spot so that after grocery buying the car could be used from which to watch others going by. Among other errands the men would drop in at the barber shop to wait for a haircut and shave (in many cases decidedly changing their appearance for the better). The younger members of a family located their friends and spent a little money on confections to their liking and walked up and down the street. If fortunate enough to have arrived in town for the early picture show, the young people often went there and afterwards knew where to find their parents "passing the time of day" with a friend or two. I am sorry to say that we often saw those who had taken "a drink" or two too many at one of the Beer Parlors or the Pool Hall. Some unfortunate hired men had little left in their pockets after a Saturday night in town. ...

We tried to spend our money wisely and therefore we enjoyed many extras that came within our lifetime. We did not use tobacco or liquor. We suffered the loss of two children. But were blessed by two very precious girls whom we tried to guide in the right ways of life, and they did not disappoint us. ...

NOTES

1. This appeared as Glenda Riley (ed.), "Eighty-Six Years in Iowa: The Memoir of Ada Mae Brown Brinton," *The Annals of Iowa* 45 (Winter 1981): 551–67.

2. Soapstone received this name because it feels somewhat like soap. Technically it is called steatite and is used for griddles, hearths, and insulation.

3. GAR stands for the Grand Army of the Republic, an organization of men and women who served on the side of the Union during the Civil War.

4. There were many women's relief groups established during the Civil War to provide clothing, bandages, food, and nursing aid to the soldiers. Annie Turner Wittenmyer, Ann E. Harlan, and Amelia Bloomer were a few of the best-known leaders of such groups in Iowa.

5. This organization was more like the Grange in its intent and goals rather than being like country clubs of today.

6. Tallow is a whitish, tasteless solid or hard fat obtained from cattle, sheep, etc., used to make candles and soap. Some women preferred to make a separate batch of tallow soap for personal hygiene along with the stronger lye and grease-based soap used for laundry. Lye is a rather harsh alkaline solution obtained by leaching (slowly running water through) wood ashes.

7. Chautauquas were public assemblies for the purpose of education and entertainment by lectures, concerts, etc.

PART THREE
Women's Public Roles and Contributions

IN addition to their domestic and family contributions, numerous Iowa women devoted untold hours to a variety of reform movements, including the abolition of slavery, temperance, and women's rights. For instance, well before the Civil War, Amelia Jenks Bloomer of Council Bluffs raised issues including temperance, abolition, and women's rights.[1] Society generally applauded women's efforts to clean up their communities by engaging in "social housekeeping," although it expected them to refrain from direct political involvement.

Women also played an active role in a plethora of other volunteer activities that accounted for thousands, or perhaps millions, of dollars of labor, ideas, and services donated to the development of Iowa. The Civil War is an outstanding instance, for women became the supply arm of the northern effort. In Iowa, from Ann E. Harlan, wife of then-senator from Iowa James Harlan, to Annie Turner

Wittenmyer, who became the State Sanitary Agent, women rolled bandages, raised funds, and transported critical supplies.[2]

After the war's end in 1865, women increased their labors. Annie Turner Wittenmyer threw herself into the temperance movement, while thousands of others joined in the campaign for woman suffrage or the assault on the emerging "farm problem" by joining agricultural organizations, ranging from farmers' wives' societies to the Grange.[3]

Besides giving their energies to reform movements and other social causes, women also worked for wages both inside and outside their homes. In 1856, a Burlington business directory indicated that women especially worked at dressmakers, milliners, midwives, and teachers.[4] In 1865, the *Iowa State Gazetteer* recorded women employed as dressmakers, milliners, music teachers, and restaurant operators. Also, a Louisa Walther owned a stocking factory, while a Mrs. Disque of Burlington operated a vineyard.[5]

Anecdotal and other assorted evidence supplies what early statistical evidence, including census-takers, overlooked. For instance, women were also novelists, notably Farmington's Rebecca Harrington Smith who wrote during the 1850s under the name Kate Harrington.[6] Moreover, in 1869 Arabella Babb Mansfield of Mt. Pleasant became the first American woman to not only pass the bar exam, but to do so with honors.[7]

More recently, photographs document women's working lives. An exceptional collection in the Research Center for Dubuque Area History at Loras College shows late nineteenth- and early twentieth-century women working in beauty and barber shops, business offices, factories, laundries, millinery and other shops, and mills.[8]

Of course, teaching especially attracted women. Through the nineteenth and early twentieth centuries, Iowans generally considered caring for children, at home or in the schoolroom, within women's "realm." Too, teaching consumed only five or six months a year—approximately three months in the summer between planting and harvesting and another three months in the winter between harvesting and planting—and was poorly paid, which discouraged many men from entering the profession and opened the way for women.

Young women, who were glad to leave the farm for the schoolroom, typically began teaching as soon as they finished their own schooling or had attended a term or two at a "female" seminary, such as the Dubuque Female Institute established in 1853.[9] After the Civil War, women teachers increasingly attended a year or more of college, enrolled in the normal [teaching-training] school of the State University of Iowa,[10] or, after its founding in 1876, went to Iowa's only separate normal school in Cedar Falls.

But women also excelled in educational administration. They gained election to school boards, as principals and superintendents, and directors of school districts. In 1870, the Iowa City Independent School District placed its first female candidates on the ticket.[11] Other districts had already done so, or were quick to follow.

The selections that follow show women as reformers, war-relief workers, teachers and other professionals, and wage-workers. It is clear that as the nineteenth century progressed, more and more women entered the public arena outside their homes and families.

NOTES

1. A sketch of Amelia Bloomer is found in Philip D. Jordan, "Amelia Jenks Bloomer," *The Palimpsest* 38 (April 1957): 139–48.

2. No author, "Mrs. Ann E. Harlan," *The Annals of Iowa* II (October 1896): 489–508 and Glenda Riley, "Annie Turner Wittenmyer, Reformer," *Iowa Woman* 6 (September 1986): 26–33.

3. For a homegrown Iowa suffragist, Mary Newbury Adams, see the Adams Family Papers, Mary Ann Newbury's letters, Special Collections, Parks Library, Iowa State University, Ames; and Louise Moede Lex, "Mary Newbury Adams: Feminist Forerunner from Iowa," *The Annals of Iowa* 43 (Summer 1976): 323–39. Also useful are Frank E. Horack, "Equal Suffrage in Iowa," in Benjamin F. Shambaugh (ed.), *Applied History* Volume 2 (Iowa City: State Historical Society, 1914), 298–305; and Louise R.

Noun, *Strong-Minded Women: The Emergence of the Woman-Suffrage Movement in Iowa* (Ames: Iowa State University Press, 1969). A discussion of women's farm organizations is found in Mary D. Taylor, "A Farmers' Wives' Society in Pioneer Days," *The Annals of Iowa* 13 (July 1921): 22–31; and Mrs. I. N. Taylor, "The Grange—Its Advantages, Social and Educational," in Iowa Department of Agriculture, *Iowa Yearbook of Agriculture, 1910* (Des Moines: Embry H. English, State Bindery, 1911), 646–48.

4. *Business Directory and Review of the Trade, Commerce, and Manufactories of the City of Burlington, Iowa, For the Year Ending May 1, 1856* (Burlington, Iowa: Hawk-Eye Power Press, 1856), 32–40.

5. James T. Hair (comp. and ed.), *Iowa State Gazetteer* (Chicago: Bailey and Hair, 1865), 518–610.

6. Marie Haefner, "An American Lady," *The Palimpsest* 12 (May 1931): 169–178.

7. M. Romdall Williams, "From Mount Pleasant: Nation's First Woman Lawyer," *The Iowan* 15 (Summer 1967): 23–24. Subsequent women law graduates are described in Teresa Opheim, "Portias of the Prairie: Early Women Graduates of the University Law Department," *The Palimpsest* 67 (January/February 1986): 27–36.

8. Mary Allison Farley, "Iowa Women in the Workplace," *The Palimpsest* 67 (January/February 1986): 3–27.

9. Nathan H. Parker, *The Iowa Handbook for 1856* (Boston: John P. Jewett & Co., 1856), 170. See also Robert E. Belding, "Academies and Iowa's Frontier Life," *The Annals of Iowa* 44 (Summer 1978): 335–58, and "The Dubuque Female Seminary," *The Palimpsest* 63 (March/April 1982): 34–41.

10. That the normal school was an early part of what is today the University of Iowa is indicated by State University of Iowa, *Circular of the State University of Iowa, Located at Iowa City, Iowa* (Iowa City: Published by the University, 1856), 14.

11. Independent School District Election Ticket, Iowa City, March 14, 1870, State Historical Society of Iowa, Iowa City.

GIRLHOOD IN
ANTEBELLUM IOWA
Joanna Harris Haines

QUAKER women especially devoted a portion of their time and energy to fighting the institution of slavery in the United States, as well as to temperance and women's rights. One Quaker woman, Mary Moore McLaughlin, recalled that abolitionism colored her early life, for she grew up in Salem, Iowa, "during the troubled days when that little Quaker town was one of the chief stations on the main line of the Underground Railroad."[1]

Another, Joanna Harris Haines, remembered that when her parents left Pennsylvania in 1852 to start over after a business setback, they settled first near Keokuk, but soon chose the new Quaker town of Grinnell. Although Joanna was only nine years old, she later described part of the journey and the family's first homes. Her recollections are similar in many ways to those of other pioneer women, yet they also indicate the degree to which reform activities influenced her family's life and experiences. She also revealed that Quakers had some prejudices of their own.

Joanna especially showed the commitment Quaker women made to the causes they espoused. Joanna's mother helped operate a "station" on the Underground Railroad, while Joanna furthered women's rights by attending, and graduating from, college. In 1928, Joanna related these and other events to her son-in-law, Frank I. Herriott, who interviewed her in Des Moines. She was then eighty-one years old and had been a resident of Grinnell since 1855, as well as a graduate of Iowa College (now Grinnell College), class of 1865. The interview appeared in the *Annals of Iowa* in October of 1945 and is used here with the permission of the State Historical Society of Iowa.[2]

MY brother, McKee, had come to Iowa in 1851 and his letters home had been so enthusiastic that my father and mother had no doubts as to whither they should journey when the financial disaster compelled them to give up the old farm. They, with my three brothers, Ephraim, James, and William J., and three sisters, Susan, Jenny, Mary, and myself started for Iowa in the forepart of 1852, going virtually all the way by river boats: first down the Allegheny to Pittsburgh; thence down the Ohio river on the steamboat "The Diadem" to Cairo; thence on the "New Englander" up the Mississippi to Keokuk.

For reasons of economy we took what was called the deck passage. One incident I recall vividly. Although but nine years old I could sing fairly well and was much given to it when by myself. My father and mother were very ardent not to say radical abolitionists. Many of my songs reflected their prejudices and public views on the heated subject of slavery. My singing soon attracted attention and I was asked to sing by the passengers. I sang the songs with which I was most familiar and one afternoon I sang the following words to the tune "Susannah Don't You Cry."

> I'm on my way to Canada
> That cold and dreary land.
> The dire effects of slavery
> I can no longer stand.
> My soul is vexed within me so
> To think I am a slave.
> I'm now resolved to strike the blow
> For freedom or the grave.

I was utterly innocent of the sorry significance of the song on board an Ohio river steamboat, with Kentucky always to the south of us and citizens of that state and other slave states farther south among the passengers. All of the anti-slavery passengers applauded my childish performance, but that song led to a rumpus. The Southerners protested in no uncertain terms to the management. My mother soon sensed the situation and told me not to respond any more to requests to sing. I can appreciate now what trouble I might have incited.

Few other events of the trip remain with me. One other incident I recall however. As we were nearing the end of our journey I remember my father looking over toward the Illinois side and pointing out the town of Nauvoo and saying to my mother in tones that imported horror and reprobation, "That is the place where the Mormons live." He dwelt on some of the then recent events which had shocked the country: the riot which led to the assassination of the Mormon leader, Joseph Smith. I had no idea of what was involved, but I got the impression that they were some sort of terrible wild animals which were very dangerous.

My impressions and those of my parents of the country and the people in Lee county were somewhat mixed. We settled on the western side of Lee county close to the then notorious "Half-Breed Tract." We had lived on a rough, hilly farm in Pennsylvania, the land of which was not very fertile. We had heard so much of the beautiful prairies of Iowa and their amazing fertility, but we found this country hilly and wooded and its roughness was not more attractive than the region from which we had come. My own disappointment was quite pronounced and I did not get over it until I came to Grinnell three years later. There were none of the vast open stretches of which we had been told. But there were bronze wild turkey, prairie chickens, and quail which my brother brought home for my mother to cook for all of us to enjoy.

The people seemed strange to us, many of them even queer. Our neighbors as I recall them were either New Englanders or Southerners. The latter were more numerous and controlled local affairs. The intense abolitionism of my parents tended to alienate us and to enhance our sense of loneliness.

My father and mother had been old school Presbyterians. When the discussion of slavery became acute in the 40's they left that church because of its attitude toward the question and joined the Free Presbyterians. They found no church of choice in Lee county. They would have joined the Congregational church of their New England neighbors, but their stout consciences and stiff notions of rectitude on the subject in controversy would not allow them to do so. The Congregationalists were patronized, if not financially assisted, by the American Tract society and that body would not publish any anti-slavery tracts, or in any manner give its countenance to the anti-slavery agitation.

It was not long before my father's strong views were well

known and of course the Southerners looked askance at him and the whole family and this increased our sense of isolation. My father did not then engage in any open or offensive agitation of the slavery question, but our home was the gathering place for abolitionists and this fact did not increase the good-will shown to us. I can remember my father and two of my sisters going to Salem in Henry county to an anti-slavery convention that aroused a great deal of interest in the family. I believe it was in 1853.

Another bright memory that does not fade is connected with Lee county. It was in our first home in Iowa that I read *Uncle Tom's Cabin*. We took the *National Era* in which the story first appeared. I looked forward to each issue of the paper with an intense interest that surpassed any I have experienced since. I was so eager to get the paper from the carrier that I would go down the road to meet him as he brought the mail. If I was lucky in getting the longed-for chapter I would go off in the woods near the old home to read its fascinating chapters before anyone could interrupt. If I was not forehanded, I was alert to get it when it was laid down and I would hie myself to the loft to read it undisturbed.

The presidential campaign of 1852 made little impression on my mind, save that following my father's views I had little interest in either of the two major parties because of their opposition to radical anti-slavery propaganda. I recall a meeting at our house at which a Wesleyan Methodist preacher, a Mr. Whitten, said without any sort of reservation, "I never trust a Whig."

In a general way we suffered none of the distress, privations and misfortunes portrayed in that story of the Dakotas thirty or forty years ago, Rolvaag's *Giants in the Earth*. We were poor as we measure worldly possessions today. On thing, however, mother always had plentiful supplies of bedding and no matter how cold the wintry nights might be, we were always warm. One matter you might be interested in, the women of the family always slept on the first floor of the cabin and the men in the upper part. This practice was due, I presume, in part to the needs of the young children. In the order of things today it would be reversed.

A characteristic or trait of my parents I want to leave on record. Although my father suffered sorry financial disaster in connection with his ventures in Pennsylvania and endured many privations of comforts, not to say luxuries, which he and my mother had been used to, during all those first years in Lee county and later in Poweshiek county I never heard either one of them, singly or together, bemoan their financial reverses or complain about the hard turns of fortune they had borne. At the table or about the fireplace, or after they had retired at night, usually their conversation was about the traffic in alcoholic intoxicants or the rights of women. We had much plain living to be sure, but always much high thinking and wholesome discussion. These memories I hold as my precious heritage.

One of the interesting experiences in Lee county was our relation to the New Englanders. Between our place and Warren was a Congregational church. The pastor was Mr. Danforth Bliss. He came to see us and wanted us to join his church as there was no Presbyterian church within reach. He was much disappointed that the strict views of my parents prevented, but it made no difference in his goodwill and graciousness to us. He was a man of beautiful spirit and a person of wide influence for good in our community. His church was not strongly supported and received much of its support from people back in New England.

Another fine influence in my girlhood was a young schoolteacher, another New Englander, a Miss Allen. She was one of the many teachers sent out from New England by Governor Slade of Vermont. She was a beautiful woman and a wonderful teacher, a graduate of Mt. Holyoke. The natives stood in awe of her. Whatever may have been the traditions as to mischief and tricks, they were never tried upon her in her administration of the school. She easily dominated the entire situation. She married a Mr. Scoville, another New Englander of marked refinement.

The Southerners among whom we lived seemed very queer to us. Their customs and manners and speech were strange to us. They were kind and neighborly if we or anyone encountered ill-fortune, but for reasons I have mentioned we had very little to do with them.

My father's discontent with the character of the land, the rough, hilly country, and the additional fact that he was living on rented land made him begin to look about for a better location. He wanted prairie land that he could cultivate more extensively and more easily. By good fortune he read one day in 1854 the advertisement or announcement of the plans of J. B. Grinnell for the planting of a colony in north-central and eastern Iowa. A church and a school of higher learning were to be established and anti-slavery principles were to be maintained. I cannot tell now whether he read it in the *National Era* or the *New York Independent,* which he may have come upon in the home of Reverend Nichols. As soon as he read the prospectus, father exclaimed, "That's the place for me."

My father and brother Samuel went up to Grinnell in the fall of 1854 to examine its prospects and, if satisfied with the outlook, to purchase a farm as circumstances might suggest. My father decided to buy of Mr. Grinnell eighty acres at $4.00 per acre, a mile west of the north line of Grinnell. My father returned to Lee county and my brother remained to prepare for our coming in the spring. He was a carpenter and built a shack for us on the corner of West street and Fifth avenue. He had it ready for us when we arrived.

We left early in the spring of 1855, or late winter, for snow was still on the ground when we started. There were ten of us, my parents, my oldest brother Ephraim and his wife, Rachel Hanlin, my two brothers, James and William J., and my three sisters, Susan, Jennie, Mary, and myself. We travelled in two covered wagons drawn by yokes of oxen, and in a two-seated buggy drawn by two spirited horses of which my father was very proud, and which were mettlesome and hard to hold, for they were in excellent condition. The weather was very cold and we had to travel with care, for my mother was suffering from a severe attack of lumbago. Save mother's distress, we enjoyed the journey. We had plenty of warm clothing and we stopped along the way at several places, among them Bonaparte and Agency City. At night, the men slept in the wagons while mother and the girls put up at hotels, or taverns as they were called. The spirited horses were hard to hold and when we were entering Grinnell, notwithstanding the long tiresome day they had, those horses went prancing along the prairie road and up to the Chambers House where we were given a warm welcome. I can still see Abbie Whitcomb, later Mrs. Horace Robbins, who welcomed us, and her sister Helen, looking from the window as our horses trotted up to the front door of the hotel.

This journey to Grinnell gave me the fulfillment of my dreams of the prairies. In 1855 there was not a tree within three miles of Grinnell. We could see for miles and all my longings for vast open spaces were satisfied. The selection of the town site, we were told, was due to Mr. Grinnell's inside information that the managers of the Rock Island railroad, then called the M & M, was to locate a station at this point.

Another thing I shall remember as long as I live with unalloyed and inexpressible pleasure was the magnificence of the wild flowers that made the prairies for miles in all directions one gorgeous mass of variant beauty. I simply cannot adequately describe it. Some three years ago I was asked to tell of my pioneer experiences to the Kiwanis club of Grinnell. I indulged in what must have seemed to the present generation utter extravagance in adjectives and I felt they would suspect me of mere exuberance. But several whose memories went back to the same days, either in Grinnell or in other parts of the state, assured me that I had not misrepresented the facts and that I could scarcely overdraw the astonishing beauty and profusion of the prairie flowers. As one looked over the stretches of the prairies, he must have been made of stone not to have been thrilled by the loveliness of it all. I cannot now name any number of species, but purple arid yellow blossoms, wild roses and sweet williams were conspicuous among them.

I learned to appreciate the extraordinary richness of the soil about Grinnell. My father came from Lee county well supplied with the latest farm implements, among them a breaking plow. He was soon in demand to break the heavy sod of the prairie. One part of the plow interested me and everyone else. In front of the plowshare and attached to the beam was a sharp knife blade reaching to the point of the share which was to cut the sod ahead of the share, thus insuring a clean cut line in the turnover and reducing the strain on the plow and the oxen pulling the plow. This plow was a matter of no little curiosity to the other residents as one of the new devices for agriculture. Because of its efficiency my father was asked to do, and did do, most of the first breaking of the prairie around about Grinnell in the next two or three years after our arrival. The extraordinary richness of the soil was a matter of constant astonishment and delight to my father. As you know it was almost coal black and as the plow turned the sod over, I recall how my father would exclaim time and time again, "How rich this is," and compare it with the poor farm land we tilled back in Pennsylvania.

Our method of planting corn and potatoes may be of interest. One of my brothers or sisters or I would follow the plow and drop the seed corn or potatoes at regular intervals and the next time around the plow turned another furrow over and so covered the seed. Was it hard work? Not to me. The new farm life was a constant delight.

One childish horror I suffered—and not exactly childish either—came from the innumerable snakes that infested the prairies.

We encountered them in all directions, and there were some very dangerous kinds such as rattlers and copperheads. My brother Will kept us in a state of terror from his irrepressible habit of killing them in a reckless manner. He was constantly doing it. His method was not with sticks or stones but by picking them up by the tails and snapping their heads off. How he could do it and how he did it so skillfully I never could understand, but he would even though my father rebuked him time and time again for his recklessness and forbade him doing it. But he brought the rattles into the house by the score.

My recollections of our first days in Grinnell prior to the Civil war cluster about several persons or incidents: first, the founder of the town, Mr. Grinnell, and the character of the people we found there or who came soon after; second, Professor and Mrs. L. F. Parker and the education I received under their teaching and the ideals they exemplified; third, the coming of Iowa college and its trustees, faculty and students; fourth, the movement for the abolition of slavery and John Brown's journey through Grinnell and conferences with those in sympathy with his program; and fifth, the onset of the Civil War and its frightful disturbance of the ongoing [sic] and progress of our peaceful life.

Each of these phases of our life constitutes a story in itself and I can give you only hints and glimpses of what actually occurred, or suggest the variant phases of the influences which remain in my memory. They are typical of the best in the beginnings of Grinnell and in the beginnings of the state. Time has worked many changes and I necessarily see many of those events through memories colored by prejudices, or marked predilections, and I hope none will ascribe to me arrogant or false assertion.

I had all the natural pride of an American. I became possessed early with the pronounced opinion that Grinnell was a very fine place in which to live and that her people were as good, or if you must have it, a little better than the average. I have since learned that there were many other communities in the state made of people precisely like my fellow townsmen of Grinnell whose culture, public spirit in public affairs and philanthropy and private and public morals were the same as ours. One does not live as long as I have and not discover that virtually all people, no matter whence they may hail, are very much the same at heart in public purpose and private virtue.

The most significant fact about Grinnell in contrast with my first home in Iowa was the predominance of New Englanders. Their ideas and ideals prevailed, but intermixed with these were emigrants from the middle states and a few Southerners. In contrast with this was the fact that in the country a few miles west and south and east of town were settlers who came largely from the south, or from the states of Pennsylvania, Ohio, Indiana, and Illinois. The difference in habits, customs and speech were pronounced and interesting. Each group was "odd" or "queer" to the others and how we laughed at the speech and ways of some of them. The New Englanders came with better schooling and higher educational ideals than those of us from the western states and in our hearts we admitted the fact, but we never got used to some of their odd phrases. Their "I want to know," "Twant so" and "Do tell" always amused me. Their nasal twang and some of their pronunciations always made us smile. Such as "idear," "caows" and "hoss."

One experience has remained bright in my memory. I was playing with one of my best girl friends about a cherry tree in the spring. I told her with pride that I had "clum" that tree. Whereupon with a reproving manner she said, "You clim the tree." We squabbled for some time as to which was correct, but in time we learned that we were both wrong.

We noticed that the New Englanders were sharper in trade and in making bargains than were the people from other parts. They were keen and shrewd. My father was a kindly man and seldom given to caustic comments, but he frequently characterized them as "blue-bellied Yankees," and never felt quite comfortable in dealing with some of them; though he was never mistreated as far as I can recall. He felt that he had to keep his wits at their best in dealing with them and he did not like it.

The few Southerners always interested us. One fine family, the Hayes, came with their emancipated servant whom we all knew as "Uncle Ned." We were impressed by their always treating Uncle Ned with such consideration. They were very kind to him and he repaid them. Their slow drawling southern speech was very charming. I always liked to hear them talk. There was a softness in their tones and enunciation which was pleasing to our ears. I cannot say so much for the speech of the mountain whites and the Hoosiers who were numerous in the township about Grinnell.

The central figure and the most interesting personality was, of course, the founder of the town, Josiah B. Grinnell. He was a man of marked ability. He was alert, energetic, quick in his actions and thinking, and incessantly active in the furtherance of his many and varied interests. He exemplified and summed up all the characteristics of a founder and promoter of a western town. Including in his program a rather elaborate and extensive scheme for the moral improvement, educational advancement and social uplift of those he sought to attract to Grinnell, his project linked at least two of the great subjects of national debate, slavery and the suppression of the liquor traffic. Because of this we became more self-conscious and contentious than we would otherwise have been.

Mr. Grinnell was the life of every social gathering. He was witty and quick at repartee. He had a fund of good stories and told them well. Whether this was because of his exuberant nature or a part of his desire to make people glad that they were in Grinnell I will not undertake to say. But I recall that as a child I was constantly watching him to see what he would do or say next for I knew that we would have a good laugh at some turn he would take.

As a public speaker he was very successful. His advocacy of the restriction or elimination of the evils of slavery was invariably interesting and at times thrilling, especially when fugitive slaves were a matter of local concern, or when the horrors of the struggle in Kansas were uppermost, or the last days of John Brown. He knew how to touch the quick of human feelings. His political opponents found him a hard one to encounter in debate. He was much sought after in campaigns prior to the Civil war and later, as his career in congress may suggest.

I recall an example of Mr. Grinnell's sagacity in scoring points in any project he was pushing—and he was always promoting some plan or other. One of the strong characters among the first settlers was Henry M. Hamilton. He and Mr. Grinnell did not pull together in their plans. Their differences were accentuated because Mr. Hamilton owned land south of the present line of the Rock Island while Mr. Grinnell's holdings were largely to the north. Mr. Hamilton, by shrewdness or by luck, got business developments, two stores, built on his side of the dividing line and this seemed to be the probable course of business, much to the chagrin of Mr. Grinnell. He offered several counter inducements but none seemed potent until he persuaded the trustees of Iowa college, then at Davenport and seeking a better or more congenial location, to come to Grinnell. He offered them as a gift twenty acres which were accepted as the college campus. With the coming of the college the tide of public interest turned and the trade began to turn north of the median line. Another item in his strategy was his gift of the present park which constitutes what in many Iowa towns is called the public square.

With the founder of the town I recall with more feeling his good wife, Mrs. Grinnell. The two were an interesting contrast. He was exuberant, vocal, and congenial, a hail-fellow-well-met always. She was reticent, serious, even severe in mein and manners and gave the impression of sternness at first. But with all her sadness of manner and restraint in words, Mrs. Grinnell is one of the bright lights of my girlhood and my later womanhood. She was very kind in doing little things that made life easier for children and neighbors. I shall never forget her gift to us of a bag of apples, the first we had in Grinnell. A kind of fruit we so longed for and could not obtain.

Among the attractions of the town to my father and mother was the announcement of the plans for schools. These were first, the common or what is now called the grade and high schools, and second in Mr. Grinnell's forecast was a university. I recall caustic comments on the extensiveness of the undertaking. Fortunately the coming of Iowa college put a stop to the talk of a university. Our first school was taught by two New England women, Miss Lucy Bixby, and then by her sister, Miss Louise.

The coming of Mr. and Mrs. Parker was a happy incident in the promotion of Grinnell as an educational center. Prior to that we had done well, but when he began his work in 1856 everything changed and a new era was inaugurated. He was a graduate of Oberlin which to my youthful mind was the radiant center of all that was best. Readers of Edward Eggleston's *Hoosier Schoolmaster* know that the pioneer schools followed a simple treadmill routine in reading, writing, and arithmetic. Professor Parker, as we called him even then, changed all that. He made us eager to learn because he made us realize that knowledge was the means of introducing us to the larger life of the world about us and to the significance of the history of the world. Recitations were not a dull round of repeating what we had memorized. He illuminated the schoolroom and made our lessons vital. They related to life and they made us see that we were individuals and how we might play a part in the progress of better things.

Mrs. Parker was then and ever after one of the most beautiful women I have ever seen. Her brown eyes and gentle ways and gracious manner of addressing young and old alike gave her remarkable influence. Professor Parker was more vigorous and electric in his work and she complemented him in the most telling way. They gave a distinction to the educational life of the community that constituted a most important part in Grinnell's fame.

It was due to Mr. Cooper, later Colonel Cooper, that Professor and Mrs. Parker came to Grinnell. He had known of them at Oberlin and their noteworthy success in teaching. Professor Parker wanted to settle in "bleeding Kansas," as we called it in anti-slavery circles, and went there to find a suitable location. Not finding just what he desired he stopped in Grinnell as he had promised and stayed.

The beginning of Iowa college, or Grinnell college as we now call it, constitutes a story by itself.[3] Mr. Grinnell had very ambitious plans for the establishment of Grinnell university. It was incorporated as such and Mr. Grinnell was president of the board of trustees. As originally conceived the university was to consist of two seminaries or schools. One was to be located on what is the present campus and was to be for the young woman. The other, for young men, was to be located in the southern part of the town, south of the present Rock Island railroad at a "safe distance" from the female seminary as the speech of those days put it. Mr. Grinnell gave twenty acres and further, as a part of his plan for establishing the university, he offered to give the proceeds of the sale of certain portions of the lots which he sold to settlers to provide a working capital or the beginning of an endowment fund. A wooden building was erected on the present site of Alumni hall (registration building).

Why was not Professor Parker made president of the university and later of Iowa college when it came to Grinnell? The answer to this question involves one of the most interesting phases of our life. While we were in fact an anti-slavery community, there were sharp differences among us as to the proper limits of agitation. Professor Parker was an "Oberlinite," and all such were looked upon by the general public as extremists and dangerous radicals. This was especially true in Iowa. Oberlin stood for abolitionism and women's rights, subjects of violent contempt in the minds of both men and women outside of the small circle of advocates for coeducation, and upon this too the majority looked with grave doubts as to its wisdom and propriety. It was common talk that Professor Parker was promised the presidency of Grinnell university, but Mr. Grinnell and others with whom he had to work soon realized that however much they might sympathize with the new thought and progressive ideas of the day, they had to reckon with the strong current of common opinion in outlying regions from which they hoped to draw popular support for the new and ambitious university. The great majority looked at our radical reforms, or innovations as they were often called, not only with disapproval but with dread, precisely as the public looks today on Bolshevism, Communism, and sundry sorts of Socialism. The people of Iowa in those days, as generally through her history, were conservative, and Mr. Grinnell and his associates soon clearly sensed this fact.

The matter of the presidency hung in the balance for several years. The Civil War kept the decision in suspense and finally Dr. George F. Magoun of Bowdoin was called. His attitude, while "advanced" was not so extreme in popular estimate as was that of Professor Parker, the Oberlinite. The relations of these two men and Mr. Grinnell constitute a most interesting study in human relationships in the furtherance of public philanthropy. Both had pronounced feelings and striking traits of character. Each was possessed with keen mentality and physical vigor and in the strenuous discussions of those days their influence on the course of events was definite and at times emphatic. They added much to the zest and picturesqueness of life in the town and constituted the major elements in its distinction abroad.

The visits of John Brown on two occasions gave to Grinnell fame, or infamy, according to one's views of his career and character. I saw and heard him on one of his trips, but was too young to appreciate the significance of his coming. When he came with the eleven negro slaves he had taken from their masters in Missouri, I saw and heard him. The town was all agog with excitement. Everyone knew he was there and there were many who did not approve of his high-handed method of invading Missouri and kidnapping the slaves. Though they abhorred slavery as an institution, they realized that promiscuous interference with the rights of the slave holders would bring on the horrors of slave insurrection and civil war would wreck the country's peace. Mr. R. M. Kellogg, an old-line Democrat, was outspoken against public sympathy with such invasion of public and private law. Brown spoke in the church where the stone church now stands. I do not recall much of what he said but he denounced the oppression inflicted upon him. I particularly remember the harsh features, the cold, relentless eye and hawklike look of the hero of the Ossawatamie.[4] He kept men and children alike in a state of awe and in this fact, I suspect, lay much of his ability to do things that most men would not dare to try to do.

The next morning Brown stopped in front of the schoolhouse with his covered wagon and hailed Professor Parker who went out to talk to him. We youngsters knew as soon as our teacher left who was out in front and one of the pupils asked if we might not go too. Either because of his sympathy with us or because he appreciated that it was useless to insist that we remain in our seats and pursue our studies, Professor Parker consented. We all scurried out and huddled about, a cluster of excited children, and saw the much talked of man sitting in the wagon seat holding the reins of the horses. Again that cold, stern eye held us in awe and silence. We were much excited to see a number of woolly heads and flashing black eyes and rows of white teeth greeting us through the cracks in the wagon cover where it had been lifted by some of the irrepressible pickaninnies crowded in the back of the wagon. We were all a tiptoe to see, and agog with suppressed excitement.

Because of my parents views on slavery we were among the conductors of the underground railway. It was a subject of little discussion, in fact, was not mentioned at the table or about the hearth. Father and mother frequently engaged in whispered conversations and we knew something was on, or up, as the phrase goes, but we were never told what it was. I believe it was not generally known that our house was a "station" because my parents were so reticent. We children knew it was a dangerous topic and talk of it might subject the family to arrest or attack and we instinctively said nothing.

One night when I came home I found a colored woman with a baby in her arms sitting by the fire. We heard mother and father whispering to one another and realized that preparations were being made. In the morning she and the baby were gone. My brother had taken them on their way. Needless to say all this gave a peculiarly exciting turn to life for us and made us all as alert as crickets to the course of public events, especially those relating to slavery.

The episode of the negro boy's education which so disturbed the peace of Grinnell was one in which my brother Ephraim was involved in no small measure. It sharply illustrates the curious phases and limitations of public and private feelings about the irrepressible negro questions. The public today is no different in such matters than it was in those exciting days.

My brother, Dr. Ephraim Harris, entered the army service as a regiment physician. In New Orleans he became in some way interested in an attractive negro lad called James. How my brother took charge of him or felt concerned to help him I do not recall. But he brought him to Grinnell. His education became a matter of concern and he was sent to the town school. His appearance in the schoolroom precipitated another crisis. Grinnell had a number of New Englanders who were idealists and friends of humanity when thinking of far-away China, Africa, or South Carolina, but their zeal in good works cooled when the actualities came into town and next door. Several citizens protested against James being put in with their children in school. Some years before the exclusion of negroes had been sought under a resolution denying "foreigners" the privileges of schools but it had been voted down with a narrow margin. Two citizens, both from New England, Captain Clark, an old sea captain, and Mr. Kellogg, were leaders of those who came to school to protest. But Professor Parker announced in no uncertain terms that anyone who ventured to take the negro boy from the school must do it over his dead body. As previous experiences with the Oberlinite indicated what his assertion implied, the lad was left alone. Nothing came from the flare-up but smoke.

Strangely I do not recall much about the political discussions preceding the election of Abraham Lincoln. My father and mother were so extreme in their views that they looked upon Lincoln with indifference, if not with positive suspicion. He did not attack slavery; he stood for the protection of the slave-holder's rights in his ownership of his slaves, even sustaining the Fugitive Slave Law. His opposition to the extension of slavery was not extreme enough for them. For years they had read the *Radical,* a paper of extreme anti-slavery views. Later it was called *Principia.* During the campaign of 1860 and in the forepart of the war it expressed most adverse opinions about Abraham Lincoln and had no respect for his program of "saving the union" regardless of the abolition of slavery. It was not until a year after the beginning of the war that my father became convinced that the abolition of slavery was one of the inevitable results of the struggle and that Lincoln's course began to interest me. The proclamation emancipating the slaves, of course, changed everything for us. Lincoln became one of our fixed stars.

My recollections of the Civil war are not so clear as it seems they should be. Four of my brothers and my father enrolled in the army. My brother, James, aged 23, and Samuel, aged 30, enlisted in Company B of the Fortieth Iowa Infantry, and served for three years. My oldest brother, Dr. Ephraim Harris, was associated with the same regiment as assistant surgeon but the major part of his service was in charge of a hospital given over to smallpox cases in New Orleans. My brother McKee also served. Their commanding officer was Colonel Cooper and they and my mother remembered gratefully his kindness and consideration. My youngest brother, William, was ordered into service, but because of my mother's need of his help with the farm he was released, and I sympathized with his disappointment.

My father's war experience was interesting. He was fifty-eight years old, beyond military age. He joined the famous "Greybeard Regiment," the Thirty-seventh Iowa Infantry, which was mustered into the national service on December 15, 1862, at Muscatine and mustered out at Davenport May 24, 1865. All of the members of the company were over forty-five years of age and were not subject to draft or other call of the government. The regiment saw considerable service of an important character at St. Louis and Franklin, Missouri, at Rock Island and Alton, Illinois, at Memphis, Tennessee, Indianapolis, and Columbus, Ohio. At Indianapolis and Columbus they guarded prison camps. My father enlisted because his conscience and earnest feelings about slavery compelled him. He was not much concerned at the outset because he felt that President Lincoln was not determined to abolish slavery. When it became clear that slavery was to be abolished, he felt no doubt as to his duty to do all that he could to assist. The achievements of the regiment and their substantial service won high praise from their officers and the government.

Our work in college was, of course, completely disturbed by the outbreak of the Civil war. We felt the same intense feeling that surged through the public at large. One incident had much of the absurd and pathetic in it. It occurred at the outset of the war. The girls of the college, mostly of my class, made a flag, or perhaps they bought it, at any rate possessed one. When Stephen A. Douglas died soon after the war broke out, Mr. Kellogg, an ardent Douglas Democrat, asked that the flag be hung at half-mast in recognition of the fact, because of his prominence and because from the time of his defeat for the presidency he had earnestly urged the South not to secede, and both the North and the South to support the Union.

We should have acceded to Mr. Kellogg's request readily, but we did not. Rather, we summarily refused to do so. Mr. Kellogg, in some heat and precipitancy, came to the college building where the flag was and undertook to lay hands upon it and himself carry out his purpose. He was anticipated and resisted by the boys. Some hot words passed and Mr. Kellogg had to abandon his plan. The next morning there was seen dangling from a tree in front of his home an effigy and attached thereto the ungracious words, "Empty barrels make the most noise." My neighbors never had much respect for college students after that. It was a silly performance. In the lights of consequent developments I know that we should have put aside our prejudices but we were such ardent youngsters, as most people are, that we could not forget that Douglas had tried to defeat Lincoln, that he started the repeal of the Missouri Compromise which we regarded as a sacred compact, and that he was a defender of slavery which we held indefensible.

Our college class work was more or less erratic just as work was disturbed in the World war [World War I], by constant excitement from news of the events, by our concern for our loved ones facing the dangers at the front, and by the intermittent reports of victories and then of defeats with horrible destruction. Systematic and serious study was very difficult, or rather impossible.

All of the able-bodied men of the classes enlisted. James Ellis and Carl Kelsey of Grinnell, John Carney whose home was near by, Hiram Cardell of Malcolm, Joseph Lyman from west of town and W. S. Kennedy, a Quaker from Sugar Creek township; all of these went to the front. From my own class of 1865 three left: Henderson Herrick, Robert M. Haines and Charles Scott. Mr. Haines was a Quaker and was constrained by his own and his mother's views as to war, but he went into service of the Christian Sanitary Commission and served as a nurse at a hospital in St. Louis. Charles Scott's name revives memories of his hard struggle. He had to work for his living while in school. He was an excellent student, a strenuous worker, and died two years after graduation.

NOTES

1. Quoted in Katharine Horack, "In Quest of a Prairie Home," *The Palimpsest* V (July 1924): 249.
2. Frank I. Herriott, "Seventy Years in Iowa," *The Annals of Iowa* 27 (October 1945): 97–118.
3. Also useful is John Scholte Nollen, *Grinnell College* (Iowa City: State Historical Society of Iowa, 1953).
4. Osawatamie was the site of a pitched battled on August 30, 1856. Approximately three-hundred proslavery supporters attacked John Brown and forty Free Soil advocates. Although Brown and his men defended the town, guerrilla warfare now raged through Kansas territory, called "Bleeding Kansas."

AN IOWA WOMAN
IN WARTIME
Marjorie Ann Rogers

THE Civil War (1861–1865) put tremendous pressure on civic-minded women who now rolled bandages, prepared food and clothing, and joined war relief associations by the thousands. Marjorie Ann Graham Rogers was among these. In 1861, the Rogers family was beginning a third year farming in Tama County, but when the news of war came Dr. Samuel C. Rogers responded. At first, Dr. Rogers recruited Tama County men and prepared his family for his departure. In late 1861, he went to the front as assistant surgeon to the Thirtieth Iowa Infantry, leaving behind not only Marjorie, but a girl thirteen, two boys eight and ten, and "baby Anna."

Marjorie Ann Rogers rented out the farm and moved her family into the town of Toledo, Iowa. Here she maintained her home and family and threw herself into war relief work, including participating in a Des Moines convention to organize "sanitary" societies, canvassing Tama County for additional workers, taking part in the State Sanitary Fair at Dubuque, and supporting the establishment of an Iowa Orphans' Home. She also hired a wagon and team to haul the produce of the Rogers's rented farm to market. Although she lacked experience driving, Rogers wrote that "I was not going to be laughed at because I was a woman."

Throughout the war—and after—Rogers continued her labors. Her comments show that women could be as politically minded, as competitive, and as combative as men. Even when facing physical danger, Rogers refused to give up. And when runaway slaves known as contraband appeared in Iowa, Rogers and her colleagues intensified their efforts. What Rogers does not say is how relief work changed women; it gave them the knowledge that they could also raise funds, organize, and lead.

Marjorie Ann Rogers's detailed recollections of the war years first appeared in *The Annals of Iowa* in 1961. An excerpt is presented here with the permission of the State Historical Society of Iowa.[1]

[Fall 1863] I had been selected to do the canvassing through the county and wished to get through this work before the weather became too cold. There were a few towns I could reach by train where I organized an auxiliary and gave instructions for packing and shipping. This was not hard to do but where I had to drive over the prairie and call at every house, it required a good deal of tact and patience, and grace even, to meet a rebuke or refusal without being, or seeming to be, impatient or surprised that anyone could refuse to aid in such a cause at such a time as this, when in nearly every house a son or husband or brother was missing, was on the battlefield or perhaps in the hospital suffering for the very things we were asking for and so anxious to receive.

I tried to remember I was asking not granting a favor, and not for myself but for those we were in duty bound to help, our suffering soldiers. I generally received kindness and courtesy and what I asked for as far as it was possible, but there were exceptions even in this work, when I would feel ready to faint from being denied or ordered out of the house with a string of abuse after me. I did not count on this when I accepted the work; we were so glad to do everything ourselves we could that we thought everyone else would be when applied to. Everyone in the county knew what we were doing and were notified they might be called on at any time and were asked to be ready with their contributions.

I was oftener insulted by women than men. The men might refuse politely but said little; they had been warned by our sheriff to keep quiet. The community would not allow any treasonable speeches from the copperheads [opponents of the war, mainly Democrats] and they became very careful where and when they showed their venom. They were rightly named. They had been holding secret meetings and making treasonable speeches ever since the war commenced, but had been warned they must desist or they would be arrested and punished for treason.

I had occasion to visit two of our auxiliaries. I left home in the morning, taking Frank [her twelve-year-old son] to drive as it was Saturday, the day I generally went in the country as the children were out of school. I could always have a horse and buggy on that day, unless there was a funeral as the undertaker had the only one I could hire for a dollar a day. He was very kind and always ready to accommodate us. The horse was gentle and Frank had been accustomed to horses when on the farm, so he drove and held the horse when I made a call. The ladies were expecting me and I gave my instructions, which did not detain me very long. These ladies packed and shipped their goods but were expected to send us an itemized bill of goods and amount of cash received, so we could give them credit for the same.

We had driven out one road and wished to come back another so as to take in some families I could visit on my way home. A tub of butter was promised and we would be ready to ship again in a few days. The ladies advised me not to make many calls on my return as I must necessarily pass several copperhead families, but time was precious and I wanted to accomplish all I could. We were going up hill and through woods, passing small farms frequently. We did not know one family from another. We had nearly reached home when we passed a very neat little white house with an orchard near. The trees were loaded with fruit. I told Frank I would venture to go in and ask for apples to dry. I noticed as I walked up to the house the front blinds were down and I knocked loud thinking the lady might be at the rear of the house. The door opened very suddenly and quickly—I had hardly stopped knocking. They evidently expected a friend and threw the door wide open, when behold, a room full of men greeted my vision.

The man was as much surprised as I was. We looked at each other a moment, then he said, "What do you want," and someone pushed the door shut. I backed down off the porch and made my way out of that neighborhood. I went directly to where I was sure of finding a friend and Frank was told to hold the horse again. As soon as I was well inside the door, I told of my escapade and said, "What does it mean?" The lady said, "That house is the headquarters of the copperheads and I am so thankful you did not make your business known, you would surely have been insulted. We hardly feel safe in our own homes and our children are often insulted in passing or while at school." She had her tub of butter ready and would send it. As we were walking out to the gate, we heard a pistol and I missed Frank from the buggy. My heart almost stopped beating for a moment and I thought, "Did they think I might report them and had shot my boy?" I called him, and soon to my relief he came running out of a grove nearby. I said, "Frank, did you hear a pistol?" He said, "Yes, mother, that was me. I fired mine off. I brought it along for fear the copperheads would hurt you."

"Where did you carry it, Frank?"

"In my coat pocket," he said. He had on a grey roundabout with deep pockets on each side. I said, "Where was it when you were playing with the children at noon where we took dinner."

"In my pocket all the time."

"What would you have done if the copperheads had insulted me?"

"I would shoot anybody that would do that; father told us all to take care of you and I will."

I was very cross with the dear boy and told him how wrong it was to carry a loaded pistol. He might have shot himself or me right in the buggy, or he might have killed one of the children accidently; in either case it would be accidental, of course. It was a very dangerous thing to do. I appreciated his love and kindness and desire to protect me, but trembled to think what might have been the consequences. ...

The other ladies engaged in the same work through the county had the same class to contend with and they were to be found as long as the war lasted. I met ladies from every county in the state at Dubuque, where a State Sanitary Fair was held, and their experience was similar to ours. This was the most aggravating thing we had to contend with in our work, so unreasonable, unnatural, disloyal to their own homes and government. It was a test of our good nature and patience.

I might fill many pages of like incidents but must speak of another class, the wives, mothers and sisters of our loyal soldiers, whom I also met in my work. We visited each of those even if we knew they could not afford to help us as they would feel hurt if we did not. It was in these homes I found the truest charity and where the noblest generosity was shown; if it was but the "widow's mite" or the mother's all, it was given freely, gladly, lovingly with a prayer for a blessing to go with it to the soldier, from a heart full of thankfulness that they could do a little if it be but a nickel or a dime. They have done what they could and they will get their reward. It was touching beyond my power to describe the stories of these Iowa women, these mothers, wives, and daughters—their endurance, their hardships, sickness, poverty and deaths, in many families doing the work of the absent father or husband on the farm, saving from his poor salary to pay off a mortgage perhaps or a debt that would soon eat up their home. Such patience, cheerfulness and christian resignation, enduring it all for their country's good, willing to suffer if they must, even more, praying for the end, but working on lovingly, loyally!

Who can tell their story? Who can feel as they felt all through these dreadful years, these grand, noble women? Where are they? God only knows. He will not forget all they endured. They were everywhere in the humblest homes in all our beautiful land. These praying, trusting, loyal, loving women were doing their work nobly, but there were exceptions even here, where occasionally a grumbler or an undeserving wife or mother might be found. In some cases the help from the county had to be withheld, but these were the exception. If these women had children and the county had been giving them aid, the children would be removed to the Home in Davenport and cared for by the State.

A very comfortable home had been established there from what was Benton Barracks. I had occasion to visit this home several times during and after the war. If the soldier's papers were proved to be correct and if the mother was not able or worthy to have the care and education of the soldier's orphans, they had a right to become inmates of this home provided for them. It was made my duty to look after these orphans, or neglected or abused children, as the case might be, and see that they were properly dressed and cared for until sent to the Home, with the consent of the mother if possible, without if necessary. A good, true wife and mother would make every effort to keep her children and they were helped to do so, but that Home was a benediction to many of the soldiers' children whose fathers never came back to care for them, for here they were educated and taught to work. I made several dangerous trips, once was caught in a flood on my return home and was gone three or four days. Mrs.

Dillman made a trip and paid her own expenses in order to visit the children, some of whom had been her pupils, as she wished to see for herself that everything was right. ...

We were very busy all this time with our sanitary work, each committee doing its own separate duties grandly. We were having entertainments, oyster suppers, and now working for a fair [money-raising bazaar]. Mrs. H. E. Crosby was on the committee on entertainments; she was a host in herself and never failed in any of her undertakings. She was excellent help wherever needed; her husband was a soldier and she was loyal, true and brave. We were anxious to make all we could at our fair. It was winter now and the long evenings were spent in work. We hoped to do as well as the other counties and a little better if we could. ...

We had our Fair and considered it a success. Some of the soldiers had brought home pictures of our generals, and my husband had sent me some Confederate money which was a curiosity and sold well, over and over, as did the pictures. When we got our receipts from headquarters in Chicago, we were more than pleased to hear we had sent $700.00 in goods and cash since our meeting, or convention, in Des Moines, and the officers of the commission assured us our donations were equal to any others and all our goods were of a superior order, which was very gratifying to our president who had been so very careful that the best only should be sent to our boys, everything else being discarded and used at home wherever needed. We all felt relieved and encouraged to go on with the good work, which must not stop as long as we had a sick, suffering soldier in a hospital anywhere, and there were many and the number increasing all the time. It was so satisfactory to know our goods reached their destination through the christian and sanitary commissions. We now saw the wisdom of changing from St. Louis to Chicago as a point for distribution, as these commissioners were posted all the time and knew where the sick were located. ...

Colonel C. had found there were so many colored people coming over into Illinois, he ordered the trains to carry them or a part of them so as to make room for others. He was on furlough and would care for two carloads. He lived west of us but left one car at Tama City and sent a message to Judge Graham, who responded as quickly as possible by calling for volunteers to go home and prepare their Sunday dinners and as much more food as possible to be ready by one o'clock. A committee was appointed to receive the contributions and deliver them to the cold, hungry negroes who must be made to feel they were among friends and welcome to this land of liberty, our own beautiful Iowa. The brother sat down a moment and the minister said, "You have heard the message and the request, who will volunteer?" Every woman in that congregation rose to her feet and all were in tears. A prayer was offered but was scarcely audible; the congregation was dismissed with this injunction, "Brethren and sisters, an opportunity has come to all of us, let us do our duty, it will not end today. We must seek wisdom from the Father who has laid this responsibility upon us. You are dismissed, God bless and help you."

We went directly to Mr. Graham's office and he selected committees from each church; our ladies would provide this day's rations. We went home and went to work while he visited the other churches, telling them our plans for this day so they might not be disturbed and could make their own arrangements after services. The ladies told me afterwards they could not even remember the text. A gentleman was selected from each church to visit the contrabands and arrange to have a committee of ladies care for the supplies.

They had all been fed in Tama City that morning, but it was a new station with only two or three families living there; they did all they could to make the poor creatures comfortable. By one o'clock we had our clothesbasket filled. We boiled potatoes, cooked meat, sent tea and sugar, and jugs of milk, bread and butter, plates, knives and spoons, towels and soap, for they must remain in the car for several days till there could be comfortable places provided for them. They were parts of several families, only one entire family of parents and children, large and small, the majority of the crowd being women and children destitute of one decent comfortable garment. I did not see them in their crowded condition in the car. My brother had appointed his committee and left me out to look after the needed supplies.

After leaving the car, the men turned out as one man to find shelter and comfortable homes for these homeless, helpless ones thrown upon our mercy without our knowledge or consent. This work was not of our seeking, but the responsibility would have to be met; we could not throw it off if we would and would not if we could. This was just a beginning of the end of what was to follow (this was before the emancipation of the slaves). They were free when they left that car and they realized it. Before they trembled for fear the next train would carry them back. Their pleadings were pathetic; they were slow to believe. They had been deceived all their lives and did not know whom to trust.

By the help of willing hands and sympathizing hearts the work was soon accomplished. Four houses were found, one near Tama City, two between Toledo and Tama and another three blocks from us. This was for the father, mother and children, the oldest of the lot and the most interesting, two grown-up girls and two good sized boys. The family left in Tama was a married daughter. They were genuine Africans. These families were to be provided with stoves and fuel, beds and bedding, shoes and stockings. Very little furniture was sufficient for their use. We found the ladies all ready to respond to our calls for help. I was given the oversight of this particular family, so I did not have any responsibility outside, and found they were all I could do justice to. The mother had once more added to her already large family soon after they were settled. We had provided a little basket for the baby, a larger one for the mother with a new comfort [quilt] on top made of bright colors. ...

[1864] Our work for the soldiers became harder as we had less and less to do with. The material we needed cost so much and we had been under such a strain so long to keep up the supplies, that we felt discouraged at times, but whenever a demand or request came for certain articles, we always found some way to get them. The Lord helped us, and we would go on cheerfully and thankfully and do the best we could. Our supply of fruit, preserved and dried, our pickles, catsup, sauerkraut, butter and beans were always found in abundance.

Our soldiers, sick and wounded, were being discharged and sent home quite frequently. They went out to serve their country in all the strength and vigor of their manhood, brave, loyal and true, but the coming back—was it possible that such a change could have taken place? Were these the strong, healthy, happy men who left all that was dear to them in life without their protection to struggle and suffer and die alone? Some had come back poor, thin and pale, scarred and bruised, lame and sick and discouraged. These grand, noble men, wrecks of their former selves, life always in the future to be a burden, with wounds that would never heal, diseases that never could be cured! But now they were at home among friends and never murmured or complained; they had done their duty and were satisfied. Many, very many never came home even to die. ...

[April 1865] The sanitary supplies we had on hand were sent to the Orphans Home in Davenport, and as we needed no more Fairs, our things were disposed of as best we could at home. My work for the soldiers' orphans continued all the next year. At the close of this year a dear little baby boy (William Sherman) was given us, but we made an idol of him and God took him from evil to come in mercy.

NOTE

1. Mrs. M. A. Rogers, "An Iowa Woman in Wartime," Part I, *The Annals of Iowa* 35 (Winter 1961): 523–48; Part II (Spring 1961): 594–615; and Part III (Summer 1961): 16–44.

LETTERS OF A PIONEER TEACHER
Arozina Perkins

Arozina Perkins took her education at the Lamoille County Grammar School in Vermont. She went west well before the Civil War as a missionary teacher of the National Popular Education Board.[1] Arozina Perkins was born in Johnson, Vermont, on March 21, 1826, the last of twelve children. The family returned to Arozina's mother's native Marshfield, Massachusetts, where Arozina's father died in 1846. It was after her father's death that Arizona decided to go west. She had taught in Johnson, Marshfield, and Fair Haven, Connecticut. In Iowa, she first taught from November 13, 1850, to March 21, 1851, in the Methodist church on Fifth Street in Fort Des Moines. The following term she moved to Fairfield to teach in a seminary. Her letters to her brother Barnabas back in Connecticut describe her situation in detail, including her recurring discouragement. She returned home to die on May 12, 1854, from a respiratory ailment at the age of twenty-eight.

The Perkins letters first appeared in *The Annals of Iowa* in 1961 and are used here by permission of the State Historical Society of Iowa.[2]

Fort Des Moines, Iowa, Jan. 2, 1851

My dear Brother,

... We have some of the most sweeping blasts here that you ever felt. The winds come all the way from the Rocky Mountains, and as there is nothing to break them here we have fresh breezes every day. This town is at the juncture of the Des Moines and Raccoon rivers.

It is mostly a level prairie with a few swells or hills around it. We have a Court House of brick, and one church, a plain framed building belonging to the Methodists. There are two taverns here, one of which has a most important little bell that rings together some fifty boarders.

I cannot tell you how many dwellings there are, for I have not counted them; some are of logs, some of brick, some framed and some are the remains of the old dragoon [military] houses. There are seldom more than one or two rooms in them, rarely three, and all on one floor. We have streets as they do in other cities. I have learned the names of few of them yet. They are numbered from the river up, a la Cincinnati. Then there is a Walnut, a Main Street, etc. etc. and a Coon row.

The people support two papers and there are several dry goods shops. I have been into but four of them. They keep "calicoes" in plenty, one piece that I asked the price of was fifty cents per yard. Then there is a variety of fringes, gimps [flat trimming usually of cord], tassals, etc. which are laid by at the East, and brought here for sale.

Society is as various as the buildings are. There are people from nearly every state, and Dutch, Swedes, etc. I am boarding in a family from Missouri. There is the man, woman, and two children which latter I have as scholars. There are three rooms, one of which, the parlor, I occupy. Shall I describe it to you? Well, in one corner stands a bed, in another a table covered with books, a clock and my accordion, between the two windows, under the looking glass is a stand—no—I happen to have it pulled out by the stove just now, to write on. Behind me is a sofa, and beneath a carpet. My two trunks are part of the furniture, and my rough box which I obtained so quickly in my hurry at Hartford is under the bed, with my go-to-meeting bonnets in it. Mr. Everly has a great taste for pictures for the walls are hung with them. I have just been up to see what they are—a portrait of Martin Van Buren and James Madison hangs just opposite my bed. I happened to notice another very particularly, 'tis of Paul and Virginia in a most tender parting scene, a declaration of independence, a mother washing her hopeful son Saturday night and another.

This is a very fine pious family and I enjoy myself very much. Mr. E. spends most of his time reading and Mrs. E. just minds her own business, as every woman ought to. The diet too just suits me, for we have plenty of corn bread, mush, and milk.

But my school—Well I am teaching in the Methodist Church as there is but one school house here, and that is occupied by Mrs. Bird, wife of the Presbyterian minister here. He preaches at the Court House two sabbaths in the month. Mrs. B. owns the school house, and has a school of about 30. The people tried to have a district school at the Court House but failed. One of the trustees, a shrewd Yankee by the name of Young, hired himself and commenced, taught two weeks then was unhoused, as the other two trustees determined to have a school on a cheaper plan than he could afford. They procured a teacher—examined him—and he proved an ignoramus— then they obtained another—little better than the first—gave him a certificate which Mr. Y. refused to sign as he did not consider him competent to teach the youth of Fort Des Moines. Of course then it was not a legal one here, but the man kept four weeks when they called a school meeting for the half dozenth time and decided that it was not a public school. It is still going on, however, but I have nearly all the girls.

I commenced on my own hook, thinking it would be better than to depend upon others. Mr. Stevens had closed his school when I came here, and things looked dark and snarled up to me I can tell you. I had made up my mind to "want for everything while I remained here" except—a school. That I had no idea would be lacking. No one here knew or cared anything about Gov. Slade's Society, and some of Mrs. Bird's friends supposed that I was got here to oppose her school. They are beginning to get undeceived by this time.

The first day I had nine scholars, now I have 25 and expect more. They are mostly girls of about 13–16. It would have amused you to have seen me the first morning in that shell of a church in the centre of a broad, open space of prairie. Judge McKay was building a fire in a tall, queer stove, and I, after sweeping out, sat down to wait for scholars. I was amused.

Well, the first two weeks I made out to live merely. I used coal, and the dirty stuff filled the room with gas and left us half frozen. Half the scholars had the chills every other day, and were first yawning, then shaking, and it almost made me shake to see them. We revolved about that apology for a stove regularly every day, and regularly every night I wrote letters and read sermons to prevent being most heartily discouraged. I was determined to like it here, tho' every one of my toes were frosted, if there was a prospect of doing any good. One night I dreamed I saw a beautiful, bright star and the next

morning I went along to school when, lo, there stood a large wood stove! You need not laugh now—for I never was more rejoiced—not for a long time. Since then I have kept pretty comfortable. I shall now think it best to remain thro the winter, perhaps longer. ...
    I'll tell you about our Christmas. At the tavern where the bell is they had a something in the evening. Some say it was a dinner, others a supper, while others call it a ball. About fifty were there. As a compliment, of course if could be nothing else, as it must have been known that I would not go, I received an invitation, printed in due form, as a "Cotillion [square dance] party." Well, that passed off, and Friday evening I had another invitation to visit with a very pleasant family. A few ladies and gentlemen were present, and we had a fine time making molasses candy. ...
    Shall I tell you how nicely I commenced the New Year? I made half a dozen calls, wrote a long letter to a friend, and in the evening went to a prayer meeting. The morning I commenced by opening to a hymn as we used to do at home. Today I went to school, found no fire, began to make one, and had the misfortune to tip the stove over; down came pipe and all; but we got it set up again, and went on as usual. How finely I began, didn't I? Well I do not intend to tip the stove over every morning for it would be too much trouble, and cease to be a variety.
    My health is very good except a cold which I took getting initiated. It has kept me coughing much of the time, but will wear away in time. ... The great excitement here is about getting the Capital located here. Whether they will succeed or not, I will not pretend to say.

Arozina

Fairfield, Iowa, May 20, 1851

My dear Brother,
    ... I had become discouraged completely—no, I saw, of tho't I saw, that it would be better for me to go to some older town and wait for young ladies and children to grow there. Therefore C. McK. wrote to know if Mr. Bill wished another teacher at his Seminary. His answer was that the condition of the school would not justify the employment of another at present. I then wrote to Mr. B. merely mentioning a few things I could teach, and requesting him if he knew of any situation where I might be useful to inform me. He then wrote

me immediately that matters had so turned about that he wished me
to come on. This was quite unexpected as I had not the least idea
when I wrote to him that he would want me, judging from his letter
to Mr. McK. Whether it was the style of the letter that interested him
(for I do not always write carelessly) or sympathy for my unpleasant
situation that caused this decision, I am unable to say; and as he
wished an answer by return of mail I wrote that I would go.

Afterwards, however, matters at the Fort [Des Moines] took a
decided turn for the better; there seemed to be a complete reaction of
feeling in the minds of many, and instead of looking upon the lone
Yankee as a speculating adventurer they seemed to understand that
she had come there for the sole purpose of doing good among them.
This change was effected mostly by visiting and calling among the
people which the winds and cold of the winter had prevented me
from doing as much as I usually do in a strange field of labor. At the
close of my second term I got up an examination [recital], which delighted the children, and had I remained I had assurances of a large
school for the summer.

Then I concluded to stay if Mr. Be. would release me. But a
couple of teachers whom he expected from the East (Miss Mary
Condit and her sister from Oswego, N.Y.) had been prevented by unexpected providences from coming on, and he urged the necessity of
my coming immediately. Then I picked up again and started. O, I
wish you could see the country in the vicinity of F. Des M. and about
Pella. I never saw as beautiful and so every one says that travels over
it. Nothing in the eastern part of Iowa, that I have seen, can compare
with it. The town I left is improving rapidly. Strangers are coming in
every day, and we passed swarms of emigrant wagons going on—
21st.

Now I must tell you about this place. Fairfield is one third the
distance from Keokuk to F. Des Moines, consequently you perceive
that I have come east more than 100 miles. It is the largest inland
town in the state at present, I think, and is said to be very healthy.
Probably by coming here for the summer I shall escape the chills
[flu] which are unavoidable on all the river towns. Rev. Mr. Bell is a
man of about 60 and has two daughters at home who with their
mother superintend the household matters. The schoolroom is in the
same buildings, and there are accommodations for about 24 young
ladies as boarding pupils.

At present there are but six boarding scholars; the session has just commenced, and more are expected, tho' the number will not be so great as in the winter, while the number of day scholars is much greater. I have the sole management of about 25 young ladies during school hours, and act the matron and lawgiver to our boarders!! What strange leaps I have ever made thro' life. Think of my hencoop schoolhouse at Fair Haven and my transit thence into the Academy. This change is even greater from such a—to this pleasant and convenient location.

The teacher Miss Wier is a western girl. She is about 30 and an excellent person. She rooms with me. The total number of the school is about 50. Each session consists of 21 weeks. I told the people at the Fort who were so unwilling to let me come away, that probably I should return there in the fall, but I shall not promise anything definite to anybody. I barely cleared my expenses there, and had just enough to take me comfortably thro' to Fairfield. There I have given six months instruction gratis. If they, or the Board require more, they must wait till I have earned enough here to repair my clothes etc., and have a few cents, at least, to resort to in case of sickness. Do you think it is wrong? and ought I to have staid there thro' all the trials? ...

Oh I have grown weary of writing letters, and tired of everything. I never was so completely low in spirits in my life as I have been for sometime past. And I have striven to appear cheerful till it almost seems a vain effort. And I cannot comprehend how you can always feel so happy. Do write me something cheerful, for I scarcely care whether I live or die. I am not homesick, neither are my feelings the result of imaginary griefs. If I ever see you again perhaps I will tell you just the truth. Till I came west I never knew much of trouble, but I like it here, and probably shall live and die here. The weather has been so dreadful for two or three weeks, that it was sufficient to cloud any one's brow. It has rained every day and there have been several long heavy tempests of lightning, thunder, hail, etc. I never knew so much thunder in the Spring before.

But I will not complain, I ought not, for only think what a comfortable little room I have, so nice and cosey [sic], with a little stove, a little bookcase for my big dictionary and its minor companions, and place for my Accordion on top with room for a vase of wild flowers. There they are blooming now—the bright, painted cup and wild phlox so sweet and modest. Then we have a little wardrobe— Oh hush! little fingers tapping at the door. Come in! And here is a large, beautiful bouquet of sweet williams and a variety of flowers I never saw before sent up by one of my young ladies. I could not live without flowers I believe.

Now it is schooltime and I must wait till noon to finish. —Noon has come and gone, and I have just dismissed school for the night. But I find myself nearly sick abed. A cold, which I felt first last night, has been increasing all day, and now I can scarcely speak above a whisper but I am delighted with my school. The young ladies were all so orderly and behaved so well that it will be nothing but a recreation to teach them, that is, if they continue so. I believe there are some pleasant spots in life after all; don't you?

Zina

NOTES

1. For a discussion of this organization, see Polly Welts Kaufman, *Women Teachers on the Frontier* (New Haven, Conn.: Yale University Press, 1984).
2. Arozina Perkins, "Letters of a Pioneer Teacher," *The Annals of Iowa* 35 (Spring 1961): 616–620. An account of a teacher's post–Civil War letters can be found in Alice Money Lawrence, "A Pioneer School Teacher in Central Iowa," *Iowa Journal of History and Politics* 33 (October 1935): 376–395.

RECOLLECTIONS OF A PIONEER TEACHER OF HAMILTON COUNTY
Agnes Briggs Olmstead

AGNES BRIGGS presented another view of teaching, this one after the Civil War. She first came to Hamilton County, Iowa, with her parents, Ulysses and Ellen Briggs, in 1856. Originally from Pittsburgh, Pennsylvania, the family had already tried Jackson and Dubuque counties. In Hamilton County, the Brigg's settled first in Cass Township, where Agnes attended a log schoolhouse with puncheon floors and a shake roof. In 1866, the Briggs's relocated to Boone Township where they built their permanent home near Briggs Woods.

In 1867 Agnes, at nineteen years of age, began teaching in a modern, white, frame structure in Boone Township. She taught for nearly twenty years—until she married attorney George C. Olmstead on October 22, 1885. Agnes continued to read and study, however, and amassed a fine private library. She prepared her recollections in 1902 or 1903. They are filled with references to two of her great loves—the classics and nature. Still, despite her tributes to nature, one finds it hard to envy her commute, especially during the Iowa winter.

On October 17, 1911, Agnes Briggs Olmstead died at the Briggs family home at the age of sixty-three. Her recollections first appeared in *The Annals of Iowa* in 1946 and are reprinted here with the permission of the State Historical Society of Iowa.[1]

IT was a lovely morning in early May, 1867, when, leaving my woodland home on the banks of the Boone, I set out on the long walk that was the beginning of a new era in my life. Hitherto I had been as a child to be taught and led; now I was to assume the responsibility of teacher and guide to others. I had no forebodings of failure nor bright visions of success. I simply planned to do with my whole might the duty that lay nearest my hand. Before me lay a broad stretch of undulating prairie, seared and blackened by the fires that had swept over it. I might almost speak of it as a trackless waste, as for the greater part of the way, there was no wagon track nor even a footpath until one was worn by my own feet.

At this time there was not one enclosed farm on the south side of my road, though there were two on the north. Seven prairie creeks intersected my path and as many times were my "hosen and shoon" removed to wade across them. They were usually from one to two feet in depth, and if I remember rightly, there was no time during that summer when any of them were low enough to cross dry-shod. Once or twice however after heavy rains I have unexpectedly plunged in chin-deep. There was no current, however, so I was in no danger of drowning.

I was to teach what was known as the Hunt school,[2] five miles east from my home, and here I arrived about half past eight, thoroughly tired out with my toilsome walk. The school house was one of the neatest, littlest structures in which I have ever been privileged to teach—"perfect and entire and clean" inside and out. Three pupils, daughters of the school director [John Hunt], awaited me. They proved to be the most docile and willing of pupils, and during the two years that I remained there, I cannot recall that they ever gave me a moment's pain or annoyance.

The settlement appeared to consist of two families. At least, there were just two dwellings that I could see as I took a survey of my surroundings. At one of these places I was to board and about six o'clock I slowly wended my way in that direction.

The house was a low, weather-beaten structure consisting of a front-room and a back-kitchen. Each of the two rooms was occupied by a separate family. I boarded with the front-room family which comprised an old man and his wife, a small son and a hired girl. I was to stay with them four days out of each week and pay them three dollars, with twenty-five cents less if I drank neither tea nor coffee. As this was but a little more than half of my salary, I considered the price reasonable and so the bargain was settled. Our bill of fare, embracing just five articles, was made out according to the laws of the Medes and Persians, which altereth not.

I did not object to this but there were "some of the customs o' the family" that I did object to most decidedly and after sixteen days of trying to adjust myself to the living conditions of the household, I finally came to myself and said: "I will go to my father's house." And so, for the remainder of the time I walked the five miles back and forth between my home and the school daily.

I was often very, very tired and at times my feet almost refused to bear me further and wading creeks grew monotonous. In the moist places the grass grew so tall [especially the prairie blue stem] that the bending tops met over my head, shutting out the sunlight. The hard rough leaves at the base of the stems would cut into my bare limbs, until I could not place a finger-tip from knee to toe, where the blood had not started. I used to feel sorry for myself as I watched the crimson drops slowly trickling down and perhaps cry a little.

And yet I would rather have paid the price it cost me than be deprived of the memory of those long walks. The real delight and satisfaction in them will be to me a joy forever.

Not the least of my pleasure was the sense of boundless freedom, of being no longer shut in. Here was elbow room, breathing space; above, the vast blue canopy of heaven; beneath, a deep gulf of billow verdure, and the great glad sun pouring its radiance over all and everything so clean, so pure, so fresh.

Many a time, as a I walked in the early morning, I watched the darkness dissolve into dawn while the stars, like weary watchers, drowsily closed their eyes. I have seen the sun rise from a cloudy bed of amethyst and gold; noted the changing landscape as it was gradually revealed in the growing light. Many a glorious sunset have I seen and how often caught the first shy glance of the evening-star. I have traced many a meteor along its fiery pathway, until it seemed to fall to earth shattered into a thousand burning fragments. I have even seen the whole Aurora Borealis drape the whole sky from zenith to horizon, with fold on fold of soft, shimmering curtains of rose and gold.

I kept a calendar for bud and flower and leaf, until they seemed to come and go as I announced the days. Morning after morning, ever with the same delight, I have listened to the matins of the meadow-lark as he celebrated earth's glory. In the evening I have waited to hear the bobolink chant his vespers and then when all the birds together sang their song of jubilee, I was present.

But birds were not my only companions. Occasionally I would see a fox trotting along. Sometimes a solitary wolf would suddenly emerge from the tall grass near my path and, after eyeing me for a moment, beat a hasty retreat with a look of intense disgust on his face. In the early winter, when more than half of my daily journey was made in the dark, I could hear the wolves barking raggedly and howling like demons as they ranged the desolate prairies, as if pandemonium were let loose.

Snakes were most abundant, principally the harmless varieties. Hurrying along one evening, I suddenly came upon the enormous body of one lying squarely across my path. Though I passed cautiously along until about five feet of his snakeship had passed under review, he never moved. As I had not the faintest idea where either extremity might be located, I made a circuit of a quarter of a mile in order to avoid disturbing him.

Another time I came a little nearer meeting with a dangerous adventure. It was on the evening of an intensely warm day in July. I had walked about two miles, was hungry, thirsty, and numb with weariness. Hardly conscious of what I was doing, I dropped down by the roadside to rest a minute. In a moment my head had dropped forward and I was asleep. I must have slept an hour when I awoke with a start. Quickly gathering myself together, I started to descend the little slope bordering a creek, when I noticed a swaying of the tall grass on my right. "There's a snake there if I am not mistaken," I thought, "and from the motion of the grass, he must be immense, and well worth seeing. I think I'll find out." Cautiously I pushed aside the grass, and there facing me, with very few feet of space between us, was the handsomest reptile I have ever seen—a lovely azure blue, with large calm eyes of black and gold that betrayed neither alarm nor hostility as they met mine. Some three feet of his graceful length emerged from the dense growth and lay half reclining on the recumbent stalks of grass. His head was raised about two feet from the ground. He was so perfectly beautiful I could not take my eyes away. Suddenly he made a spring. The shock was terrible, but, quick as he was, I was quicker and with one great leap I cleared the slope and fairly flew over the next half mile. I had heard of blue racers before but had never seen one. And I had no mind to try the tender embraces of this one.

The oddest part of the adventure was yet to come. Twilight was deepening into dusk and I was nearing home when my sister, Thirza, unexpectedly appeared in my path. "O," she cried, "what has been the matter with you? What trouble have you met with?"

"None at all," I replied, "I've had no trouble."

"Then why did you call?" she asked.

"I didn't call, and everything has been remarkably still. I've scarcely heard a sound but the chirp of a grasshopper."

"But you did call. We all heard you. Three times the call came, distinct and clear. It was your voice and you spoke my name as no one outside the family ever speaks it." We never knew who called that night, but I have a vague impression that my curiosity came near costing me dear—but that snake was a handsome fellow.

Another evening I came across an enormous geometric spider. I never saw a finer specimen. The body as nearly could measure it with my eye, was two and a half inches in length, while the legs had a span of eight inches more. The cephalo-thorax was a vivid yellow, bright as the petal of a buttercup; the abdomen was striped alternate velvety bands of jet black and snow white. She was balanced in the center of a magnificent web some four feet square attached to two tall stalks of compass plant or gum weed. As I stood watching, a heedless katydid landed in the lower edge of the snare. Like a flash the spider swooped down upon her helpless victim, and in a moment it was so firmly bound, wing and foot, that further struggle was impossible. When I returned on Monday morning both queen spider and palace had alike disappeared.

But all the time I was growing familiar with these wild creatures, I was making human acquaintances as well. Among the earliest and truest of these were the members of the Hunt family. As Mr. Hunt was the director and for a time, the daughters, my only pupils, I was soon on friendly footing with them all. Thus early began a friendship, which, for thirty years, has continued without change. They were unique. Each was a strong and decided character, reminding me in many ways of the old New England Puritans. Husband and wife were one in struggle and aspiration, one in sympathy and burden bearing, and the daughters accorded them a trustful and loyal devotion, beautiful to see.

If ever a man was fashioned to pioneer a forlorn hope, or live wholly within his own resources, that was John Hunt. Firm of purpose, energetic and persevering and possessed of remarkable mechanical ingenuity, he was a whole colony of mechanics and trades people within himself. Few indeed were the needs of the average pioneer family which his industry and skill could not supply.

Their own farm produced the flax which, woven in their own loom, furnished table linen, bedding, towelling, and underwear. Wool used for winter clothing was raised, spun and woven in the home. If shoes were needed, Mr. Hunt would don his leather apron and shape a shoe but little inferior in appearance to a factory made article and far superior in durability.

A small blacksmith shop stood near the house where he repaired machinery and shod horses. He was an excellent carpenter, and no man could do better cabinet work. In short, if there was any branch of mechanical labor in which he did not excel, I failed to discover it; while Mrs. Hunt was as skillful and thorough in her departments as he was in his.

Huldah, the eldest daughter, was a most exemplary girl; the pride and comfort of her father, the stay and support of her mother, the guide of her younger sisters, a faithful friend and a model pupil. At the end of my two years of work here she took charge of the school, when I accepted a position a little nearer home. For two years she did the work of a faithful teacher. Then, just four years from the day on which we first entered upon the mutual relations of teacher and pupil—"God's hand beckoned unawares. And the sweet, white brow was all of her."

Happily the family circle was not again broken in upon by death until twenty years later, when the father was called. Jessie, the second daughter, prepared herself for a teacher, but precarious health compelled her to resign this work. Doretha, the youngest, has for many years been one of Hamilton county's most successful and efficient teachers. The little mother, now in her eighty-third year, is calmly waiting a joyful reunion with the husband of her youth.

Immediately after the close of the fall term in the Hunt district, I began teaching the winter term of the home school, now known as the Woodleaf school [on the Kamrar Road]. I remember this as a particularly disagreeable winter. The weather was severe, the schoolhouse indescribably forlorn and dilapidated. The desks were in all stages of demoralization. The dictionary had been used for a billiard ball until it was a handful of shreds and patches. The few scattered bits of plaster, which still adhered to the wall, furnished small protection from the keen northwest winds that played hide and seek through a thousand crevices. The snow drifted in through the roof. The outside walls were guiltless of paint. Here and there one wing of a shutter flapped back and forth groaning and creaking most dismally. We used to sit around the stove to study or recite, one division making way for another as we alternately scorched or froze. It was the pursuit of knowledge under difficulties but we made the time count for all that.

In this school six families were represented by twenty-three pupils. With the exception of Biernatzki brothers William, Henry, and Albert, and my own brothers, Charles, Ulysses and Frank, I have lost trace of them. Albert Biernatzki, as bonnie a brown-eyed laddie as ever blessed a mother's heart and home, was first inured to alphabetic toils, while his brothers had already attained to the dignity of the third reader and a primary arithmetic. William is now in business in Webster City; Henry died in 1893 and Albert is now Judge Biernatzki of Salem, South Dakota.

The next spring (1868) I returned to the Hunt school. New settlers had increased the number of pupils to seventeen. The road was less rough and wild than the year before, and ere the summer had passed, four of the seven creeks had well nigh disappeared.

November 9th found me again at my post ready to commence the winter term. The first week I got along pretty well, but by Tuesday of the second week, the first blizzard of the season was on— snow, frost and wind, each contending for the mastery. I started for school half an hour before daylight. Brother Ulysses with a lantern went along to help me over the nearest creek, which we crossed on stepping-stones. But my feet slipped on an icy boulder and I fell through the ice, filling my shoes with water. There was no time to go back so I struggled on through the storm over that long, weary five miles. When I reached the schoolhouse I found no one there. Even those living nearest had been unable to face the storm. I went on to Mr. Hunt's, where as ever I found welcome and good cheer. My courage had all oozed out of my frozen finger tips and for the remainder of the winter, I stayed with this kindly family.

When school closed on January 9th (1869), the snow lay heavy and deep through all the surrounding country. On the last day my brother Stephen and one of the neighbor boys came to visit the school. My brother strongly opposed my going home that night so we concluded to wait until the next morning, leaving there about nine o'clock. What a getting home it was! Hannibal crossing the Alps was a mere circumstance in comparison. At least three miles of the way lay through trackless snow that might be anywhere from two to six feet deep. An incipient January thaw had honeycombed the mass just sufficiently to let us sink through at every step. I am not quite positive as to what experiences befell my two companions in tribulation, for we were seldom within hailing distance of each other. Where the snow was not more than two feet in depth I tried to walk; when deeper I could make more progress by creeping on my hands and knees. When neither way would do, I drew my garments close about me, holding them fast with my hands and feet, then rolled over the ground like "Slow-solid and Stickly-prickly" after their metamorphosis. When we reached home, a little after two, we were as wet as they after they had "soaked all night in the turbid Amazon."

That summer (1869) I took charge of the Pleasant Hill school, about four miles south of my home. We had some sunshine that summer, but every day we had rain sometime during the twenty-four hours. Happily my previously formed aquatic habits had made me proof against such trifles and I bore my frequent duckings and drenchings with commendable philosophy.

One lovely evening in June—we had had our morning shower—a party of young people insisted on my joining them for a walk over to the Sternberg Mills. Our road lay through deep woods, and the rank foliage produced by the abundant rains was massed everywhere in almost tropical profusion. Bright flowers gave a touch of color and from green depths came a trill of some belated bird, and over all the glory of the waning day. The old mills were nestled down among the hills in one of the most picturesque localities along the Boone. Some of the workmen were still there and piloted by them, we explored every nook and corner of the place.

The miller, John Ross, whom the early settlers of Hamilton county remember well, was especially courteous and painstaking. Our researches ended, we stopped to rest on a great nearby log which made a convenient seat. The river, dark, deep and silent as the tide of eternity, lay at our feet, and above lay,

> The last high upward slant of sun upon the trees
> Like a dead soldier's sword upon his pall.

We chatted a while of old times and when I rose to go, Mr. Ross said, "You must be sure to come to see us some day. At least you might come when you can't find any other place to go." "I shall come," I answered, whether I can find another place to go or not." Little more than a week later as I was on my way to school, I met a messenger with the tidings, "John Ross was murdered last night." How strange and awful it seemed! I kept my promise and went to see him; but the closed eyes gave me no look of recognition, and the poor discolored face no smile of welcome.

The winter of 1870–1871, I received a very pressing invitation to preside over the Randall school [the Sheldahl school in Scott Township], at the then extravagant salary of thirty-five dollars per month. Such a temptation was not to be resisted, though the school was more than twenty miles from home. Here I had fifty pupils of all ages from four to forty-five; several men recently from the old country having come to learn English. During this term I boarded with Mrs. Rasmus Sheldahl, a daughter of Lars Henryson, who was for many years a member of the Hamilton county board of supervisors. Modern luxuries were not much in evidence here, but the people were very kind and did their best for me and that was good enough.

I had been teaching seven weeks when the director informed me that the school would expect at least a three days' vacation for the Christmas holidays, to which they were looking forward with eager anticipation. I could not refuse, though as a rule, I object to holidays. This one happily would give me the wished for opportunity of spending Christmas under the home roof-tree. Though how to get there— it would be easy enough now—but that was long before the shriek of the whistle echoed across the fields and the rushing train roared by. The weather was severe and the snow deep; I could not ask anyone else to make such a trip. I had never before attempted so long a walk but felt certain I could manage it.

Friday evening came clear and cold. I left the school house unusually early for me but the twenty-third of December is not a long day, and the sun was already sinking into a cloud sea of gold and amethyst when I started across the fields, thinking to reach Lakin's Grove, spend the night with Mrs. John Cooper and then go on in the morning.

It was a difficult matter to make much speed through that trackless waste of snow. The scene grew graver. The somber night shadows settled over all and before I had gone a mile I knew I was lost. Hungry and tired I realized I must give up my plan of reaching Mrs. Cooper's that night and content myself with trying to find the nearest place of shelter. I plodded along watching eagerly—as the lost traveller always does—for a light in some window. At last I saw a faint glimmer through the trees and with nervous haste pressed on towards it. I found that it proceeded from the tiny window of a tiny cottage in the woods. I rapped at the door; nobody came and I rapped again; still no response. I drew off my glove in order to emphasize the raps with unpadded knuckles. Inside an Indian "ghost dance" or something equally exciting and vociferous seemed to be in progress, but I hoped that in course of time some one would hear the outside disturbance. I peeped through the little window to see what my chances were. The house had one small, unfinished room and the only visible furniture was a small, rough table on which stood the light that had attracted me—a bit of rag in a dish of grease. The place swarmed with children, eight or ten, as nearly as I could count, for they were all engaged in the wildest, maddest revel that untamed child nature is capable of. By and by a man came with a pail of milk in his hand. To him I stated my case and asked to be directed to Ambion Anderson's. With much difficulty I gathered an idea of the direction I must take and reached the place without further mishap. Their kindness, as always, was unfailing and I was warmed and fed to my heart's content.

Morning dawned clear, cold and still and by sunrise I was again on my way. A keen northwest wind was blowing and it was nearly noon when famished and chilled I reached Lakin's Grove with seven miles of my journey accomplished. I felt very reluctant about stopping, though I was acquainted with several families here. However, I feared my feet were freezing cold, so by the time I had reached the last house in the grove I dared not go by without stopping to thaw out. I was not unacquainted with the lady of the house, having often met her at church, where she had as often urged me to call. I was certain it would be no intrusion to do so now. In response to my timid rap she came to the door. I explained how I happened to be there and asked permission to come in and get warm. It was grudgingly given and on entering I drew up a chair to the stove and tried to warm my poor chilled feet. She had just taken a large pan of bread out of the oven; a big kettle of "that delicious American beverage known as porkinbeans" simmered on the back of the stove; and a pan of dried apples was bubbling on the front. True, these things were not dainties, but how good that food smelled. Like Esau, I was faint, and would have sold my birthright for a mess of pottage, but none was offered. I suppose the woman resented my interfering with her dinner hour. So in a few moments I took my departure relieved to find myself outside her door again. The bitter northwest wind was warm compared with her charity.

Eight miles of snow-covered prairie lay between me and the next house, which was Mr. Darrin's, but I pressed forward with that pitiless blast cutting my face and beating me back at every step. What a weary way it was! My feet moved like lead, but I reached the place at last. Miss Ella, the dark-eyed daughter of the house, met me at the door and seizing my arm, she whisked me in without ceremony and in an instant she and her mother had my wrappings off. I was placed in an arm chair by the stove and kind-hearted, motherly Mrs. Darrin tried to fit my feet into the oven by the side of a brown turkey that lay there comfortably sizzling. In vain I protested that I could stay only long enough to thaw out for it was late and I was far from home. Mr. Darrin gave me most positive assurance that I could not cross his threshold again until I had had my dinner. I shall not try to tell how good that dinner was. People who were never hungry could not be made to understand. I do not recall meeting Mr. Darrin's people again, as they removed to another county shortly after that. But, in grateful remembrance, I number them with the guests which I have with me always.

Another hour of precious daylight had faded and it was four o'clock again when I set forth on my pilgrimage. In the meantime the weather had changed. The sky was overcast and a storm seemed imminent. The snow was falling thick and fast before I reached the place where I must turn out of the highway into the old path that I had so often traversed during my first two years of work but the track was quite obliterated. Darkness came on apace, no landmarks were visible. Still undismayed I plodded on, thinking I could not lose my way on such familiar ground. I even remembered singing in the storm:

> Haste, traveler, haste! the night comes on,
> And thou art far from home and rest;
> The storm is gathering in the west
> And thou art far from home and rest;
> Haste, traveler, haste.

Another hour of weary wandering, when just as I had decided that I was rapidly reaching nowhere, I once more caught the glimmer of one of those ever-welcome lights in the window. I was sure it was Mr. Bauer's. I knew the place well and once reaching it, I could easily make my way home from there. On nearing the house I was surprised to find that it had an entirely unfamiliar look, and a closer survey satisfied me that I had never seen it before. I dreaded losing more time but felt compelled to stop and enquire "where I was at." I was most happily surprised when the face of an old friend appeared in the doorway—one whom I had often met though I had never visited her. It was the home of Mr. and Mrs. Samuel McComb, two of our courageous, enterprising pioneers.

All the while I had thought myself going north, good angels were guiding me south. Mrs. McComb would not wait for a word of explanation until she had drawn me into the house and removed my snow-covered wrappings. In spite of my remonstrances she insisted on preparing me a lunch. What a delicious little tea it was. Pioneer she might be but no table could be more dainty than hers. Mrs. Mc-Comb was a thoroughly womanly woman and a genuine homemaker. Given a drygoods box, a bit of cheesecloth and a paper of tacks and she would furnish you a home so cozy and comfortable that you would have no desire to exchange it for any other in the world. Lunch disposed of, like poor little Joe, I realized that I "must be movin' on," and prepared to do so, but they firmly insisted on my remaining with them that night. But I was reluctant to trespass further on their hospitality, especially when I was so near home. So I would not consent to stay.

At this crisis an idea dawned on Mr. McComb and he pleaded on his own behalf—"Wouldn't I stay and read a novel to him? I was such a beautiful reader and he so loved to hear me." Of course if I felt that I could favor them I would stay. But I have long suspected that the reading was a cunningly devised plot to keep me in out of the darkness and the storm.

It was well for me that I stayed for even in the bright light of the next day it took me nearly three hours to reach home, which was little more than two miles distant. The face of the country was so changed I could not recognize it. The broad tract of land that three years before had been open prairie was now enclosed in cultivated farms. Everything was strange and I well knew that had they permitted me to venture forth that night, I must either have wandered through the fields until morning or perished in the storm. Life's fitful fever is over for these two friends of mine, but the memory of their generous, thoughtful kindness deepens as the years pass by. As I think of them like a whisper comes the prayer for departed souls—

> Eternal rest grant unto them, O God
> And may light perpetual shine upon them.

The early spring of 1871 found me plying my vocation at Rose Grove. This place will be remembered by the pioneer settlers of Hamilton county as one of the divisions of the old stage line between Webster City and Marshalltown. Even at this day there are not lacking those who recall the time when as travellers they stayed their weary feet at the hospitable doors of the old wayside inn nestled among the trees. ...

We were a busy family with little leisure and less inclination to seek recreation in accustomed ways or by conventional methods. Still we had our times of relaxation for whenever a brother came with the imperative behest—"Girls, girls! come quick! we've made another discovery!"—no matter how opportune or inopportune the time, away we all went to see the wonderful thing that had come to pass. And we were never disappointed. There was always something well worth seeing—some new species of plant or flower; or some remarkable development of animal or vegetable life; a strange bird or a peculiar fossil from the stone quarries. Nothing new or strange ever escaped their notice.

Our eldest brother, Stephen, was gifted with a marvelous insight into Mother Nature's mysteries. I had a curious impression that in some weird fashion, he walked and talked with her as friend with friend. He knew the favorite haunts of every species of native bird or plant. He seldom failed to find the earliest of its kind and always, those first shy blossoms were gathered in the early morning into a tiny dew-gemmed cluster for one of his sisters. Sometimes he brought us flowers of peculiar varieties. I remember one cluster that resembled lilies of the valley and another time a bouquet of immense pink and white lady-slippers. Not only were we (his sisters) initiated into the mysteries of bird and insect housekeeping but the haunts of fishes and reptiles came in for a large share of our wondering admiration. We came and went as silently as the spirit of the woods without the timid creatures having been as much as aware of our presence.

Through this home woods I passed each morning and evening during the time that I was teaching twenty terms of school. Just beyond the southern limit stood the little schoolhouse (now rebuilt) whither the precious mother sent her whole nest of overgrown broodlings during the winter of 1879–80. It was our last winter all together and was perhaps the happiest of our lives.

NOTES

1. Agnes Briggs Olmstead, "Recollections of a Pioneer Teacher of Hamilton County," *The Annals of Iowa* 28 (October 1946): 93–115.
2. The Hunt school lay on the prairie about five miles east and a little south of the Briggs home. John Hunt, the school director and recorder of Hamilton County, lived across and down the road about one-half mile.

EARLY DAYS IN
CLAYTON COUNTY
Amelia Murdock Wing

D URING the closing decades of the nineteenth century, women increasingly combined their domestic roles with public ones. Amelia Murdock's descriptions of her early life demonstrated this duality. She remembered numerous women with admiration for their housewifery and mothering skills, but also for the intellectual abilities and "strong-mindedness." She particularly admired her sister Marion, who became a Unitarian minister with a pastorate in Humboldt.

Amelia herself spent many years as a talented teacher, even working at Jane Addams's Hull House in Chicago. She also mentioned other women teachers, a journalist, a station-agent, and a medical doctor. She did not point to these women as exceptions; rather, they ran through her narrative as commonplace.

Like many other writers in this collection, Amelia gave a sense of the difficulty and extent of women's work, yet she also revealed a life of the mind. She remembered the presence in her home of discussion, speeches, literature, and music. In addition, contrary to popular myth, she observed that women often loved the outdoors. Nor did they meekly accept social restrictions, gender expectations, and current fashions. Instead, they fought back and expressed themselves.

Amelia Murdock was born in May, 1852, the third child of Judge Samuel Murdock and Louisa Patch Murdock of Garnavillo, Clayton County, Iowa. As a young man Amelia's father, Samuel Murdock, had migrated from Ohio to Iowa City, the territorial capital, after Iowa separated from Wisconsin territory. There he continued to study law and, with a young physician named Dr. Andros, walked north to find available government-owned farmland.

At a Fourth of July celebration Samuel Murdock met Louisa Patch from McGregor, Iowa. The couple married on September 11, 1845, and Samuel took Louisa to the log cabin he had built for her on his homestead, about one and a half miles from Garnavillo.

It was here that Amelia, as well as three other girls and a boy, were born. Because their father became a judge and landowner, the Murdock children enjoyed more advantages and a higher social class status than the average pioneer.

Between 1942 and 1944, Amelia Murdock Wing, then of Santa Monica, California, dictated her story. She noted that, "When one has reached the age of ninety-two, however clear her pictures of the past may be, she meets extreme difficulties in getting them put into words and transferred to paper. As I am unable to hold a pen and, further, have poor eyesight, I must depend upon dictation." She feared her narrative would seem disconnected as a result, but in fact, she related her memories with care and continuity.

Amelia's memoir first appeared in *The Annals of Iowa* in 1946. A slightly abridged version appears here with the permission of the State Historical Society of Iowa.[1]

AS the years went by, my father improved the farm with evergreen trees which he dug from the timber in great number and planted about his home. The farm became known as "Evergreen Farm." Although my father later had his law office for a time in McGregor, the town from which my mother came, and where Mr. Stoneman was his partner, he looked on the farm as his home until 1876. He was much interested in the cultivation of this place and planted many rare trees and shrubs. Among the native growth were Tamarack, the American black larch, and the sumac which the Indians used as tobacco and which they called kinnikinic. ...

John Murphy, who lived close to Jimmy Ryan, worked faithfully for my father and was such a friendly soul that he endeared himself to our family. He was especially kind to us children, ever ready to harness the horses or do anything that we desired. Once after my sister, Marion, became an Unitarian minister, she was invited to fill the pulpit in a little town in Minnesota. As she stood there speaking, she suddenly spied an elderly man sitting in the congregation gazing up at her. Although she had not seen him since she was a child, she recognized him as John Murphy. She was so overcome at the thoughts that because of their old friendship he, a strong Catholic, had come to a Protestant church to listen to a woman and an Unitarian, that she could scarcely go on with her speaking. Her meeting with him after was quite affecting.

Down in the timber back of Evergreen farm was the pretty little home of Dennis McCarthy, a charming bit of cultivation, the garden gay with beautiful flowers raised by the mother of the family. Although I did not know Mrs. McCarthy, I was convinced that she was a devoted home-maker, whenever I saw her two little girls playing about the garden, dressed so neatly, or when they started off to school, dressed as if for church with starched frocks so immaculate and crisp.

One of our neighbors whom I remember particularly on account of her extreme industry was Mrs. Derby, who lived on a farm belonging to my father, situated across the road east from Evergreen farm. The house was a half or three-quarters of a mile from ours. Mrs. Derby was a tall, slim woman, always neatly dressed in a freshly-ironed calico. When she would come to spend an afternoon visiting us, which she frequently did because she was lonely on the farm, she knitted all the way over and all the way back and also every minute of time she was there. She was adverse to losing a minute of valuable time. I believe it was socks for the soldiers that she was knitting.

Further back in the deep timber, lived the Vedo family. Although they were in a most attractive spot on Cedar creek, they were far distant from neighbors as well as from town. But, if one felt sympathy for them as being so isolated, he need only recall that they had eighteen children. (People had families in those days!) At one time they all had the small-pox and four of them died of it. The children never went to school. No compulsory education law to touch them!
...

On the east of town lived Mr. Ben Schroeder with his large family. One daughter, Lucy, married one of the interesting Beckman boys. Her sister, Mahala, always lived with her, as they were devoted to one another. They were buried on the same day, having passed on in the prime of life. The Beckman boy was one of three brothers, whose mother was one of the most industrious housewives and devoted mothers in the vicinity. As the boys would trudge along to the German school, they were always dressed so immaculately that one would think that it was Sunday school instead of day school to which they were going. ...

About a mile north of town, Ben Fox and his wife with their large family settled on a large farm. Mrs. Fox was greatly admired for her literary ability, consequently was an agreeable neighbor of the Porters. At times she wrote for the county papers. ...

Let us turn our attention within the town of Garnavillo. In the early days, the two-story schoolhouse had but two grades, one on the first and one on the second floor. These accommodated all the pupils. There is one teacher I remember very vividly—a Miss Sarah Prince—for there seemed to be some mystery about her. Although the pupils were more or less fond of her, we felt this mystery. She left Garnavillo, and some years afterward some girls from the town were in Dubuque. They went to consult a fortune teller. Although she was partially disguised, they recognized Miss Prince. We never heard of her again.

There was no high school in Garnavillo. Students who wished to continue their education beyond the lower grades attended the private school of Prof. Jonathan Briggs. This rather eccentric bachelor was a deep thinker, high respected, and highly educated. The school he built also contained his own living quarters, which we young people called "Bachelor's Hall." No one—not even his most intimate friends—was admitted to these living quarters. Since Prof. Briggs and my father were both interested in scientific and historical subjects, they were fast friends and he was a frequent visitor at our home. He was a very timid man and did not like to meet strangers. He would come in without knocking and, if he saw none of the family, he would just sit down and begin to read; but if he heard company in the parlor, he would immediately leave without speaking to any of us. Once I saw him in the dining room and started in to greet him, but he had become startled and went running out of the back door, through the barnyard, and down into the timber. He usually dropped in just about the right time to get a good dinner, but never remained if there were others there.

One of my recollections of student days with him was the clever tricks the pupils would play on him if they had not learned their lessons. Some boy would ask him a question on a theme in which he knew the professor was intensely interested, and that would start him to talking; since he then became oblivious of the passage of time, he would consume all the recitation period and the pupils would save themselves from discovery of their illy learned lessons. My sister, Marion, had her first experience in teaching as an assistant of Prof. Briggs. ...

Jessie Brown and I were chums from early childhood. She was a frolicsome girl and always wanting some new adventure. Since we were inseparable and she was at our house a great deal, we had many escapades. As little girls, we rode upon the same horse—our dear old Jennie—and explored the timber thereabout, always seeking for new roads. Jennie seemed almost human as proven by one incident which happened when we were riding on the highway. A load of young men passed, driving from Guttenberg to some place northward. They had been imbibing too freely of intoxicants and so, as they passed us, they gave our horse a quick lash with a whip. I tried to keep my seat by holding to the horse's mane, but I slipped down in front of her legs. Instead of being fractious, our dear Jennie stood perfectly still and tried to caress me with her soft nose.

One day when Jessie was visiting me, she exclaimed, "Let's hitch up and go to town." I replied, "The buggy box is off, so we can't go." She said, "Oh, never mind the box. We can go without that." We did, and whom should we encounter but her uncle, Mr. Crosby! The honorable gentleman was much shocked and said, "You girls go right home. Jessie, I am ashamed of you for riding in that ridiculous looking vehicle!"

My mother was never worried about us girls no matter how long we were gone, for there were no wild animals about and tramps had not yet made their appearance. One day, Jessie and I went for a long walk in the timber to the east of our farm. When we became a little hungry, we ate May-apples which happened to be ripe. We wandered farther and farther and at last became completely confused as to which way we should go to get home. As our hunger increased, we ate more May-apples, until I became so satiated with them that I never wanted to see another afterward. At last, to our amazement, we found ourselves in Garnavillo, a mile and a half from Evergreen farm. We were very tired little girls when we got home.

An example of my father's kindness is that once when some girls came for me to go horseback riding with them, I told them I could not go because the horse, Jennie, was being used in the field. They told my father what they wanted, and he went to the field and told the man who was plowing to let me have the horse, and he could go and do some work in the garden.

Previous to the opening of the new cemetery, which [was] surveyed by Emmett Brown, the only cemetery in Garnavillo was just west of the Lutheran church. Under a large pine tree there, is the plot of the Murdock family, where lie the remains of my father, his parents, three of my sisters, and a brother who died when a baby. So, that spot has ever been sacred to me, one which I always loved to visit. At the time my father passed away at Elkader, January 26, 1897, his remains were taken to Garnavillo for burial. Although it was extremely cold—the thermometer was 20 degrees below zero—a long procession of friends accompanied Marion and me and followed the hearse the distance of ten miles. It was Mr. Crosby who entertained eighteen of us with a fine, hot dinner at the hotel. Such courtesies are appreciated at a time of bereavement. ... Mr. Crosby and father had been pals for many years.

The Lutheran church and its schoolhouse were built before my recollection. Helmuth Brandt, a tall, fine looking man, was teacher of German for many years. Before we ever attended the English school, my sister, Marion, and I were sent by our father to this German school. We had many German neighbors and father was anxious to get us started early in that language. To this day, I can remember the long pointer used by Mr. Brandt when he had us repeat the a-b-ab's in concert. Our walk to school was a mile and a half, but the trip home we made a pleasant one, stopping to play in the corners of the old rail fences.

The Methodist church was the first one in Garnavillo for Americans. My principal recollection of it, in addition to the fact that we attended its Sunday school, is the socials to which our mother used to take us. She was considered an expert in making rice pudding, for plenty of rich cream, many eggs, and plump raisins went into the making. So, she always took a large milk pan of this toothsome dessert.

An outstanding man in Garnavillo was Dr. Linton. He built a large two-story building with his office on the first floor, which served also as the town's drug store. He remained a bachelor until late in life, when he married Mrs. Mary McCraney. This union was of short duration. After his death, Dr. Charles Hamilton occupied the building with his family.

One of the very old buildings was the carpenter shop of old man

Barnes at the east end of town. I shall diverge to say that in those days, elderly people had the appellation "old" or "grandpa" or "grandma" or "grannie" attached to their names. These were sometimes applied even to people who had no children. So, Mr. Barnes was called "old" although he was strong and well and went faithfully to his carpenter shop to work every week day. Further illustrating the use of the word "old," there was the mother of "old lady Weber" to distinguish her from Mr. Weber's wife. Then there was "old lady Rudsell" or "grandma Rudsell," and "old lady Scudder," an English woman who had a flower garden which she was spry enough to keep in beautiful order and which gave us children great delight.

There were reasons for the word "old" seeming applicable in those days. People had teeth pulled and had no artificial ones to replace them, and so cheeks sank in and mouths became wrinkled. Since then, the study of foods from a scientific viewpoint and the discovery of vitamins have helped to keep people young looking though old in years. Then, the older women were expected to dress old and to sit in the chimney corner knitting or making patch-work. Many of them who were so relegated were no older than a great many women of this day, who are constantly active, going to bridge parties, indulging in other amusements, or helping at Red Cross center.

But, to return to Mr. Barnes, he was such a quiet man that, although I was at their home often, I never heard the sound of his voice. He had lost his two oldest sons in the Civil War. His fine wife died early, leaving five daughters and one son. Maria, the oldest of the daughters, married my mother's brother, Wallace Patch. Eugene, the son, married Minnie Maurer. He died young, leaving his wife and two small daughters. After a time, she married Helmuth Brandt, the German teacher. She proved herself a devoted mother to his large family of children.

Jake Maurer, the brother of Minnie Maurer Barnes Brandt, and one of those boys who had got training in the Sunday school class of Mr. Crosby, was head of the public schools at one time and was also postmaster. He was a genial man and beloved by his pupils. He and his wife had three sons and a daughter. The two oldest sons, while yet in school, started a little newspaper which was called the Garnavillo *Sentinel,* and which is still published. They were most studious and both became Congregational ministers. One, Irving, was called to be president of Beloit college, of which school the state of Wisconsin is very proud; and there he remained until his recent demise. The other, Oscar, became pastor of the Congregational church in Hartford, Connecticut, located near Yale college. The third son became a physician and the daughter married a physician.

An interesting incident happened after my sister, Marion, had become an Unitarian minister. Yale college gave the use of its buildings for an Unitarian conference which lasted for a week, and she was one of the speakers. What was her delight to find that the Rev. Oscar Maurer had been one of her interested listeners, and her further delight in being entertained in his home after the meeting. They had not seen each other since Oscar was a lad.

My father used to take great pleasure in discussing scientific subjects with Prof. Briggs, head of the private school, Mr. Crosby, the lawyer, and Dr. Linton. Dr. Linton and my father were greatly interested in research into pre-historic lore. They excavated mounds in Clayton county that had been made by the Mound Builders, and they were successful in assembling the complete skeleton of a man. They found a great many of the Mound Builders' axes, which were considered great trophies. My father sent a quantity of them to a museum in the east.

Another man much interested in these early relics was S. H. Smart, whom I mentioned earlier as superintendent of schools in Clayton county. In his later life he lived in Minnesota, with his daughter, Emma. I was invited to visit his family there, and another guest at the time was Alma Rodgers. One day Mr. Smart said, "Amelia, I want to take you out to see a Mound Builders' mound. I want you to be able to tell your father about it." Accordingly, quite a group of us started to walk out to the spot, which was some distance from town. A part of us loitered behind the rest to look into a deserted, dry well, located on vacant land which we had to cross. Kneeling down, we gazed into the well, and to our horror we saw a mass of writhing rattlesnakes. Needless to say, the wonderful mound was forgotten as we fled through the deep grass back to the road, fearing at every step that we would meet a venomous snake. The other groups went on and paid a placid visit to the mound, knowing nothing about the nearness of the reptiles until we told them later. I never got to describe that mound to my father! . ...

When I summon to my mind all of my old friends in Clayton county, my own life seems to unroll before me like a panorama, starting with my early childhood and continuing until my recent visits with old friends now living in California.

In the days of my early childhood, people did not send their children to school as young as they do now, and the children in the country did not attend school as early as those in town. Our mother taught Ellen, me, and Marion at home until we were old enough to go to town to school.

Mother used to enjoy telling us, later, of these experiences. My older sisters, Ellen and Marion, would stand and spell, and so keen was the competition between them that sometimes one of the girls would cry if she missed a word.

Marion was never inclined to what was known as "Woman's work." Indeed, she preferred weaning the calves and breaking the colts to any kind of housework. One of her particular detestations was sewing, and she decided she simply would not learn to sew. After she started to school, her teacher had a class for sewing and the girls were told to bring some article on which to practice. Mother cut out a garment and had it ready for Marion. She started with it all right, but on the way to school hid the package in a corner of the rail fence. The teacher finally became completely discouraged about teaching her to sew and said, "You may take a book and go over there in the corner and read." Of course, this was no punishment, for nothing could please her more.

Marion was always ready with her tongue. Since we lived a mile and a half from town, we were glad to catch a ride as we went back and forth. One day as Marion, still a little girl, was walking to school, a man gave her a ride. He expressed admiration for a half-mile of beautifully shaped trees along the road. My sister said, "They are my father's trees." He inquired the name of the trees and she replied that they were ash. He then asked what kind of ash, and she answered glibly, "I'm not exactly sure of the name, but I think they are potash." She had an answer!

One of the studies of our early childhood I have said before was German. We had so much help both in the house and in the field, that we began to pick up the language. It was not always words which were fitting for us to use. I well remember once when I was still small enough to sit in a high chair, I was eating a belated breakfast at the dining room table while the German hired girl was ironing at the same table, and she taught me the words of a song. I, of course, did not know why she laughed so much when she heard me say them and had me repeat them for all the German help that came around the house. When I was older I found out that they were vulgar words. I could see a good reason why my father thought it best that we should learn German at Helmuth Brandt's school.

One of the immigrants about our home was a young Austrian who was a "man-of-all-work" for my father. He became very fond of us five little girls, and decided to give us a Merry Christmas at Yuletide. The custom of Christmas trees, which was imported to America from Austria, had not become common at that time. The young man went to the woods, brought back a little evergreen tree, and hid it in the granary so that even our father and mother would not know about it until Christmas. He bought and made various little trinkets with which to decorate it and fastened on candles to light it up. About daybreak, Christmas morning, our parents saw a light that startled them, and when they found what it was, they were as much surprised and delighted as were we children.

Other foreigners that we saw at least yearly were the Hungarian peddlers. They were about the countryside with packs on their backs filled with trinkets, ornaments for dressing, and household utensils. We children got a real thrill when the pack would be opened and we saw all the gay and exotic things.

Something else in the way of personal adornment that my mother got was some real cameos. She bought quite a number of books and with each one came one of these pins. They were very beautiful and some of them are still treasured by relatives to whom they were handed down.

It was not such a delight to see the gypsies come as it was the peddlers, for we were much afraid of them. Their errand was not to sell, but to beg; and because we feared what they might do if we displeased them, we saved every old garment that we no longer wished to wear, hanging it in the attic ready for the day when the gypsies would come.

One of the pleasant pictures of my childhood is patriotic rallies held at the public square in the center of Garnavillo. My mother would dress her five little girls in their freshly laundered frocks and stiff white sunbonnets and would take us to hear the stirring music. To this day at ninety-two, on hearing martial music, my thought reverts always to those happy days. The value of patriotic music to children can hardly be over estimated. Brave soldiers were made of the little boys who listen and keep time to this music and to the beloved old-time songs.

When an epidemic of diphtheria came to do its deadly work and in its course reached Evergreen farm, the five little daughters of Judge and Mrs. Murdock were all stricken at the same time. All recovered except Carry. She was my constant companion and our devotion was intense. One night when she was very low, they left her just long enough to get her a drink. She jumped out of her bed, ran to my bed, and when they came back we were in each other's embrace. They took her arms from about me and carried her back to her room. The next morning, they told me she was gone. At that moment my life seemed blighted; I felt no longer a carefree child.

My mother felt that she could no longer remain on the farm after losing this little girl, who had seemed such a remarkable child for her brief six years. So the family moved to McGregor where my father had his law office—the firm of Murdock and Stoneman. I was about nine years of age and my youngest sister, Laura, was four. My oldest sister, Ellen, joined the Baptist church and we all attended that Sunday school, including Laura. She had such a captivating manner and was so beloved that many gifts had been put on the Christmas tree for her when the school had its annual observance. I can still picture her as she joyfully marched up the aisle to get them. She was concerned lest Amelia would not get so many as she did. She whispered to me, "Never mind, Melie! Your name will soon be called."

Two years were spent by the family in this pleasant town. It was a new experience to live by the Mississippi river and watch the large steamboats go up and down. The town was named for the McGregor family. There were two brothers, James and Alexander, between whom there was a lifetime feud. Although James, at that time, was an old man, he was a much admired figure in the town. Gregor McGregor, Alexander's son, was a rich bachelor and also a striking figure. There were very few amusements to occupy his time, so his favorite sport was driving his spirited horse up and down through the streets of the town. The two principal streets were Main and Ann. Going up the hollows there were some short streets (for this reason the town was called the "pocket city"), where, for the most part, the aristocracy of the town lived.

The Killingers lived near us on Ann street. Rosetta Killinger was a playmate of mine. At one of the Iowa picnics here in California in recent years, I met her and we renewed our acquaintance that had been interrupted about seventy-five years before. Libby Bass was another of my little friends. We afterward chummed together in Chicago when we were both attending Kindergarten college. Georgia Bowers was an intimate of Ellen and Marion. She was the sister of Dr. Bowers. After Georgia lost her sister by death, her brother-in-law wished to marry her, but, although she returned his affection, she refused, for she was a Catholic. She remained unmarried.

One of my constant playmates was Lina Burlingame, who lived next to a large lumber yard. We played house in the rooms made by the piles of lumber. One of our sports was climbing up high on the lumber and then dropping down to the ground. In later years, I obtained a position for Lina in the Elkader public school where she was then teaching. Lina had a sister, Jennie, who passed away suddenly while she was mailing a letter to her parents. She had filed on a homestead in Dakota and was living there. ...

Those two years in McGregor were pleasant ones, but alas, our little Laura became ill with scarlet fever and after long weeks of illness passed away. Needless to say, the family were disconsolate and my father especially seemed broken-hearted. A short time later small pox broke out in the house next to ours. That settled it! The next day we began moving back to the farm. I might say here that our house in McGregor was burned to the ground in a few years after we left there.

My mother was glad to get back to the farm work to help her throw off her grief at losing her little girls. There was plenty of work—the making of butter, cheese, soft soap, candles, and the canning of fruit. My older sisters, Ellen and Marion, were away at school and I was the only child at home, but I too tried to drown my grief for my little sister by occupying myself with the chickens, my dog, Mungo, my horse, Jennie, and my swing under the pine trees. I loved the roses and other flowers and the shrubbery. There were strawberries, raspberries, currants, and other small fruits, and there were two large orchards.

At one time there were sixty-seven varieties of apples in our two orchards. We also had many kinds of grapes, and yearly my father exhibited his apples and grapes at the county fair, which was one of the great gatherings of people in that day. It used to be my duty to take charge of his exhibit. My father developed a new variety of grape from the Delaware and Concord grapes. Once father noticed a bunch of grapes hanging on the trellis, which had the size of the Concords but the color of the Delawares. Now, the Delawares were small and red, and the Concords were large and blue. He took the seeds from this bunch and propagated them and then sent samples of them to various horticulturists, asking what was the name of them. The answer came back each time that no variety of that kind had ever been known. My father was honored by having them named the "Murdock" grapes.

One thing was a great drawback to me when I went among the fruit and flowers, and that was the fact that I was allergic to bees. They would light on me, and I would run wildly and stick my head in the lilac bushes. Father had many hives and we were well supplied with honey which we all loved, including myself. I recall at one time some cousins from Minneapolis were planning a visit to us. In every letter they urged us to have plenty of honey on hand. On the night of their arrival, my mother told father there was no honey in the house. He was always ready to comply with any request made of him, so he took a lantern and went out and got a few cards of honey. He said, "I will bring more in tomorrow." But, alas, some passing thief had spied the lantern light and been attracted to the spot, and when morning came, there was no honey left.

One of the domestic jobs that pleased us children was mother's candle making. Sometimes in an emergency, when she ran out of candles, she would use some molds which made just six at a time; but, once a year she made a large supply. She filled the wash boiler with tallow; then, she put wicks over some little round sticks and dipped them in the hot tallow and hung them in a row above the boiler. By the time the last stick was hung up, the first sticks were cool enough to dip again. Thus the work proceeded until the candles were of the right size. We thought it great fun to help with this work, and then view the result of such a fine supply of candles ready for use.

Making of soft soap was another process we enjoyed. Into an immense iron kettle, which was kept in the back yard, mother put lye, made from ashes, and to this she added waste grease which had been carefully saved for the purpose. This concoction was boiled over a fire in the yard. The soap was put away in kegs.

Cellars, in those days, were storehouses in themselves. A barrel of kraut was made in the fall; chunks of pork were salted down; fruit was canned and kept in long, heavy wooden boxes; many kinds of vegetables could be kept there throughout the winter (canning of vegetables had not yet begun); apples were stored away. The apples that looked perfect we would wrap in pieces of newspaper and pack away. Cared for thus, they would last into July without decaying. In our cellar there was a floor of rock, always cleanly scrubbed. There was a long table for use in handling the milk and butter, and a wooden dash-churn stood beside it. We children used to like to help make the butter and then enjoy the fresh buttermilk. I always wanted to take out some of the butter before it was salted, as this seemed to me a tempting morsel. There was a large cupboard whose tin doors had holes for ventilation, and this was where the milk, cream and butter were kept. No one had ice in those days, but our cellar was cool.

Another one of the labors for the adults and joys for the children in those days was the making of maple sugar. We had some friends who had a maple sugar camp and used to invite us to come when the "sugaring-off" was going on. I recall them saying once when we arrived, "Now, you children may help yourselves and eat all the syrup and sugar you want." They were safe in saying this, for they knew we would soon get satiated. I, like the other children, soon had to stop, but afterward I could not help wishing I had eaten just a little bit more, for it seemed to me that the sugar at the camp was someway so much better than the syrup and the sugar we had at home.

But life was not all work, even for mother. She used to take us children down to Cedar creek about a mile in the woods back of Evergreen farm, and there we would enjoy wading in the pretty, rocky stream. Marion, being a born orator, would run up onto the bluff and speak pieces to us below. "Barbara Frietchie" was one of her favorites.

Another pastime was to go exploring in the deep woods. In our childhood, no timber had been cut west of the road south of Garnavillo. I can recall a day when my oldest sister, Ellen, took some of us into a seldom seen part of the woods which was a fairyland of lovely wild flowers at that time. We were thrilled with the yellow lady's slipper, that exquisite orchidaeous flower, the Indian candlestick, and the quaint Jack-in-the-pulpit, which were in a riot of abundance. Sometimes on Sunday afternoons, my father would at my request go off with me into the woods to hunt for the lovely lady's slipper or other flowers that were in season. I never saw any of the pink and white lady's slipper in Iowa, but they were profuse in Minnesota timber. I recall once, while traveling on the train there, a change of cars was made at a station located in timberland. The station agent was a woman, and she had the windows full of Indian candlesticks and those fragile pink and white orchids. We were thrilled by the charm-

ing picture. "The train is not due for some time, and you will have
plenty of chance to go get some," she said. Into the timber we hurried and found that the patches of flowers were so thick that we could
not walk without stepping on them.

Children show their trends of thought very early in life, and
Ellen and Marion showed their independence of thought when yet
very young. That characteristic remained with them their whole
lives. Now, in those days, a woman who had very decided opinions
of her own was frequently sneeringly called by some men "a strong-
minded woman." Once a man, talking to Marion about a certain
woman, remarked in a derogatory tone, "Oh, she's a strong-minded
woman." My sister replied, "Well, I am afraid she would not return
that compliment to you."

Ellen and Marion even had the bravery to disapprove of the
fashions, which most women never question, but meekly conform to.
They thought hoops were an abomination, even though our mother
did wear them. At last hoops were put on the market for little girls.
They, of course, refused to wear them, but since they liked to play
jokes and especially on me, their younger sister, they bought some
for me, although they knew I would not want to be bothered with
them.

One day, father invited me to drive with him to Guttenberg. My
sisters urged, "Now is your chance to wear your hoops," but I remonstrated. "But you must not go unless you wear the hoops," they
said. "What would the people in that town think of you, if you were
not dressed in the style?" I said no more and let them put the hoops
on me. But after we had driven about a mile, I said to father, "I do
not want to wear these hoops." He replied, "Just stand up and I'll
help you take them off." Off they came, and I went to Guttenberg
comfortable, if not stylish.

By the time I was in my teens, hoops were so universally worn
that all of us—mother, sisters, and I—had succumbed to the dictate
of Madame Fashion. To be seen without hoops endangered a
woman's standing and she was liable to be called eccentric.

Another fashion which we had to adopt eventually was the bustle. Men of today seem to take the eccentricities of women's styles
much more meekly. Even the adoption by women of man's distinctive garment—pants—does not seem to arouse them.

Even pastors say nothing against it; and this despite the fact that
the scriptures strongly admonish women not to put on men's attire.

In connection with the bustle, I remember an incident that happened at a teachers' institute, where each one was expected to answer roll call in the morning with some quotation or sentiment. A young man by the name of John Bagley had a black mustache of the latest fashion, of which he seemed extremely proud. One morning, this spruce young man answered roll call with a verse which quite offended the girls. He said:

> Mary had a little lamb;
> When it began to rustle,
> She cut the wool from off its back,
> And made herself a bustle.

When the girls were sputtering about this, I said, "Never mind. We shall get even!" The next morning my response to roll call was this:

> Johnnie had a little lamb;
> Its fleece was like the ash;
> He cut it off and colored it,
> And made a fine mustache.

There were no more slurs on bustles by him.

For a female to be seen in pants was considered a disgrace. When girls clandestinely purloined a boy's suit, they tried to be careful not to be seen by the other sex. My sister, Marion, enjoyed donning a suit belonging to Glen, a boy who lived with us. This he resented, but still was good natured about it. Marion liked to ride horseback astride, which was considered quite a breach of etiquette. The rest of us, of course, rode sidewise on side-saddles, but some became expert enough to ride sidewise without a saddle. Riding astride was safer than riding sidewise, and Marion did not see why she could not choose that way.

When I mention girls wearing pants, I recall an incident that happened after our family sold Evergreen farm in 1876 and moved to Elkader, the county seat, where my father now had his law office. A group of us girls were together for a jolly evening in the home of Dr. Chase, where we frequently congregated. The Chases' lovely home was near the bridge over the Turkey river. Someone suggested that half of us should dress in boys' clothes and go out walking in the town in company with the other half in their feminine attire, and we would make the boys of the town think that the girls were accompanied by out-of-town boys. Although it would be quite a disgrace if the girls so dressed should be recognized, it was evening and rather dark, and the girls thought they would take the chance.

So half of the girls went to their homes and managed to slip out with boys' suits. When all were dressed, we marched over the bridge into the other part of town. But some of the young men who saw us were suspicious and began to follow us. We all got panic stricken and started to run, never stopping until we got back into the Chase home. It would appear laughable to a girl of today that any female should be so fearful of being seen in pants, but it can be understood when one remembers that women, with their full skirts over wide hoops showed no more of their lower appendages than the toes of their shoes. In fact the proper term was "lower limbs," and it was even in better taste to act as if women were made in one piece from the waist down!

Discussion of the fashions has carried me far ahead, chronologically, of my story. I want to record an incident which happened in the early 60's. My father, Judge Samuel Murdock, on the supplication of a man distantly related to us, went to Washington, D.C., to see President Lincoln and attempt to get him to pardon this man. The facts were these: the man had a store in the south which was entered by soldiers who proceeded to take anything and everything they wanted without any payment. The man remonstrated with them, and a violent altercation took place, culminating finally in physical violence on the part of the soldiers toward the storekeeper. The latter, fearing for his safety, shot, and one of the soldiers was killed. Accused of murder and convicted, the man lay in prison awaiting execution.

Father outlined his view of the case to the president and asked a pardon. Lincoln heard him through and then picked up a paper outlining a case which resembled the one in which my father was interested. Lincoln said, "Here is a paper I want you to read. You are a lawyer and a judge. Now, what would be your decision in this case?" My father looked through the paper, then said, "Well, Mr. President, I could scarcely presume to insist that you should decide as I would, but if I were the judge in this case I would consider myself unjust if I did not release the man." Lincoln said, "Well, do you think I would be less just than you would be? The man, for whom you plea, is pardoned."

When I was at the age of sixteen, we three sisters attended Fayette university. "University" was a misnomer, for it was really only a small college. Prof. Brush was the president of the institution. It was through his influence and that of Dr. Parker, a personal friend of my father, that father was induced to let us enter this college. My pleasurable days there stand out in my memory. My chum was Mary Parsons, who later married Val Scrayer. My friendship with her has been kept up through all the years by letter, although we never met again.

Dr. Parker had two sons, the older of whom was Daniel N. Parker, who became a Methodist minister. The friendship between him and myself has been kept up ever since those early days. He happened to be pastor of the Methodist church in Lansing, Iowa, when I was there studying German. It was very pleasant to renew our intimacy of school days. The principal of the high school in Lansing was Prof. Eugene Merritt.

Once when my mother visited me there, Rev. Parker and Prof. Merritt, with the latter's girl friend, invited my mother and me to take a ride in a skiff on the Mississippi river. Mother was always ready for sports and quickly accepted. As we were floating down the river, a raft passed us and we all transferred from our skiff to the raft, towing our skiff along with us. The raft seemed to be going very slowly, but was really going faster than we realized. When we transferred to our skiff again and started upstream, the young men had to row against the strong current, which they found very difficult. We soon realized that we had gone much farther than we imagined. It was midnight when we again landed in Lansing. ...

As I had gone to the town to continue my advanced work in German under Prof. J. J. Rhomberg, I desired to live in a German family in order to perfect myself in conversation. Some of my friends disapproved of my being on such intimate terms with the Germans. But I followed my own inclination and secured board with a Mr. and Mrs. Nachtway. Mr. Nachtway had a drug store. He was highly educated and had in his home a large library of German books to which I had access. Further, I was invited to join a club of German young people which had been started by Prof. Rohmberg and which was called "Lese-kreischen," meaning "little reading circle."

There were eighteen members and we read eighteen German plays that school year. Another training I had was through reading to Mrs. Nachtway, which I did at her request. She was a typical German hausfrau, keeping her home immaculate, getting up excellent meals, milking the cow, caring for the horse, and doing numerous other duties. Since she had a taste for literature and had little time to read, she had me to read plays to her while she was sewing. She, in turn, would explain the meanings of words I did not know and correct my pronunciation. This was a great advantage to me.

There was an outdoor location where I loved to study. It was high on the bluff overlooking the river. There I would sit on a rock and enjoy both my books and the view of the Mississippi with the big steamboats plying up and down. One day, glancing up from my book, I was horrified to see coiled by my side a very large rattlesnake. Anyone can imagine my terror and the speed with which I scampered down from that bluff. That was my favorite spot no longer!

One day, after I had been in Lansing about a year, I received a letter from my father telling me that I had been offered the position of teaching German in the public schools of Elkader, the county seat, which was then our home. We had removed there from Evergreen farm in 1876, as I have mentioned before. When I read the letter, I went weeping to my teacher and told him that I could not presume to take that position for I was not capable of filling it. However, he said that I could do it, and must accept. So I did, and, after I got started, it became a real pleasure, although the teaching was very heavy. The children came to me as soon as they were in the first reader, and I had them through all the grades into the high school, using the conversational method. For three years I did this strenuous work, in the third year having eighty pupils each day. As salary I received $40.00 a month, which was about the same paid the teachers in the grades.

Although I hesitated to give up the work and leave my father and mother, I at last decided to make a change. My sister had graduated from Meadville, Pennsylvania, Unitarian Theological Seminary and had taken her first pastorate in Humboldt, Iowa. She requested me to come and live with her and assist in the parish work. This was a pleasant period of my life. My sister started literary clubs and other cultural activities which were both enjoyable and educational. The people became our loyal friends.

Since I had always been attracted toward the idea of doing kindergarten work, after three years in Humboldt, I went to Chicago and entered Miss Elizabeth Harrison's Kindergarten college. There, I received broad training, for we were required to practice teaching in the various kindergartens of the city, now in those of the most aristocratic people, and again among the people of the slums. The latter appealed to me very much, for in teaching those forlorn little tots, I felt as if I was doing work especially needed. I recall one kindergarten in the vicinity of Armour's meat-packing plant where three of us girls had charge for a time. The neighborhood was considered such a dangerous one for nice young women that the windows had bars. We taught there in the morning, but never ventured to eat our lunch in that neighborhood, but delayed it until we could get back to the college vicinity, where we had classes in the afternoon. The class of children in that school can be well illustrated by a conversation which was overheard between two of the pupils. A little boy exclaimed in a rather boastful voice, "My dad came home drunk last night!" The small girl to whom he said it was not to be outdone and announced in an equally boastful tone, "So did mine!" As yet, there were no public kindergartens and these schools were all private, either pay schools or charity schools, designed for pupils from three to six years.

When I finished my two years' course, I was offered, through the recommendation of Miss Harrison, the position of teacher of the kindergarten at Hull House. This appeared a most attractive offer as the whole country looked upon the Work of Jane Addams at Hull House as one of the greatest philanthropies of the day. But I had two years of strenuous study and practice teaching without a vacation and was greatly in need of a rest. Needless to say, the position at Hull House would not be a restful one. My parents felt I should come to them and have a vacation before going on with my teaching, and I acceded to their desires.

Many interesting amusing incidents happened during my teaching in private kindergartens in various places. Small children are, as a rule, alert and active and want to try new things that come to their attention. Once in my teaching in Elkader, I was talking to the children on kindness to animals. One of the things I mentioned was that they could do kindnesses to birds, and among these would be the putting out of material with which the birds could build their nests. I pointed out that the birds used bits of string, cotton, and cloth in making the nests. A mother of one of my pupils, returning home from an afternoon out, found the front lawn strewn with rags. She said to her little daughter, "My dear Blanche, why did you scatter rags all over the grass?" The child answered, "Teacher told us that we should put out things for the birds to use in making their nests." Well, her work was not entirely wasted, for, amusing to relate, in the fall when the leaves had fallen from the deciduous tree in the front yard, there was seen a bird's nest with quite a good-sized piece of cloth hanging from it.

Later I became a teacher of the primary grade in the public schools of Elkader. One summer I decided to teach a term of school in the country. In those days, country children went to school in the summer time so that they could help with the farm work in the spring and fall. During that country teaching in Highland township, I was once a guest in the home of some of my pupils. Between the house and the barnyard was a little stream crossed by a bridge. As I walked over this and looked down into the water, I discovered, to my delight, that there was a bed of white clay in it, just such as we had bought at a large price for our kindergarten work in Chicago. I had enjoyed that clay modeling so much and was proud that some of our pieces had been at the World's Fair in Chicago in 1893.

So, I dug out a quantity of the clay and took it to the country school. Of course, at that time I would never have dared introduce handwork as is done in progressive education projects of today, but I did take the time at recess and noon to teach the children to make articles from the clay. Seeing the work of their children, even some of the mothers became interested enough to take clay modeling as a pastime. The school room had a wainscoting about four feet high with a ledge at the top of it, and it was there that we set up the finished figures, making a decoration all around the room. Some of the children showed great skill and we put on an exhibit at the county fair, which attracted much favorable comment.

At another country school where I taught through the summer, I found the school grounds perfectly barren. I made my project there the beautifying of those grounds. There were woods nearby and at the close of school in the afternoons we would make excursions to them and bring back plants and shrubs, which we planted about the school building. The children entered into this heartily, and it is to be hoped that they kept up their interest after my departure and that other schools followed their example.

Speaking of the clay reminds me of other peculiarities of soil in our community. Pictured Rocks cave was the pride of McGregor. Many years ago a young man in McGregor, a deaf-mute with an artistic talent, began scraping different colored sands from the sides of the cave and filling bottles with them all arranged in patterns—emblems, flags, and even words. It appeared like an almost impossible feat, and these bottles were in such demand that he made considerable profit from his labor. A small cave similar to the Pictured Rocks was located several miles east of Prairie du Chien, Wisconsin. It was called Batavia cave. When a party of us picnicked there, I brought home a red rock of sandstone so heavy that it was a task for a man to lift it.

On the West Union road a few miles west of Elkader was another curious cave that was worth a trip to see and was much frequented by picnickers. Among the other natural curiosities near Elkader was Table Rock, a granite formation. One could imagine it was made for a giant's table, for it was too high for ordinary people to sit at it. However, it made a platform onto which four people could climb with their picnic baskets and there enjoy their lunch. Of benefit to picnickers in Humboldt county was a spring situated in the woods by the Des Moines river, which was peculiar in that it gushed from the top of a rock about five feet high. It seemed to have been put there by old Mother Nature just for our benefit.

The recreations and amusements of those days were all very simple ones, and frequently were an outgrowth of our work. I recall a trip one summer to Strawberry Point for teachers' institute. A number of us made the trip of twenty miles or so in a big wagon. In those days farmers had great crops of melons in their fields and passersby were welcome to help themselves. Some of the boys in our crowd climbed the rail fences and brought out to us luscious melons on which we feasted during the rest of the drive. When we arrived in Strawberry Point, the girls of our party wanted to find a boarding place all together. A family had built a new house but the upper floor was not quite ready for occupancy. The lady of the house kindly put up beds for us there, and we had a week of fun together, permeated with the frolicsome spirit of a girls' boarding school. It was at that institute where the war of the bustle and mustache verses took place.

Since there was no speedy transportation that permitted of people going many miles and staying for only a few hours, as is possible today, visits usually covered several days. Once when Marion was home on a vacation from the Boston School of Oratory, where she had been studying, we received a letter from gentlemen friends that they would like to come and spend the week-end before my sister's return to Boston. Miss Maggie Vaupel, who later became Dr.

Margaret Clark of Humboldt, Iowa, and still later of Long Beach, California, was at the farm spending a few days before she too would go with my sister to Boston. We assured the young men that they would be most welcome and at once set about planning entertainment for them. But on Saturday morning, the day on which they were to arrive, I felt so ill that I could not get up for breakfast. Later I managed to get dressed and went down to where father, mother, Maggie, and Marion were playing croquet. After watching them for awhile, I told them that I felt ill, and so they helped me into the house and put me to bed. The young men arrived as scheduled, but I did not see them, for I had picked up a typhoid germ and was unable to raise my head from my pillow for ten weeks and was confined to the house for seventeen weeks. This was disastrous to the plans of Marion and Maggie, for they were compelled to postpone their departure for Boston for many weeks.

When I was quite well again but did not dare venture outdoors because of the severity of the cold weather, Kate Vaupel, Maggie's sister, came to spend a week with me. Kate later became the wife of Prof. Hossfeld. One day Kate said, "Amelia, let us have a party." Accordingly, we wrote to my cousin, Will Gilbert, of Elkader, to bring over a load of young people. Mother made a dishpan full of doughnuts containing rich cream, and prepared other tempting foods. When in the evening we heard sleigh bells ring, Kate ran out to greet our friends, but it was not the crowd she had expected. Instead, it was a surprise party from Garnavillo. Soon we heard sleigh bells again, and now Kate ran out with assurance that it was the Elkader party. But no, it was another surprise party from National, about six miles distant. The Elkader friends never did arrive, for they had not received the letter in time to arrange the trip. Of course, mother's doughnuts were eaten.

A sequel to this incident happened more than sixty-five years later. After Marion and I had taken up our residence in Santa Monica, California, I was standing in the hall one day when a feeble old man came up the stairs to our apartment. I hesitated about inviting him in and asked him if there was anything he wanted. He replied, "Well, let me in and I will tell you who I am." After coming in, he said, "I want you to try to guess who I am first." There was not the slightest resemblance to anyone I had even seen and I could not guess. He then said, "Do you remember when in 1874 you had two surprise parties on one evening at your home on the farm? I was in that crowd from National, and I remember every detail about it, and how you let me go down cellar with you to get apples." He was Ransom J. Bixby, of Edgewood, who at one time served in the Iowa legislature.

I presume it is an almost unheard of thing for anyone to reach my age—ninety-two—and be able to say she had never been injured. But that has been my good fortune, despite the fact that I have had many experiences which might so easily have resulted in a serious accident.

Once when, as a little girl, I was visiting my mother's sister, Mrs. Marion Patch Russell, in Minneapolis, I was riding to school in a sleigh with my little cousins. The snow was four feet deep and there was only half the road opened. When the boy who was driving met a team, he turned out into the deep snow and we all thought we were going to be tipped over. One of the girls cried, "Hop out, hop out!" I was the only one who hopped. The driver went on some distance before he realized that anyone had jumped out. This seemed to me, as a child, a very serious experience, for I seemed to be sinking down in the snow to the point of suffocation. Indeed, it cannot be said what the result might have been if he had not soon returned for me.

We had many terrific thunder storms and wind storms in Iowa. One of my early experiences was to see a large tree near our front gate and only a few rods from the house struck by lightning and completely shattered. After that I was much terrified whenever a storm threatened.

I had not realized how terrible a sandstorm could be until I once went through one in Lyon county, Iowa. I had been invited to supper at the home of Ed Parch, formerly of Elkader, and when I started to walk to their home a most violent sandstorm was raging. I did not wish to forego the pleasure of visiting these old-time friends, so I struggled forward in the face of a force almost devastating. It was the faculty of perseverance habitual to the Murdock family that helped me to succeed in reaching the home of my friends.

Once I was driving with an elderly lady who drove a very spirited horse. There were three of us women on the seat of the carriage and a little girl was seated on a box at our feet. Suddenly, the top of the carriage began to come down slowly and would soon have crushed us. Instantly, I wrapped my long skirts about my ankles tightly, lifted my heels close to my body, and jumped over the wheel without being injured. I ran to the horse's head and caught his bridle to stop him so that the others could get out. Fortunately, a man drove by at that instant and helped us and adjusted whatever was wrong about the carriage top.

At another time I was driving with an elderly woman, when to my horror she suddenly drove the buggy up on an embankment at the side of the road. My first impulse was to grab the lines and turn the horse back into the road; but I did not, and on that instant I realized her purpose, for I had my first disconcerting view of an automobile, as one filled with intoxicated young men sped by us on the road. How lucky that I did not turn the horse back into the road. ...

It may not be unfitting to close these wandering memories with a view of Marion with [a] beautiful rose in her hand. Her little figure always stood so erect and alert, her smile was so bright, and her eyes so keen. Left the only two of our family, we spent so many years together in pleasant companionship. Marion passed from this life in January, 1942, at the age of ninety-four. Now, the visits of dear friends must keep me company.

As I sit at the wide west window of my apartment with the sun pouring in its warmth and golden color, making beautiful the days I walk the sunset trail, my thoughts flit back to all the many scenes and activities that have been crowded into my ninety-two years. And they have been so many! In this story, I have included, for the most part, only those that center about the early Iowa home. "Nearly a hundred years! Do they not seem long?" you ask. No, they seem short.

The prevailing influences in my life have been those bequeathed me by my pioneer parents: energy, thrift, perseverance, and upright living. Seeming to prove the accusation that all old people harp upon "the good old days," I close with the opinion that no modern slant on life, based on loose and easy living, can equal the spirit I saw demonstrated daily in my pioneer family.

NOTE

1. Amelia Murdock Wing, "Early Days in Clayton County," *The Annals of Iowa* 27 (April 1946): 257–96.

WOMEN IN IOWA
Jennie McCowen, M.D.

T HE closing selection is especially appropriate because it was written *by* an achieving woman *about* achieving women. During the early 1880s, the Iowa Commission for the World's Exposition, to be held in New Orleans, asked Dr. Jennie McCowen to review the Census of 1880 and summarize what Iowa's women had accomplished outside their homes. McCowen, who supplemented the census data with figures she collected, her own observations and wide reading, and an occasional nineteenth-century belief about women, found a great deal of activity and efficiency by women. Consequently, she concluded that Iowa demonstrated a "progressive and liberal attitude ... toward women." One might also conclude that late nineteenth-century Iowa women continued the pioneering tradition of their mothers and grandmothers, albeit it in a slightly different way.

In writing about her own profession, McCowen stated that, "The medical profession of Iowa, as a body, is noted for its justice, courtesy and liberality towards women practitioners." Although she admitted that "occasional hostility" had once existed, she claimed that it had "almost entirely disappeared" and that women physicians enjoyed "perfect professional equality." Whether McCowen was simply putting the best face on Iowa for the World's Exposition or whether she truly believed what she wrote is unknown, but her review of the census statistics cannot be doubted; one only has to check the census to verify them. She found that, in addition to their heavy domestic and family cares, Iowa women had entered virtually every job (working both inside and outside home), business, profession, club, charity, and reform activity.

McCowen's report, which is excerpted here, first appeared in *The Annals of Iowa* in 1884.[1]

The census of 1880 reveals the fact that over eighty thousand women are at work at various gainful occupations. Women have money invested in almost every kind of industry and business enterprise in the State, and inquiry reveals an unexpected number of women managing business enterprises of various kinds; among which may be mentioned millinery, wholesale and retail (one wholesale house alone, reporting 800 firms of women in Iowa on their books), groceries, glove and hose factories, jewelry, wholesale and retail, hotels, confectionery and fruit stores, market gardening, etc. In the Street Railway Company of the State Capital, a woman, Mrs. Mary Turner, who is also a very considerable stockholder, is secretary and treasurer of the company, and in the same city a woman stockholder, Mrs. McMurray, is secretary of the Dey Mountain Mining and Milling Company.

In the pursuits popularly supposed to be monopolized by men, the census returns reveal women workers as follows: boiler makers, boot and shoe makers, makers of brick and tile, brooms and brushes, cutlery and edge tools, foundry and machine shop products, furniture, chairs, glass, dressed furs, lead-bar, pipe and shot, leather, marble and stone work, mattresses and spring beds, buggy tops, linseed oil, paint, saddlery and harness, surgical appliances, windmills, window blinds and shades, agricultural implements, awnings and tents, looking glass and picture frames, iron, tin and copper ware, shingles and laths, washing machines and wringers, wooden ware, wire work, drugs and chemicals, mineral and soda waters.

Women are also enumerated as millers, miners, pork-packers, shippers, stock-raisers, barbers, blacksmiths, weavers, commercial travelers, detectives, gold and silver workers, printers, lithographers, stereotypers, editors and publishers. Women are engaged also in the canning of fruits and vegetables, the roasting and grinding of coffee and spices, in the manufacture of artificial flowers and feathers, cigar and cigar boxes, fancy paper and wooden packing boxes, soap and candles, starch, paper, hats and caps, masquerade costumes, men's and women's furnishing [clothing and accessories] goods. In agriculture women are named in considerable numbers as laborers, farmers and overseers, gardeners and nursery women, vine growers and florists. The raising of poultry, the keeping of bees and the raising of silk-worms furnish supplementary employment to many more.

There is a constant increase in the number of saleswomen in stores and shops of all kinds, with a decided increase in the number of bookkeepers and cashiers. We have two women who are presidents of banks, Mrs. L. A. Weiser, of Decorah, and Mrs. L. B. Stevens, of Marion; three who are brokers of money and stocks, four who are clerks and book-keepers in banks. An increasing number of young women have found employment in short-hand and type-writing. The number attending schools of this kind have increased rapidly. In nineteen schools in the State from which I have been able to collect statistics, almost one-half the students are now young women. An increasing number of women are employed in verbatim and professional reporting, including the reporting of law suits, taking depositions, reporting speeches, conventions, lectures, etc. Ladies can qualify themselves for court-reporting, but the duties are not so agreeable as the work in an office. We have one woman, however, Mrs. Fannie Harrison, of Clarksville, Iowa, who is doing most excellent and satisfactory work in this direction. Fifteen ladies are empowered to act as notaries public, there are five county recorders and various clerks, deputies, etc. The post-office and the offices of enrolling and engrossing clerks for both the House and the Senate have been filled by women for a number of years. The State librarian, the librarian of the State University, of many colleges and of many, if not most, of the city libraries are women. Some of the telegraph and most of the telephone operators are women. We have our share, too, of book agents, peddlers of lace and fancy notions, and during the past year another field of activity in this direction has been opened to women—that of insurance agents, in which new field their efforts are meeting with success, I am told. And lastly we have *manicures,* whose foothold in the list of our business enterprises ought certainly to gain us immunity from the further reproach of being "wild Westerners."

Recapitulation of All Workers	Men	Women
Agriculture	302,171	1,386
Professional and Personal Services	103,933	69,575
Trade and Transportation	50,212	660
Manufacturing, Milling and Mining	61,449	8,442
Total	597,879	80,065

These figures, however, give only approximately the number actually engaged in productive [paid] labor. A large number of women working in conjunction with husband, father or other male relative are not reported as workers for wages.

Again it must not be forgotten, in making any comparison in regard to the relative numbers of men and women engaged in various industries, that Iowa has 71,000 more men than women, while in many of the eastern manufacturing states, there is a large excess of women.

But very few children, comparatively, are engaged in business occupation, the total number, by the census of 1880, being but 1543. Our population is largely rural, about 14 per cent only of the total population living in towns having 4,000 inhabitants or over. And our children are in school, the last report of the State Superintendent of Public Instruction showing 75 per cent of children of school age in school.

COMPARATIVE WAGES AND EFFICIENCY OF WORKERS

Our public school teachers have an average salary of about $30 per month, one-fifth less than the average salary of men, not so great a disparity as formerly and chiefly accounted for by the fact that most men are principals or superintendents, while the lower grades with a corresponding diminution of salary are filled chiefly by women. In many, if not most places, there is no difference in the salaries paid men and women for the same grade of work. The County Superintendents have $4 per day, the same as men. The lady court reporter has $6 per day for every day in attendance upon court, and six cents per folio for transcripts, the same as men. As short-hand secretaries ladies receive from $50 to $100 per month. There is practically no difference in the compensation to young men and women for a specified amount and quality of work. Men are often paid a few dollars per month more than ladies for the reason that they stand in readiness to perform certain kinds of work in emergencies for which a lady would not be called upon.

Among the public school teachers [in efficiency], if there is a difference, it is in favor of the women. As County Superintendents of schools, women are by testimony of those teaching under them, generally more efficient in their work. They are acknowledged to be faithful as examiners and in their clerical work, but are said to be rather less exact in statistics and less quick in comprehension of legal matters than men. In convention work they have done equally well with men, the papers they have presented being sound and progressive. As short-hand secretaries ladies are usually preferred unless there are other duties which it is not supposed a lady would care to perform. It is said "they do better, that is cleaner, work than men, make neater transcriptions, etc., and are contented to remain the same place longer and in this way become better acquainted with the duties of the place and render their employers more valuable services."

In schools of every kind, where prizes are offered for excellence, young women have always taken their full share. In the business colleges they have taken prizes for best penmanship, neatest ledgers and best composition until the newspapers have cried out: "What is the matter with the boys?"

In the medical schools women have taken prizes in excess of their proportionate numbers for theses, clinical records and dissertations.

In the inter-high school oratorical contest girls have always carried off the lion's share of the honors. In the collegiate oratorical contests prizes have in a number of instances been awarded to young women, in virtue of which they were entitled to represent their colleges in the State oratorical contests. On two different occasions in the State contest the first prize has been awarded to a young lady, in 1876 to Miss Evelyn M. Chapman, of Simpson Centenary College, and in 1881 to Miss Minnie Brunson, of Upper Iowa University, entitling them to represent the State of Iowa in the inter-state oratorical contests. On both these occasions Iowa's representative took high rank and reflected credit upon their *alma mater* and their State.

In business circles we have yet to hear of one woman guilty of embezzlement or defalcation [embezzlement]. As cashiers they are said to count more rapidly and accurately than men and have a superior ability to detect counterfeits. As bookkeepers they are more careful and painstaking in their work. In independent business enterprises women seldom "fail."

PATENTS

Patents have been issued to Iowa women as follows: To Miss Flora Grace, of Webster City, for a thermometer; to Miss Eugenie Kilbourne, of Cedar Rapids, egg beater and griddle greaser; Mrs. I.T. Lamborn, attachment to door screen; Viola J. Angier, of Spencer, album for photographs; Mrs. L. S. Avory, of Manson, an ironing board.

EDUCATION IN IOWA

Education in Iowa has had a vigorous and natural growth. Co-education everywhere prevails naturally and as a matter of course, there being but one female college in the State. With the exception of the Catholic and Episcopal schools, girls are admitted on equal terms with boys into all schools of all grades, from the Kindergartens to the State University. Equal privileges are accorded women in all the medical schools—regular, homeopathic and eclectic—in all the Law schools, in all the Business Colleges, in the Dental College and in the College of Pharmacy. The most noticeable advance of the past year has been made at the Agricultural College (a State institution with a large national endowment) in establishing in connection with the college a school of Domestic Science fully equipped and having as its head a woman as professor of Domestic Economy. So far as is known, this is a step which no other State has taken.

The first woman in America to be elected to a full professorship with all the honors and emoluments thereunto pertaining was Miss H. J. Cook, of Cornell College. Now one or more women are occupying positions on the faculty of twelve of our higher institutions of learning. The professorships so held are Greek (3), Mathematics (2), English Literature (5), Natural Sciences (2), Modern Languages (2), Domestic Economy (1). In three of these colleges the secretary of the faculty is a woman. Not being unaware of the shrug of the shoulders and the smile which any mention of Western universities and colleges is wont to excite in certain quarters, it may be added that Iowa is entirely willing to abide by a comparison of *results,* as shown by the census.

Of the public school teachers of the State, two-thirds are women; of the superintendents and principals of graded schools, eighty-one are women—more than one in five; of the County superintendents eleven are women—one in nine; of teachers in normal [teacher training] institutes during the past year eighty-one were women—more than one-third; of the principals of secondary institutions of learning thirty-seven are women—about one-third; of the tutors and instructors in college and universities one-half are women; of the educational journals published in the State, one, *The Iowa*

Normal Monthly, of Dubuque, has, until recently, had a woman, Mrs. J. W. Shoup, for associate editor and business manager; another, *The Central School Journal,* of Keokuk, had a woman, Miss L. G. Howell, for sole editor and proprietor. Houghton & Mifflin, the Boston publishing firm, in writing of the former, have taken occasion to express their "hearty appreciation of the intelligence and discrimination of her book notices," affirming that "they were superior to those of almost any other journal of the class in the country."

During the last session of legislature, a woman was appointed secretary of the senate school committee. Of the State board of examiners one is a woman. In an increasing number of places over the State women are serving efficiently and satisfactorily on boards of education. Six women are now serving as presidents of such boards, thirty-five as secretaries, while fifty are vested with the responsibility of treasurer. ...

LITERATURE AND THE ARTS

All over the State literary, historical, and conversational clubs are increasing in numbers, in membership, and in amount of active methodical study accomplished, and are from year to year becoming more truly the centers for intellectual improvement. Most of them are well-organized, many have published constitutions and by-laws, courses of study, programs, etc. and some have club-rooms fitly furnished and equipped with still a balance in bank. ...

It we accept the dictum of Morris, in his recent Oxford lecture, that "art includes not only painting, sculpture and architecture, but the shapes and colors of all household goods, nay, even the arrangement of the fields for tillage and pasture," in short that "art is the beauty of earth," we in Iowa may indulge a comfortable complacency over the display in the out-doors art studies of our State.

Within more conservative limits, we have a multitude of amateurs with varied and varying gifts, and a few professionals with a reputation not confined to the State. There are within the State thirty-seven women who have studied art abroad, and women in almost every town of consequence, who have studied in the various American art schools. There are a number of Decorative Art clubs in the larger cities and a greater number of clubs for the study of art. Aestheticism as cultivated by the disciples of the "green and yellow melancholy" has never found much favor in this part of the West, but there is a growing taste for things good and beautiful in art. There is, however, little concerted action as we have no great art center or art schools. There are 144 women teaching art classes, sixteen teaching artistic embroidery and fancy work. The number of pupils receiving art instruction is given as 1,754. These figures do not include convents or Catholic schools and are known to be very incomplete. The only woman in the West who makes pretensions to the plastic art is an Iowa woman who has been commissioned to make the busts for the new State Capitol at Des Moines. There are a number of women who do creditable china painting; several who do their own firing, etc., and find a market for their wares in New York.

THE SCIENCES

A deserved reputation in science is a matter of slow growth and our State being comparatively new, the conditions have not been favorable to the development of a taste purely intellectual, which appeals neither to the emotional nor sensational side of us. Nevertheless, many of our women are making collections in the various departments of Natural History, and a number are quietly pursuing different lines of scientific research, though they are not yet to any great extent formulating results for publication. There are seven women in the State, however, thought worthy of mention in *Cassino's Directory of American Naturalists,* their specialties being biology, paleontology, botany and entomology. In addition to these ladies, the teacher of natural science at the State Normal School is a young woman; in two of our colleges the professorship of natural science is held by a woman, and the professor of botany in the College of Pharmacy is a woman. About one-tenth of the meteorological observers for the Iowa Weather Service are women.

A young lady of Davenport is doing most valuable original work in tracing the life history of the insects of the State, rearing and sketching the larvae in all stages. Her drawing, plain or colored, on wood or grained auto-type paper for photo-engraving, are most accurate and life-like. Until interrupted by ill-health she did work of this kind for eastern naturalists, who, desiring illustration for their text, sent larvae to be raised and sketched. Similar work is being done by a young lady of sixteen in Keokuk, who gives promise of a brilliant future in this line of original research. A young lady of Princeton has prepared the illustrations for a new work on zoology by one of the professors of the State University. The drawing were made from live and alcoholic specimens, dissections and shells. This is the first time a woman has been employed here in this capacity, and the verdict was that they had never before had so good work done in the University. This young lady has also illustrated botanical articles in the *Popular Science Monthly*. A lady of Muscatine, whose specialty is entomology, has been for several years studying the insects injurious to vegetation in this section of the country, and has written a number of papers upon this subject, which have been read before the State Horticultural Society and printed in its reports. For three years past she has been entomological editor of the *Iowa State Register.*

The Davenport Academy of Science, with a total regular membership of 206, has on its roll the names of fifty-nine women, more than one in four. The working membership is in about the same proportion. In the published proceedings, Vol. III, p. 13, credit is given to the women workers in the Academy in the following language, which occurred in the speech of Dr. Parry, the well-known botanist, nominating a woman for the presidency:

> It is quite unnecessary to explain to any one here present that the actual success and present prosperity of the Academy has been co-incident with the interest taken in it by woman. It was a Woman's Centennial Association that first inaugurated and successfully carried out the publication of the proceedings, on which more than any other one thing, the scientific character and standing of the Academy abroad has been firmly established. The very ground beneath our feet is the spontaneous gift of a generous woman, and this commodious building, which affords us a permanent home, from lowest foundation stone to highest rooferest, if not the direct work of woman's hand has been wrought out and completed under the inspiring influence of a woman's heart. It has been proposed and I doubt not will meet the spontaneous approval of all present to recognize this obligation in a very appropriate way as well as add a crowning glory to the institution by electing Mrs. Mary L. D. Putnam, President of the Academy of the ensuing year.

Mrs. Putnam was unanimously elected. This occurred in 1879 and was the first, and so far as I am aware, the only instance on record of a woman being chosen president of an Academy of Science. From year to year the names of women appear in the list of of-

ficers of this Academy, and at present the recording secretary, who is
ex-officio one of the Board of Trustees, the librarian and the chairman of the publication committee are women. The summer classes
in practical botany sustained by this Academy are two-third women,
and last winter a course of lectures on the Physiology and Hygiene
of Womanhood, given under the auspices of the Academy by one of
its members, a lady physician, was attended by from 100 to 125
ladies.

HEALTH PRACTITIONERS

Year by year an increasing respect for and confidence in the ca-
pabilities of the woman practitioner of medicine is shown in the most
matter-of-fact way—by the balance in her bank account. In 1880
seventy-three women physicians were enumerated and, to my
knowledge, the number is now considerably greater. The medical
profession of Iowa, as a body, is noted for its justice, courtesy and
liberality towards women practitioners. The occasional hostility of
earlier years, in certain localities, has almost entirely disappeared,
and there is now no part of the State in which educated and capable
women are not received by their brothers in the healing art, on terms
of perfect professional equality. Not only are they freely admitted to
all the medical societies—county, district and state—but in many
cases are acceptably occupying official positions as secretaries, trea-
surers, or on the Board of Censors. Last year, one of the most able
and influential societies in the State chose a woman (who had first
served three terms as secretary) to preside over their deliberations, a
thing before unheard of in the medical world. This year she was re-
elected without a dissenting voice, no other nomination being made.
It is the rule rather than the exception for the lady members of the local societies to be among the delegates sent to the State Society and
this year two ladies were given credentials to represent the State Society in the American Medical Association, the highest body in the
profession.

At the meeting of the State Society this year a number of ladies
were in attendance, not on sufferance, but with all the rights and
privileges of members, taking part in the proceedings, serving on
committees, etc. "No members took more prominent part or received
more courteous attention than they. That utmost harmony and good
will prevailed throughout the sessions and that there has been no let-

ting down of the high masculine standard to accommodate the mental or professional calibre of the ladies may be inferred from the remarks of one of the oldest members present, who said he had never before attended a meeting where so many able papers had been read." One of the leading dailies in the State, in commenting on the *personnel* of the Society, says: "It was a splendid gathering of *men* and *women,* which would do credit to any State in the Union." The president-elect in his address expressed gratification at the presence of so many ladies, and declared that they had "not only done credit to themselves as medical practitioners, but had reflected honor upon the Society."

Last year the annual address before the Alumni Association of the Medical Department of the State University of Iowa was given by a woman, and this year the Alumni have elected a woman to the presidency of the Association.

Although pharmacy is one of the vocations supposed to be scarcely yet opened to women, there were in Iowa, in 1882, no less than forty-three women enrolled as registered pharmacists, the law in this State providing rigid tests as to fitness. The State Pharmaceutical Society includes women in its membership, who have taken an active part in its proceedings, serving on committees, taking part in debate, etc.

There are in the State, according to the last census, 110 nurses, many of whom are graduates of the various schools for nurses, and twenty-six midwives; though it is believed that this latter figure falls far short of the actual number.

The census gives us but one lady dentist, but there are now three in the State, one at Mt. Pleasant, one at Grinnell, and one at Council Bluffs. Almost all dentists have one or more lady assistants in their offices.

OTHER PROFESSIONS

Five ladies have graduated from the University Law School and two from the Des Moines Law School. But four, however, are now practicing with the State, one at Cedar Rapids and one at Iowa City are practicing in partnership with their respective husbands. These ladies confine themselves to office-work, preparing pleadings or papers, looking up cases, etc. Another at Delhi does similar work in connection with her father, and the fourth, has for several years past, as an officer of the National Woman's Christian Temperance Union, devoted herself chiefly to the legal aspects of the temperance question, in which field of work her reputation is not confined to the State. The first woman ever admitted to practice in the U.S. Courts was Mrs. Emma Haddock, of Iowa City.

Friends or Quakers have here as everywhere been pioneers in giving freedom to women in ministerial work. Believing that the essential qualification for the work of the ministry is the immediate teaching and influence of the Holy Spirit, their practice has ever conformed to their doctrine, and if a sister felt moved by the Holy Spirit to minister unto them, *no man said nay.* They also hold, however, that as the gift is divine, the service is to be freely and faithfully performed without any view to reward from man, hence their ministry is not set apart from worldy avocations as are those of other denominations.

Of these latter, the census mentions ten. These ladies are capable, talented and successful workers. As pastors and preachers they will stand honest and fair comparison with any of the brethren. Some of them have been set over peculiarly trying parishes, and they have even here achieved a goodly degree of success. Where brethren have failed leaving the "desolation of destruction" they have been called to go and rebuild the "old waste places."

The denominational affiliation of these ladies is Unitarian, Universalist and Christian.

CLUBS, CHARITIES, AND REFORMS

... The Reform Schools have a woman on the Board of Trustees, and the Reform School for Girls has been in charge of a woman until recently, failing health having compelled her resignation. The State Hospital for Insane at Independence has a woman on the Board of Trustees and also on the medical staff. One member of the Visiting Committee to inspect the State Hospitals for the Insane is a woman.

Women in this State are growingly efficient in the various benevolent and philanthropic enterprises of the day, as is evidenced by the good work of the Ladies' Christian Association, Relief Corps, Aid Societies, etc., in almost every city. The thoughtless and indiscriminate doling out of alms is giving place to an intelligent and conscientious study of the causes of pauperism, crime and wretchedness with a view to reducing them to a minimum. In several places, sewing schools for neglected girls, managed entirely by ladies, are in successful operation. From year to year one or more ladies in conjunction with gentlemen (usually an equal number of each) have been delegated by the governor to represent Iowa in the National Conference of Charities. On two different occasions ladies so delegated have read papers before that body which attracted widespread attention, and on several occasions the report for the State has been made by one of the lady delegates.

The Woman's Christian Temperance Union, an incorporated organization with a membership of 5,000 earnest, consecrated women cannot be overlooked in any statement purporting to sketch the work of women in this State. With dauntless courage these mothers of Iowa banded themselves together to wage a hand-to-hand contest with the powers of darkness for the peace, purity and protection of the home. Operating through 230 local Unions with their thirty-one different departments of organized work—evangelistic, educational, social, hygienic, scientific, legal, etc., this society of women has been a force felt from the center to the circumference of one State, and co-operating with the great central organization, whose membership stands shoulder-to-shoulder from Maine to Texas and from the Atlantic to the Pacific, they have made a record unparalleled by any other existing organization. In the National W.C.T.U. convention at St. Louis the Iowa members distinguished themselves by boldly taking a stand against casting the weight of the organization in favor of St. John and the prohibition party. With but two exceptions the Iowa delegation voted solid against the measure.

One of the practical features of their organization in the State has been the establishment and maintenance of a state refuge for erring women known in honor of Mrs. Benedict, as the Benedict Home. During the past year twenty-five women, with ages ranging from thirty-one to *thirteen years,* have sought this refuge; six have been restored to their friends, three have married, two have died, one had been transferred to an insane asylum, a wreck for life, and five only have gone back to a life of sin. The Board of Managers, representing five different churches, have worked together as a unit in this most unpromising of all faith work.

The Iowa Equal Suffrage Society has adopted the motto of the State with the change of a single word, thus: "Our liberties we prize, our rights we will *secure.*" An amendment to the constitution giving women the right of suffrage was passed by the 19th General Assembly, and it remained for the 20th General Assembly to ratify that action before it could be submitted to popular vote. All honorable means were used to secure favorable action, but notwithstanding the Governor in his message favored its submission to the people, and notwithstanding the thousands of petitions, it was lost by a vote in the House of 50 to 44, the vote in the Senate standing nays 26, yeas 24.

The first protest against equal suffrage ever presented to an Iowa legislature was presented this year, signed "many ladies." The Senate objected to receiving a document with no names attached, but finally it was referred to the library committee, of which the Senator presenting it was chairman. The advocates of the measure are defeated, but not dismayed, and with 150 editors in the State who have signified their willingness to give space for suffrage articles, they do not propose to give up the fight.

The great fraternity of Free Masonry, whose doors have been closed against women for three thousand years, now in the nineteenth century, in organizing the modern degrees of the Chapter, Council, Commandery, and Scotch Rite have provided also an adjunct to their ancient and honorable organization for their wives, sisters and daughters; and the order of the Eastern Star with five degrees, first established in 1850, now extends into thirty-two states and territories with a membership of fifty thousand. The Most Worthy Grand Matron who stands at the head of this organization in the United States is an Iowa woman, who, previous to her election to this high office at San Francisco last year, had as Grand Matron of her own State, won for herself a national reputation as one of the foremost workers in the cause in the United States.

There is in Iowa a Grand Chapter, forty subordinate lodges, and a membership of 1,500 or more active and earnest workers. The code book for the use of the order was compiled and published by two of the Iowa sisters, and is now going through its third edition.

The Daughters of Rebecca, who sustain a similar relation to the I.O.O.F. [Independent Order of Foresters], have over one hundred lodges with a total membership of about two thousand.

The Association for the Advancement of Women, an organization whose object is "to consider and present practical methods for securing to women higher intellectual, moral and physical conditions, with a view to the improvement of all domestic and social relations, though not yet very thoroughly organized in the West, has a growing membership in this State. Iowa is represented in the management of this organization by a vice-president from Davenport and a director from Dubuque.

The National Association for the Protection of the Insane and the Prevention of Insanity is a society whose title sufficiently indicates its character and scope. Its plan of organization contemplates a corresponding member in each state and territory of the United States and in each country in Europe and eventually in the world. Although its membership includes both men and women, the direction of the work in this State is entrusted to a woman.

SUMMARY

While enumerating the work of women in connection with the world's progress in the arts, the sciences, the industries, the professions, we cannot overlook the fact that much of woman's best work cannot be recounted, tabulated or set forth in columns of figures. Hundreds of women, in every avenue of life, some sheltered from the sterner struggle for bread, others themselves workers, are "lending a hand" to the great needs of the world without publicity. Neither can we overlook the 310,896 women who are heads of families. No work can be more ceaseless, more taxing, more deserving of appreciation at the hands of the commonwealth than the training up of the future citizens into healthful, useful and moral men and women; and many are the women to echo the sentiment of a mother of ten boys, who, when interviewed in regard to her public efforts, replied, "*I would rather be known as the mother of my boys.*"

NOTE

1. Jennie McCowen, M.D., "Women in Iowa," *The Annals of Iowa* 2 (October 1884): 96–113.

Conclusion

After reading Iowa women's words and memories, it is easy to understand why so many people have developed an interest in women's history. Iowa women's writings and reminiscences offer a unique, firsthand look into a pivotal era in Iowa's history—and into the history of the American West. Their words also indicate what mettle, determination, and inventiveness Iowa women showed as they helped found and develop the state.

Indeed, in their writings and other documents Iowa women wove a engrossing tapestry of words. It is my hope that current scholarship will fill in those parts of the design that have faded from view; that in a decade I will be able to revise this collection by including material by, or about, uneducated women, non-English speaking women, and women of color. I am optimistic that the collection and study of such sources as census records, family Bibles, marriage licenses and wills, and similar resources will widen our understanding of the female frontier in Iowa.

I also trust that such topics as spouse and child abuse, alcoholism, divorce, prostitution, rape, and murder will be elucidated as we continue to search out and analyze police ledgers, divorce records, doctors' accounts, and other similar chronicles. Perhaps we can then not only expand our picture of Iowa's female frontier, but add an even larger portion of realism to it.

In the meantime, we can continue to admire and honor the women who did leave their stories behind and gave us a glimpse of what life was like in pioneer Iowa. Although the term "gutsy lady" was not coined until well into the twentieth century, it certainly applied to many women of earlier generations.